7

Christ Jesus, the Way

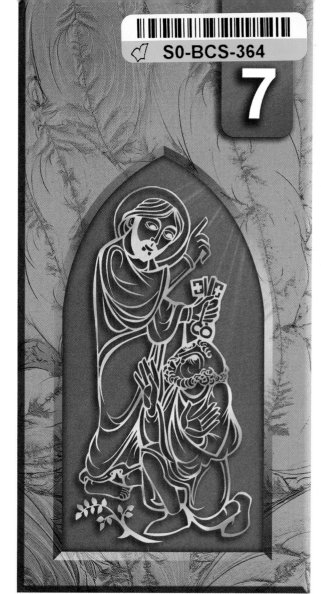

Parish Edition

General Editors

Sister Catherine Dooley, O.P.
Rev. Berard Marthaler, OFM Conv.
Rev. Gerard P. Weber

Consulting Editors

Monsignor Thomas McDade, Ed.D.
Irene Murphy
David Michael Thomas, Ph.D.

Benziger

Woodland Hills, California

Credits

Consultants: Clare Collela; Dr. Peter Gilmour, Ph.D.; Rev. Robert Hater, Ph.D.; Sr. Ann Laszok, CSBM (Eastern Catholics); Sister Eva Marie Lumas, SSS; Rev. Ronald Nuzzi, Ph.D.; Daniel Pierson; Rev. Peter Phan, Ph.D.; Art Zannoni (Sacred Scripture)
Contributors: Sylvia DeVillers, Joanne McPortland, Margaret Savitskas, Susan Stark
Mission Education: Maryknoll Fathers, Brothers, and Sisters
Liturgical Catechesis: Sr. Catherine Dooley, OP (General Editor); Sr. Miriam Malone, SNJM; Joan Vos; Sandy Lauzon
Liturgy: Rev. John Gallen, SJ
Music Editors: Gary Daigle, Jaime Cortez

Design: Bill Smith Studios, Monotype Composition, Visual Education Group
Production: Visual Education Group
Cover Design: Robert Hyre and Logan Design
Cover Art: Br. Stephen Erspamer, SM
International Photography: Maryknoll Magazine

Nihil Obstat: Sister Karen Wilhelmy, CSJ, Censor Deputatus

Imprimatur: † Roger Cardinal Mahony, Archbishop of Los Angeles

The nihil obstat and imprimatur are official declarations that the work contains nothing contrary to Faith and Morals. It is not implied thereby that those who have granted the nihil obstat and imprimatur agree with the contents, statements, or opinions expressed.

Send all inquiries to:
Benziger
21600 Oxnard St., Suite 500
Woodland Hills, CA 91367

ISBN 0-07-821776-8
Printed in the United States of America
1 2 3 4 5 6 7 8 9 073 08 07 06 05 04 03

Christ Jesus, the Way

Contents

Contents

While Jesus was having his last meal with his disciples, he said to them, "Do not let your hearts be troubled. You have faith in God; have faith also in me. In my Father's house there are many dwelling places. I am going to prepare a place for you. And I will come back again and take you to myself, so that where I am you also may be. Where I am going, you know the way."

Thomas said to Jesus, "Master, we do not know where you are going; how can we know the way?"

Jesus said to him, "I am the way, the truth, and the life."

From *John 14:1–6*

Know Love Serve

A Youth Catechism

Who do people
say that the
Son of Man is?
Matthew 16:13

Welcome!

Peter had gone through so much in the past few weeks. Jesus had singled him out as the leader of the Christian community—and then, almost immediately, his fear made him deny knowing Jesus. He had watched from a distance as Jesus suffered a terrible death, and he had stood stunned at the sight of the empty tomb.

During the long days of waiting and praying that followed Jesus' return to his Father, Peter had wondered how he would ever find the courage and the words to share all the Good News that was in his heart.

But now, this morning, everything was different. Filled with the Holy Spirit, on fire with faith, Peter rushed outside with the other Apostles. Standing before crowds of people visiting Jerusalem from every corner of the world, Peter had no problem at all putting his faith, his hope, and his love into words that everyone understood:

Jesus was a man commended to you by God with mighty deeds, wonders, and signs, which God worked through him in your midst, as you yourselves know. This man you killed, using lawless men to crucify him. But God raised him up, releasing him from the throes of death, because it was impossible for him to be held by it. God raised this Jesus; of this we are all witnesses. Exalted at the right hand of God, he received the promise of the holy Spirit from the Father and poured it forth, as you both see and hear.

From *Acts 2:22–33*

Your Book

You are a member of the Church. Everything you do as a Catholic Christian flows from the life and teachings of Jesus Christ. This year, you are invited to come to know Jesus better and to grow in your mission as his follower. A lot of your learning will take place in the time you spend and the ideas, hopes, and questions you share with the other members of your group and with your adult companions on the journey.

You will also have two books to guide you. One is the Bible, especially the New Testament accounts of Jesus' life and the mission of his disciples. The other is your religion book, which is designed to help you come to know, love, and serve God better and follow Jesus more closely.

Your religion book has four parts.

1. Know, Love, and Serve: A Youth Catechism

Become familiar with this useful treasury of Catholic beliefs, traditions, and practices. You will come back to this section all year long.

2. Your Lessons

Each week, as you learn more about Jesus, you will have many opportunities to put what you learn into practice.

3. Seasons of Faith

This part of your book invites you to celebrate the seasons and feast days of the Church Year with the whole community.

4. Glossary

This list of words to know will help you develop a level of ease with the vocabulary of your faith.

Follow Jesus

When Jesus asked his Apostles that most important question—"Who do you say that I am?"—there must have been a moment of silence in which everyone waited to see who would speak first. In that moment, Peter had time to recall the events of the previous twenty-four hours. He remembered standing in the hot sun, holding one of the baskets overflowing with leftover bread and fish. Thousands of people had just shared a picnic like no other, where moments before there had been only a few small loaves of bread and a couple of fish in the whole wilderness. Peter didn't know exactly how this great miracle had taken place, but he did know it had something to do with the confidence and love with which Jesus had thanked his Father in heaven for the meager scraps. Jesus had treated the food as if it was a banquet, and it became one.

There were so many moments like that, beginning with the time Jesus had called Peter and his brother Andrew from their father's fishing boat. Peter had seen with his own eyes how Jesus fed not only people's stomachs but also their empty spirits and their hungry hearts. Peter knew there was really only one answer to Jesus' question, an answer that Peter and all the people of Israel had been waiting to say for thousands of years. Peter didn't have a clue about what the consequences of speaking would be, and he didn't care. His let his heart speak as he said, simply: "You are the Messiah, the Son of the living God" (based on *Matthew 16:13–18*).

Wisdom of the Ages

According to Church tradition, Peter was the first bishop of Rome. His successors in that office are the popes, who inherit the authority Jesus gave to Peter on the day that Peter professed his faith. Many traditional symbols of the papacy can be traced to this connection with Peter. The papal ring, which serves as an official seal on Church documents, incorporates images of both fish and the sign of the cross; it is traditionally known as the Fisherman's Ring after Peter, who was a fisher before being called to follow Jesus. Jesus told Peter, "I will give you the keys to the kingdom of heaven." The banner of the pope shows two crossed keys, symbolizing power over both temporal (earthly) and spiritual matters. When a new pope is elected, the ancient Latin anthem *Tu est Petrus* ("You are Peter") is chanted at his first Mass, repeating Jesus' words to his faithful friend.

You, like Peter, profess your faith in Jesus. When people ask you who Jesus is, take a moment to recall the many ways you have experienced Jesus' nurturing, saving, healing, and loving presence in your life. Then, your answer, like Peter's, will be simple and heartfelt.

This year you will continue to grow in your knowledge of your faith and in the wisdom it takes to make good moral decisions. The resources in this section will remind you of what you already know. Use these questions and answers to review key teachings.

Important Questions

1. **Who is God?**
   God is the one, divine Being who created all things and rules over all creation. God is eternal, all-powerful, all-knowing, and all-good. No human language can fully describe God, who is beyond all imagining.

2. **What is meant by the title *Blessed Trinity?***
   The Blessed Trinity is the mystery of one God in three divine persons: Father, Son, and Holy Spirit. The title *Blessed Trinity* describes the way God has revealed himself to humans, as a community of love in perfect unity.

3. **How do Catholics view the Bible?**
   For Catholic Christians, the Bible is the revealed Word of God, set down in human language through the inspiration of the Holy Spirit. The Church's living tradition and teaching authority help Catholics interpret the Bible, which does not need to be read literally to give the Sacred Scriptures the deep respect they are due. Scripture is an integral part of every Catholic liturgy, and familiarity with the Bible is an important part of growing in faith.

4. **What do Catholics believe about human nature?**
   Catholics believe that humans, like all God's creatures, were created in goodness and right relationship with God. But the first humans chose to turn away from God's love in an act of disobedience. This original sin had consequences for all humanity, bringing death into the world and leaving humans subject to temptation and sin. God's grace is stronger than sin, however, and God calls all people into right and loving relationship through the saving actions of Jesus.

5. **Who is Jesus?**
   Jesus Christ is the Son of God made man, the Second Person of the Blessed Trinity. Jesus is fully divine and fully human. He shared fully in every aspect of humanity except the inheritance of original sin. Though Jesus was tempted, he never yielded to sin because his will was completely joined with that of God, his Father.

6. **Who is the Holy Spirit?**

   The Holy Spirit is the Third Person of the Blessed Trinity, the love of God sent forth by the Father and the Son to be with the followers of Jesus forever. The Holy Spirit is the source of grace and truth and keeps the Church's teaching authority faithful to the message of Jesus. The Holy Spirit came to the Apostles in a dramatic way on Pentecost, filling them with the joy and courage to carry out their mission.

7. **What is the Church?**

   The Church is the gathered community of the followers of Jesus in every age and place, the Body of Christ on Earth. The Church is one (united in diversity), holy (sustained by the Holy Spirit), catholic (universal, open to all), and apostolic (sent to share the Good News of Jesus). Although the Church is made up of all baptized Christians, there are divisions in the Church on Earth. Catholic Christians belong to the Roman Catholic Church, headed by the pope, the Bishop of Rome. The Catholic Church also includes a number of other non-Roman Rites, or Catholic communities that celebrate according to their own cultural and religious traditions.

8. **Where do most Catholics experience belonging to the Church?**

   For most Catholic Christians, the Church means the local faith community, the parish—a number of individuals and families who gather for worship, education, and witness in the same neighborhood or town. The parish is headed by a pastor or administrator. The Catholic parishes in a given area form a diocese, a territorial community under the guidance of a bishop. (A large diocese is known as an archdiocese, and its bishop an archbishop.) The bishops of each country meet at a national conference for administrative purposes, but each bishop is directly responsible to the pope as head of the universal Church.

9. **What do Catholics believe about other Christians? About people of other faiths?**

   Catholics regret the divisions that mar the unity of the Body of Christ, and they work for a return to wholeness. Catholics are called to work and pray for Christian unity. While Catholics, like all Christians, believe that salvation comes through a relationship with Jesus Christ, the Church teaches respect for people of other faiths and religious traditions, recognizing that the yearning to relate to God is universal. Catholics have a special regard for Judaism, which was the faith of Jesus. Catholics share the Hebrew Scriptures with Jews. Many Catholics are involved in interfaith efforts to promote understanding among members of the world's religions, especially Judaism, Christianity, and Islam, which all trace their origins to Abraham.

10. **How is Jesus Christ present in the Church today?**

    Jesus is present in the sacraments, seven powerful signs and sources of God's grace that celebrate the relationship between God and humans. Through the Sacraments of Initiation—Baptism, Confirmation, and Eucharist—people become part

of the Church and enter fully into sanctifying grace. Through the Sacraments of Healing—Reconciliation (Penance) and the Anointing of the Sick—Catholics celebrate God's forgiving and healing love. Through the Sacraments of Vocation—Marriage and Holy Orders—Catholics celebrate God's call to live the life of faith in relationship with and service to others.

11. **Why is the Eucharist the heart of Christian life?**
The night before he died, Jesus instituted the Eucharist by sharing himself, body and blood, with his friends as bread and wine. Jesus continues to be present today in the Eucharistic celebration, the Mass—in the gathered assembly, in the Word of God proclaimed, in the person of the celebrant, and especially in the consecrated Bread and Wine. In Holy Communion, Jesus unites, heals, strengthens, and forgives. Active participation in the Mass on Sunday prepares you to live your faith all week long.

12. **Why do Catholics give special honor to Mary, the mother of Jesus?**
Catholics honor Mary as the Mother of God and Mother of the Church. She is the best model of human faithfulness to God. Mary put her trust in God by agreeing to be the mother of the Messiah. She reached out to others in loving care. With her husband, Joseph, she raised Jesus to be faithful, loving, and just. She stood by her Son throughout his life, endured his terrible death, rejoiced in his resurrection, and was reunited with him in heaven, body and soul, at the end of her life on Earth. Throughout the Church's history, Mary has been honored under various titles and depicted in various images by Catholics around the world.

13. **Who are the saints, and how do Catholics honor them?**
The word *saints* means "holy ones." In one way, all followers of Jesus (including you!), whether or not their names are known, are part of the Communion of Saints, the assembly of faithful Christians throughout the ages. The Church honors the memory of many named saints by following the example of their lives and including their feast days in the liturgical calendar. The process by which saints are officially recognized and added to the Church calendar is known as canonization. Mary is the greatest of the saints. Saints are generally grouped into *martyrs*—people who witnessed their faith by dying for it—and *confessors*—people who lived their faith in a special way every day. Catholics honor the saints but do not worship them; worship belongs to God alone. When you talk to the saints in prayer, you are not praying to them, but asking them to be companions in prayer. You have a patron saint (often the saint whose name you received in Baptism). Patron saints are invoked by individuals, nations, organizations, members of professions, or people needing special help in an aspect of life with which the patron is particularly associated.

14. **What is prayer? How important is it for Catholics?**
Prayer is, very simply, communication with God. Prayer can be public or private; formal or spontaneous; spoken, sung, or

silent; using words or actions, talking or listening. Prayer is an integral part of life for Catholic Christians. Traditionally, prayer is categorized by motivation: you can pray to praise God, to thank God for blessings, to express contrition and ask God's forgiveness, to intercede (ask God's help for the needs of others), and to petition God's help for yourself. The Church's public prayer and worship, or liturgy, is at the heart of Catholic life. The Mass is the central act of public prayer. Each day, many Catholics celebrate the Liturgy of the Hours, public prayer conducted at regular times of the day. The Church has a rich history of traditional prayers and prayer forms, such as the rosary, also known as devotions. Scripture, especially the Book of Psalms, also plays a central role in the Church's public and private prayer.

15. **How do Catholics live a good moral life?**
Catholics believe that God created each person with free will—the ability to choose between right and wrong. Such choices are known as moral choices, and living a good moral life means making choices that are directed toward loving God and others. Choices that demonstrate a lack of love for God and others or disobedience to God's laws are known as sins. You have been gifted with a conscience, the ability to use your reason and rely on God's grace to make the right moral choices, but you have the responsibility to form your conscience properly.

16. **How is the conscience formed?**
A well-formed conscience is *in*formed, meaning that you have done everything you can to learn all you can about what God asks of you. Becoming familiar with God's law as expressed in the commandments and the teachings of Jesus, reading the Scriptures, listening to and following the direction of the Church's teaching authority (known as the *magisterium*), participating in the sacraments, following the example of the saints and of faithful Christians you know, and praying regularly for the help of the Holy Spirit are all important means of forming your conscience so that when you are called to make a moral decision, you will know what to do.

17. **What is the difference between mortal and venial sin?**
Mortal (or deadly) sin is a seriously wrong action or choice that disrupts the relationship of grace between the sinner and God and separates the sinner from the community. To be mortal, the sin must be seriously wrong, you must know that it is seriously wrong, and you must have freely chosen to do it anyway. Mortal sin prevents the sinner from participating in Holy Communion and must be absolved through the sacrament of Reconciliation before the sinner can be restored to full communion with God and the community. Venial sin is less serious wrongdoing, but a pattern of venial sin and bad habits over time can lead to more serious wrongdoing. Although sacramental confession and absolution are not required for venial sin (which can be forgiven by sincere contrition and participation in the Eucharist), regularly celebrating the sacrament of Reconciliation is one of the best ways to stay in right relationship with God and others.

Statements of Belief

If someone were to ask you what you believe as a Catholic Christian, you might struggle to find the right words. At every Sunday Mass, however, you proclaim what you believe in the words of an ancient profession of faith, the Nicene Creed.

The chart on these two pages will help you connect the faith statements of the Nicene Creed to their foundations in Scripture and reflect on what these beliefs mean in your life.

In the Words of the Nicene Creed	In Scripture	In Your Life
We believe in one God, the Father, the Almighty Maker of heaven and Earth, of all that is seen and unseen.	James 2:18, Ephesians 4:6 Ephesians 4:6, Genesis 17:1 Genesis 1:1, Isaiah 40:28 Colossians 1:16	You are the child of one all-good, all-powerful, all-loving God, who created and sustains all things. You share with all people the dignity of having been created in God's image. You share in God's creativity and are called to care for the Earth.
We believe in one Lord, Jesus Christ, the only Son of God, eternally begotten of the Father God from God, light from light, true God from true God begotten, not made one in Being with the Father. Through him all things were made. For us and our salvation he came down from heaven:	Ephesians 4:5, Philippians 2:11 Acts 8:37, 2 Corinthians 1:19 John 1:14, John 3:16, John 4:9 1 John 1:5, John 1:4–9 John 17:3, 1 John 5:20 Hebrews 1:5 John 10:30 John 14:10–11 Ephesians 3:9, John 1:1–3 John 16:28	You belong to the community of followers of Jesus Christ, the eternal Son of God. Jesus is fully God and fully human, and he came into the world to save you and all people from the power of sin and death.
by the power of the Holy Spirit He was born of the Virgin Mary, and became man.	Luke 1:35 Luke 1:30–31 Philippians 2:7–8	Jesus graced human life by becoming human. Your human life is precious because Jesus, your brother, chose to share in its sorrows and joys. His mother, Mary, is your mother, too.
For our sake he was crucified under Pontius Pilate; he suffered, died, and was buried.	John 19:15–16 John 19:28, Acts 17:2, Hebrews 2:18, 1 Peter 2:21, Matthew 27:59–60, Mark 15:46, Luke 23:53, John 19:41–42	The price of human selfishness and sin is suffering and death. Jesus chose to pay that price for you, so that you would know that no suffering is meaningless and no one dies alone.
On the third day he rose again in fulfillment of the Scriptures;	Matthew 28:6, Mark 16:6, Luke 24:6–7, 1 Corinthians 15:3–4	God raised Jesus from death to show you that love always triumphs, and death is not the end.

In the Words of the Nicene Creed	In Scripture	In Your Life
he ascended into heaven and is seated at the right hand of the Father. He will come again in glory to judge the living and the dead, and his kingdom will have no end.	Acts 1:9 Acts 7:55–56, Luke 22:69, Hebrews 1:3, Colossians 3:1, 1 Peter 3:22 Matthew 24:30, Mark 13:26, Luke 21:27; 2 Timothy 4:1, 1 Peter 4:5, Revelation 20:12 Luke 1:33	You do not live for this life only. There is an eternal life of happiness and union with God; Jesus shows you the way to that life of unending justice, love, and peace. Your life will be judged and will have meaning based on how well you have loved others.
We believe in the Holy Spirit, the Lord, the Giver of life, who proceeds from the Father and the Son. With the Father and the Son he is worshiped and glorified.	John 14:26, 2 Corinthians 3:17, John 3:5 John 15:26, John 16:14–15 Matthew 28:19, 1 John 5:7	God is a community of love, three Divine Persons in One. The Holy Spirit is the presence of that loving community of grace in your life, which draws you into holiness, wholeness, and loving relationships with God and others.
He has spoken through the prophets.	2 Peter 1:21	The Scriptures and the teaching authority of the Church speak directly to you, carrying the Good News of God's love. The Holy Spirit helps you grow in love and truth.
We believe in one holy, catholic, and apostolic Church.	Ephesians 4:5, Ephesians 5:27, Colossians 1:5–6, Ephesians 5:27, Colossians 1:5–6, Ephesians 2:20,	You are not alone. You are part of the Christian community, the Church, journeying together in faith, hope, and love.
We acknowledge one Baptism for the forgiveness of sins.	Acts 22:16, Ephesians 4:5	You have been freed from sin through Baptism and called to live a new life in the grace of the sacraments. God's forgiving love is always there for you.
We look for the resurrection of the dead and the life of the world to come. Amen.	John 5:28–29, Acts 24:15, Revelation 21:3–5, Revelation 22:1–5	The future is not to be feared. You can work for justice, love, and peace in this life and look forward in joyful hope to the life of everlasting happiness to come.

The charts on these two pages will help you remember the structure and contents of the Bible.

The Old Testament

Selection/Type	Books	Description
The Torah or Pentateuch	Genesis, Exodus, Leviticus, Numbers, Deuteronomy	The Books of the Law, the story of God's People from the creation of the world through the covenant on Mount Sinai
Historical Books	Joshua, Judges, Ruth, I Samuel, 2 Samuel, I Kings, 2 Kings, I Chronicles, 2 Chronicles, Ezra, Nehemiah, Tobit*, Judith*, Esther**, I Maccabees*, 2 Maccabees*	The religious history of biblical Israel from the arrival in the Promised Land through the return from Exile and the time of the Second Temple
Wisdom Literature	Job, Psalms, Proverbs, Ecclesiastes, Song of Songs, Wisdom*, Sirach*	Poetic works of prayer, practical advice, and religious philosophy
The Prophets	Isaiah, Jeremiah, Lamentations, Baruch*, Ezekiel, Daniel**, Hosea, Joel, Amos, Obadiah, Jonah, Micah, Nahum, Habakkuk, Zephaniah, Haggai, Zechariah, Malachi	The words of the prophets called to speak God's message of reform, justice, and hope before, during, and after the Exile

Why Your Bible May Look Different From Your Friend's

The Old Testament is also known as the Hebrew Scriptures, although the Catholic canon or version of the Bible contains several Old Testament books that are not included in the Jewish Scriptures and are therefore not considered canonical by some Christian denominations. These books are marked with an asterisk (*). Books that contain additional material beyond that in the Jewish canon are marked with two asterisks (**). The organization of the books of the Old Testament in Christian Bibles also differs from that of the Jewish Bible, the Tanakh.

The New Testament

Selection/Type	Books	Description
Gospels	Matthew, Mark, Luke (the Synoptics), John	The life and teachings of Jesus
Acts	Acts of the Apostles	The story of the growth of the early Christian community
Pauline Letters	Romans, I Corinthians, 2 Corinthians, Galatians, Ephesians, Philippians, Colossians, I Thessalonians, 2 Thessalonians, I Timothy, 2 Timothy, Titus, Philemon, Hebrews	Letters by or in the name of Saint Paul, the Church's great missionary to the Gentiles, mostly directed to specific communities or individuals, containing reflections on early Christian theology and advice on living the Christian life
Universal Letters	James, I Peter, 2 Peter, I John, 2 John, 3 John, Jude	Letters directed to the Church as a whole, in the name of the Apostles, conveying key teachings about Christian life
Apocalypse	Revelation	A visionary glimpse of the kingdom of God in its fullness, written to bring hope to early Christians who were suffering persecution

Things to Remember

You should be familiar with these lists—not just the words, but what they mean and how you can live them. Use these pages to refresh your memory.

The Great Commandment

You shall love the Lord, your God, with all your heart, with all your being, with all your strength, and with all your mind, and your neighbor as yourself.

Luke 10:27

The Ten Commandments

Based on the Decalogue, or "ten words," of the Sinai covenant as found in the Book of Exodus:

1. I am the Lord, your God. You shall not have other gods besides me.
2. I shall not take the name of the Lord, your God, in vain.
3. Remember to keep holy the Sabbath day.
4. Honor your father and your mother.
5. You shall not kill.
6. You shall not commit adultery.
7. You shall not steal.
8. You shall not bear false witness against your neighbor.
9. You shall not covet your neighbor's wife.
10. You shall not covet anything that belongs to your neighbor.

The Rules of the Church

1. Take part in the Eucharist every Sunday and holy day. Do no unnecessary work on Sunday.
2. Receive the sacrament of Penance at least once a year.
3. Share in Holy Communion on Sundays, especially during the Easter season.
4. Do penance on the appointed days.
5. Contribute to the support of the Church.

The Gifts of the Holy Spirit

This traditional list of seven gifts is based on Isaiah 11:1–3. The names by which these gifts are known in the contemporary English liturgy are in parentheses.

Wisdom
Understanding
Fortitude (Courage)
Knowledge
Council (Right judgment)
Piety (Reverence)
Fear of the Lord (Wonder and awe)

The Beatitudes

Blessed are the poor in spirit,
    for theirs is the kingdom of heaven.
Blessed are they who mourn,
    for they will be comforted.
Blessed are the meek,
    for they will inherit the land.
Blessed are they who hunger and thirst for righteousness,
    for they will be satisfied.
Blessed are the merciful,
    for they shall be shown mercy.
Blessed are the clean of heart,
    for they shall see God.
Blessed are the peacemakers,
    for they will be called children of God.
Blessed are they who are persecuted for the sake of righteousness,
    for theirs is the kingdom of heaven.

Matthew 5:3–10

Corporal Works of Mercy

Feed the hungry.
Give drink to the thirsty.
Clothe the naked.
Visit the imprisoned.
Shelter the homeless.
Visit the sick.
Bury the dead.

Spiritual Works of Mercy

Admonish the sinner.
Instruct the ignorant.
Counsel the doubtful.
Comfort the sorrowful.
Bear wrongs patiently.
Forgive all injuries.
Pray for the living and the dead.

The Virtues

Virtues are gifts that help you live a moral life. The word *virtue* is rooted in a Latin word for "strength"; virtues are good habits and practices that strengthen your ability to live your faith. Of the many virtues, seven are key.

Cardinal Virtues

Prudence, justice, temperance, and fortitude are called *cardinal* (meaning "hinge") virtues because all other good habits and practices hinge, or depend, on these four. These gifts are also called moral virtues. The more you practice them, the better able you are to live a good moral life.

- **Prudence** is the virtue that helps you make wise choices. A person who is prudent sees the big picture, looks ahead to the consequences of choices, and refuses to be distracted by negative peer pressure. When you are prudent, you take time to weigh your actions and choices.
- **Justice** is the virtue that helps you treat others as you would be treated. A person who is just makes sure that others get what they need and deserve as children of God, even when it means sacrificing their own desires.
- **Temperance** is the virtue that helps you live a life of balance and moderation. A person who is temperate makes proper, not wasteful or abusive, use of God's gifts. When you are temperate, you avoid the temptation to be self-indulgent and to go for instant gratification.
- **Fortitude** is the virtue that helps you stay faithful to your Christian values. A person with fortitude hangs in for the long haul instead of giving up in times of trouble.

Making Moral Decisions

Making the right moral choices is not always easy. The STOP sign can be a reminder of a simple, four-step process that can help you when you are faced with a moral decision.

- **S**top. Take time to consider the choice with which you are faced. Don't just act on impulse or follow the crowd. Take responsibility for your actions.
- **T**hink. Recall what you know about right and wrong. Listen to the guidance of your informed conscience. Use your reasoning ability. If possible, ask the advice of a trusted family member or adult counselor.
- **O**rder your options. You may have several choices; moral decisions are seldom clear cut. Look at the whole picture. What will be the consequences of each choice for you and for others? Which is the best choice given what you know to be right and what the consequences might be?
- **P**ray. Ask the help of the Holy Spirit in making the best moral decision. Then, act on your best choice, taking responsibility for the consequences.

An Examination of Conscience

Use these questions based on the commandments to help you review the moral choices you make each day. You can also use this examination of conscience to prepare for the sacrament of Reconciliation.

1. How well do I show love for God? Is God first in my life, or do other people or things take precedence?

2. How well do I show respect for God's name? When I make promises, do I take them seriously? Is my language respectful?

3. How actively do I participate in the Eucharist? Am I part of my parish community? Do I make time for prayer, spiritual reflection, rest, and renewal?

4. What contribution do I make to my family's happiness? Am I obedient and responsible to parents and other adults who have authority over me? Do I demonstrate love and respect for sisters and brothers and other family members?

5. How well do I show respect for God's gift of life? Do I take care of my health and the well-being of others? Do I steer clear of violence, fighting, alcohol, and drugs? Do I respect and care for people who are ill, disabled, or elderly?

6. How well do I show respect for God's gift of sexuality? Am I modest and chaste in my thoughts, words, and actions? Do I avoid companions, situations, and entertainments that demonstrate disrespect for God's gift of sexuality? Do I show respect for people regardless of their gender?

7. Do I speak and act honestly? Am I a person of integrity? Do I avoid and discourage gossip and teasing? Do I take care of my possessions and respect the property of others? Am I careful to make sure that others receive what is justly theirs?

8. How well do I show gratitude? Do I rejoice in others' successes or run them down out of envy? How generous am I with my time and talents? How strong a hold do material possessions have over me?

You grow in love for God through prayer, worship, and celebration. The resources in this section will help you continue your practice of personal prayer and the communal celebration of the sacraments, especially the Eucharist.

Christian Prayer

Prayer—talking and listening to God—is one of the best ways to show love for God. As a Catholic Christian, you have many opportunities for communal prayer in Mass, the sacraments, and other public liturgy. But you need to make room in your day for personal, private prayer, too. Here are some reminders to help you nourish and develop your prayer life:

- Make use of the whole range of Christian prayer forms. You can talk to God spontaneously, in your own words, or more formally, in the words of a traditional prayer. You can pray by reading Scripture or by singing a hymn. You can pray by working, or playing, or dancing, or crying with your mind on God. You can pray with silence.

- When you pray, find a quiet place in your heart. You do not need to worry about getting rid of all distractions and stray thoughts—that's not possible—but you can learn to simply let them go.

- Take time to get to know God. Your prayer, whether spoken or silent, may be short, but you can still give God your full attention. Allow some time for silence, too, because that is where God often speaks to your heart.

- Talk to God as you would talk to anyone you love. Share the joys and sorrows of your everyday life. God already knows you "by heart," but it can be helpful for you to express your feelings, questions, and reactions to the events of your life in prayer.

- Ask God for help. Remember that God may not answer your prayer in the way you might wish, but God always gives you the answer you need most. Be open to signs of God's presence in your life, seen most often in the loving actions of others. Don't forget to ask God's help for other people, too. You may be the answer to someone else's prayer!

- Remember that you can ask Mary and the saints to join their prayers with yours. You may sometimes feel more comfortable expressing your prayerful request through Mary's motherly care, or asking your patron saint or a saint known for a special activity to intercede for you.

A Treasury of Prayers

The Sign of the Cross

In the name of the Father,
and of the Son,
and of the Holy Spirit.
Amen.

The Lord's Prayer

Our Father, who art in heaven,
hallowed be thy name.
Thy kingdom come.
Thy will be done, on Earth as it is in heaven.
Give us this day our daily bread,
and forgive us our trespasses
as we forgive those who trespass against us.
Lead us not into temptation,
but deliver us from evil.
Amen.

Hail, Mary

Hail, Mary, full of grace,
the Lord is with you.
Blessed are you among women,
and blessed is the fruit
of your womb, Jesus.
Holy Mary, Mother of God,
pray for us sinners,
now and at the hour of our death.
Amen.

Glory to the Father

Glory to the Father,
and to the Son,
and to the Holy Spirit,
as it was in the beginning,
is now, and will be for ever.
Amen.

Prayer to the Holy Spirit

Come, Holy Spirit,
fill the hearts of your faithful
and kindle in them the fire of your love.
Send forth your Spirit and they shall be created,
and you will renew the face of the Earth.
Lord, by the light of the Holy Spirit,
you have taught the hearts of your faithful.
In the same Spirit,
help me to know what is right
and always rejoice in your comfort.
I ask this through Christ the Lord.
Amen.

Morning Prayer

I give to you, my God, this day
all I do or think or say.

Meal Blessing (Grace)

Bless us, O Lord, and these your gifts,
which we are about to receive from your bounty,
through Christ our Lord.
Amen.

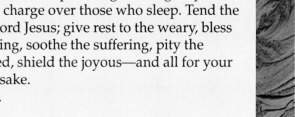

Evening Prayer

Keep watch, dear Lord, with those who work
or watch or weep this night, and give your
angels charge over those who sleep. Tend the
sick, Lord Jesus; give rest to the weary, bless
the dying, soothe the suffering, pity the
afflicted, shield the joyous—and all for your
love's sake.
Amen.

An Act of Contrition

My God, I am sorry for my sins
with all my heart.
In choosing to do wrong
and failing to do good,
I have sinned against you
whom I should love above all things.
I firmly intend, with your help,
to do penance, to sin no more,
and to avoid whatever leads me to sin.
Jesus Christ suffered and died for us.
In his name, dear God, forgive me.
Amen.

An Act of Hope

O my God, relying on your almighty power
and infinite mercy and promises,
I hope to obtain pardon for my sins,
the help of your grace, and life everlasting,
through the merits of Jesus Christ,
my Lord and Redeemer.
Amen.

An Act of Love

O my God, I love you above all things,
with my whole heart and soul, because
you are all-good and worthy of all love.
I love my neighbor as myself for the
love of you. I forgive all who have
injured me and ask pardon of all whom
I have injured.
Amen.

The Jesus Prayer

*This prayer is based on the scriptural pleas
of those who asked Jesus for healing or
forgiveness. Among Russian Orthodox
Christians, these words are prayed as a
silent, repeated invocation timed to the
breathing.*

Lord Jesus Christ,
Son of the living God,
have mercy on me, a sinner.

The Franciscan Peace Prayer

*This popular prayer was composed in the spirit of
Saint Francis of Assisi.*

Lord, make me an instrument of your peace.
Where there is hatred, let me sow love;
    where there is injury, pardon;
    where there is doubt, faith;
    where there is despair, hope;
    where there is darkness, light;
    where there is sadness, joy.
O Divine Master,
grant that I may not so much seek
to be consoled as to console;
to be understood as to understand;
to be loved as to love.
For it is in giving that we receive;
    it is in pardoning that we are pardoned;
    and it is in dying that we are born
        to eternal life.

An Act of Faith

O my God, I firmly believe that you are One God
in three divine Persons, Father, Son, and Holy
Spirit; I believe that your divine Son became
human and died for our sins, and that he will
come to judge the living and the dead. I believe
these and all the truths that the holy Catholic
Church teaches, because you have revealed them,
and you can neither deceive nor be deceived.
Amen.

Scriptural Prayer

The Bible's Book of Psalms is a collection of prayers and hymns flowing from every possible human emotion. As a faithful Jew, Jesus knew and prayed the psalms, as the Christian community continues to do today. You can draw on this great scriptural prayer book for yourself, praying whole psalms or using just a line or two to express thanksgiving, praise, contrition, petition, or intercession. Here are some examples.

In times of joy
You make me jubilant, Lord, by your deeds;
at the works of your hands I shout for joy.
(Psalm 92:5)

In times of trouble
Lord, hear my prayer;
    listen to my cry for help.
In this time of trouble I call,
    for you will answer me. *(Psalm 86:6–7)*

On your birthday
You formed my inmost being;
    you knit me in my mother's womb.
I praise you, so wonderfully you made me;
    wonderful are your works!
(Psalm 139:13–14)

When you have done wrong
Wash away all my guilt;
    from my sin cleanse me. *(Psalm 51:4)*

In thanksgiving
I thank you, Lord, with all my heart;
    I praise your name for your fidelity
    and love. *(Psalm 138:1a, 2b)*

For learning
Lord, teach me the way of your laws;
    I shall observe them with care.
Give me insight to observe your teaching,
    to keep it with all my heart.
(Psalm 119:33–34)

A questioning prayer
Why, Lord, do you stand at a distance
    and pay no heed to these troubled times?
(Psalm 10:1)

For guidance
Show me the path I should walk,
    for to you I entrust my life. *(Psalm 143:8b)*

In injury or illness
I am very near to falling;
    my pain is with me always.
Forsake me not, O Lord;
    my God, be not far from me!
(Psalm 38:18, 22)

At night
Praise the Lord from the heavens;
    give praise in the heights.
Praise him, sun and moon;
    give praise, all shining stars.
(Psalm 148:1, 3)

In fear or sorrow
Fear and trembling overwhelm me;
    shuddering sweeps over me.
But I will call upon God,
    and the Lord will save me.
(Psalm 55:6, 17)

A daily prayer of praise
From the rising of the sun to its setting
    let the name of the Lord be praised.
(Psalm 113:3)

Marian Prayers

In Catholic tradition, Mary offers a mother's listening ear and loving care to all followers of Jesus. These ancient prayers, commonly known by their Latin names, ask Mary to intercede with her Son on behalf of those in sorrow and distress.

Memorare (Remember)

Remember, O most gracious Virgin Mary, that never was it known that anyone who fled to thy protection, implored thy help, or sought thy intercession was left unaided. Inspired by this confidence, I fly unto thee, O Virgin of Virgins, my Mother. To thee do I come, before thee I stand, sinful and sorrowful. O Mother of the Word Incarnate, despise not my petition, but in thy mercy hear and answer me. Amen.

The Angelus

This responsorial prayer is traditionally prayed at dawn, at noon, and at dusk. Church bells mark the hours of prayer.

V: The angel of the Lord declared unto Mary.

R: And she conceived of the Holy Spirit. *(Hail, Mary)*

V: Behold the handmaid of the Lord.

R: Be it done unto me according to your Word. *(Hail, Mary)*

V: And the Word was made flesh.

R: And dwelt among us. *(Hail, Mary)*

V: Pray for us, O holy Mother of God.

R: That we may be made worthy of the promises of Christ.

V: Let us pray. Pour forth, O Lord, your grace into our hearts, that we, to whom the incarnation of Christ, your Son, was made known by the message of an angel, may by his passion and cross be brought to the glory of his resurrection, through the same Christ our Lord.

R: Amen.

Praying the Rosary

The traditional prayer form known as the rosary combines prayers counted off on beads with meditation on the mysteries, or key events and themes, of the lives of Jesus and his mother, Mary.

The Mysteries of the Rosary

The mysteries of the rosary are traditionally grouped by theme. These themes and events can also be found in your own life, as this chart shows. You may find it helpful to connect your praying of the rosary to the "mysteries" of your life.

The Joyful Mysteries

Mystery	What It Recalls	In Your Life
Annunciation	Mary says yes to God's call to be the mother of Jesus.	Beginning a new ministry, finding a new way to use your gifts
Visitation	Mary visits her cousin Elizabeth.	Visiting a relative or friend, helping a neighbor, cheering someone who is ill
Nativity	Jesus is born in Bethlehem.	Celebrating a birth or a birthday
Presentation	Mary and Joseph take their baby to the Temple for the first time.	Celebrating a baptism or baptismal anniversary, caring for a baby
Finding in the Temple	Jesus is reunited with his family after leaving them to teach in the Temple.	Recovering a relationship you thought was lost, forgiving and being forgiven

The Mysteries of Light

Mystery	What It Recalls	In Your Life
Baptism in the Jordan	Jesus is baptized by John and begins his public ministry.	Celebrating confirmation, taking on new responsibilities
Wedding at Cana	Jesus performs his first public miracle at Mary's request at a wedding.	Celebrating a wedding or anniversary, enjoying family life, having a party
Proclamation of the Kingdom	Jesus teaches, heals, forgives, and proclaims the coming of God's kingdom.	Sharing faith, teaching and learning, making good choices, healing
Transfiguration	Jesus is revealed in glory as God's Son to the disciples Peter, James and John.	Gaining insight into yourself and others, supporting one another's gifts
First Eucharist	On the night before he is to die, Jesus institutes the Eucharist.	Celebrating community, sharing meals and banquets, reaching out to those in need

The Sorrowful Mysteries

Mystery	What It Recalls	In Your Life
Agony in the Garden	Jesus prays and commits himself to his Father's will just before his arrest.	Praying for your own needs and the needs of others, learning to trust in God
Scourging	Jesus is whipped and beaten.	Living with the reality of suffering
Crowning With Thorns	Jesus is painfully mocked and humiliated.	Dealing with embarrassment; working to end gossip, exclusion, and harassment
Way of the Cross	Jesus carries his cross to the place of execution, followed by angry crowds.	Bearing your own and others' burdens, standing up for your beliefs in public
Crucifixion	Jesus suffers and dies on the cross.	Letting go, mourning loss and death

The Glorious Mysteries

Mystery	What It Recalls	In Your Life
Resurrection	Jesus is raised from death and appears to his friends in his glorified body.	Celebrating new life and fresh starts, being hopeful, sharing joy and peace
Ascension	Jesus commissions the disciples and returns to his Father in heaven.	Living your faith every day, listening for your vocation
Pentecost	The Holy Spirit comes to the Apostles, who carry Jesus' message to the world.	Having courage, being spirited, sharing good news, communicating across boundaries
Assumption	Mary is taken body and soul to heaven at the end of her life.	Caring for and nurturing human life and bodily health
Coronation	Jesus acknowledges his mother as Queen of Heaven and model of Christian life.	Having healthy self-respect, celebrating others' accomplishments

The Liturgical Year

Liturgy is the public prayer of the Church. Catholics celebrate according to a liturgical calendar that divides the year into seasons and feasts that commemorate the great events in the life of Jesus and of Mary, his mother. Each Sunday, major feast, daily Mass, or commemoration of a saint has its own readings and prayers, so that throughout the year, Catholics celebrate the whole cycle of faith. The Church Year begins not on January 1 but on the First Sunday of Advent and runs through the last Sunday of Ordinary Time. Ordinary Time, by the way, isn't ordinary in the usual sense; this two-part season of the year gets its name from the fact that the Sundays are numbered in sequence (using ordinal numbers).

Church Feasts

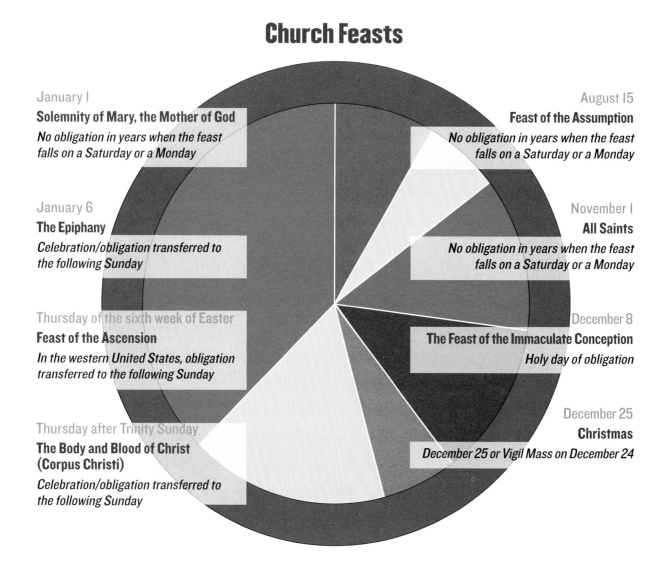

January 1
Solemnity of Mary, the Mother of God
No obligation in years when the feast falls on a Saturday or a Monday

January 6
The Epiphany
Celebration/obligation transferred to the following Sunday

Thursday of the sixth week of Easter
Feast of the Ascension
In the western United States, obligation transferred to the following Sunday

Thursday after Trinity Sunday
The Body and Blood of Christ (Corpus Christi)
Celebration/obligation transferred to the following Sunday

August 15
Feast of the Assumption
No obligation in years when the feast falls on a Saturday or a Monday

November 1
All Saints
No obligation in years when the feast falls on a Saturday or a Monday

December 8
The Feast of the Immaculate Conception
Holy day of obligation

December 25
Christmas
December 25 or Vigil Mass on December 24

Holy Days of Obligation

Easter is always a Sunday, but there are other great feasts of the Church that fall on various days according to the calendar. Catholics are obliged to participate in the Eucharist on these feasts, known as **holy days of obligation.** Conferences of bishops in various countries and regions have the authority to determine which feasts (Easter and Christmas) are to be celebrated as holy days of obligation, when they are to be celebrated, and when the obligation applies. In the United States, the holy days of obligation are shown in the chart.

Advent

The season of Advent is three-dimensional—it celebrates the past, present, and future of faith. The word *Advent* means "coming," and Advent is definitely a season of anticipation. During the four weeks of Advent, Christians prepare prayerfully for the coming of Jesus.

The Three Dimensions of Advent

Past   Readings from the Hebrew Scriptures recall the longing of God's People for the coming of the Messiah promised by God. Christians believe that the words of the prophets foretold the coming of Jesus.

Present   By making time for prayer, reflection, and works of justice amid the rush and commercialization of the season, Christians prepare to celebrate Christmas, the Feast of the Nativity of Jesus.

Future   New Testament readings and the prayers of the Mass look forward "in joyful hope" to the Second Coming of Jesus, when God's kingdom of justice, love, and peace will be established in its fullness.

Advent Feasts

Three important feasts fall within the Advent season:

• The feast day of Saint Nicholas (December 6) honors the Turkish bishop whose goodness and charity toward young people made him acclaimed as the patron saint of children. According to Dutch custom, Saint Nicholas brings gifts to children in honor of the Christ Child. Dutch immigrants to the United States brought the custom of gift giving in the name of *Sinter Klaus*—now known far and wide as Santa Claus.

• The Feast of the Immaculate Conception (December 8) honors Mary as the Holy Mother who was preserved from original sin from the moment of conception in her mother's womb.

• The feast day of Our Lady of Guadalupe (December 12) honors Mary under the title by which she is especially honored in Mexico and the southwestern United States. According to tradition, Mary appeared to a Mexican Indian named Juan Diego, declaring her special love and protection for those suffering under colonial oppression. Under the title of Our Lady of Guadalupe, Mary is the Patroness of the Americas.

The Christmas Season

Christmas—the celebration of the birth of Christ—is more than just one day in the year. Rather than signaling the end of a season of material hype and frenzy, Christmas Day is the beginning of a season that celebrates God's living Word made flesh.

The Christmas season begins with the Vigil Mass on Christmas Eve. Here, the message of Jesus' birth is proclaimed as it was to the shepherds.

The celebration continues on Christmas Day, the Feast of the Nativity of Jesus, and goes on even longer than the "twelve days of Christmas" celebrated in the old carol.

Among the feasts that fall within the Christmas season are

- The feast day of Saint Stephen (December 26). As the Church's first martyr, the deacon Stephen is honored on the day after Christmas. This is the "feast of Stephen" mentioned in the carol "Good King Wenceslaus"; December 26 is traditionally a day to show gratitude for God's blessings by giving material help to those in need.

- The feast of the Holy Innocents (December 28). This feast honors the nameless children killed by Herod's armies in a vain attempt to eliminate Jesus. On this day, Catholic Christians pray and work for all innocent victims of violence, including refugees, orphans, and the unborn.

- The Solemnity of Mary, Mother of God (January 1). On the calendar New Year's Day, Catholics celebrate Mary, whose Yes to God's will made every year a new year.

- The Feast of the Holy Family (the Sunday after Christmas). This feast celebrates the love and faith of Mary, Joseph, and Jesus and of families everywhere.

- Epiphany (January 6). This feast, now celebrated on the Sunday following January 6, recalls the visit of the Magi to Jesus' family. The word *epiphany* means "revelation"; this feast recalls one of the first revelations of Jesus to the world, symbolically represented by the "wise men from the East."

- The Baptism of the Lord (Sunday after Epiphany). This feast recalls another revelation of Jesus' role and mission, his baptism by John in the Jordan River.

Lent

This forty-day period of penitential preparation recalls the time Jesus spent in the wilderness, praying and fasting in preparation for his public ministry. During Lent, the followers of Jesus prepare for their great work of proclaiming the Good News of the Resurrection by spending time in prayer, practicing the spiritual disciplines of fasting and abstinence, participating in the sacrament of Reconciliation, and taking action to meet the needs of the poor and the oppressed.

The timing of Lent, like that of many other seasons and feasts, depends on the date chosen for Easter. Lent begins 40 days before Easter, on the day known as Ash Wednesday, from the custom of being signed with blessed ashes as a mark of penitence.

The word *Lent* comes from an old English word for "lengthen," because Lent occurs as the winter days begin to get longer and the Earth moves toward spring. Just as spring is often a season of housecleaning and physical refreshment, Lent is a season of spiritual renewal.

During Lent, adults and children of catechetical age who are preparing to celebrate the sacraments of initiation at the Easter Vigil participate in a special series of liturgies, accompanied on this last stage of their faith journey by the whole parish community.

The last week of Lent is known as Holy Week. Passion Sunday, the sixth Sunday of Lent, begins in joy with the commemoration of Jesus' triumphant entry into Jerusalem. The assembly waves palm branches and walks in procession. But the mood quickly turns somber as the gospel account of Jesus' Passion is proclaimed, recalling the last days of Jesus' life.

The Sacred Triduum

These three holiest days of the Church Year begin at sundown on the Thursday of Holy Week and continue through Evening Prayer on Easter Sunday.

- The Mass on Holy Thursday evening recalls the institution of the Eucharist at the Last Supper. Following the example of Jesus, parish ministers wash the feet of those whom they are called to serve.

- On Good Friday, the Church commemorates the day Jesus was crucified with a solemn liturgical celebration that includes prayers for the needs of the world, penitential hymns, Holy Communion, and veneration of the cross.

- On Holy Saturday evening, the sorrowful reflection of Good Friday moves into the joy of the resurrection with the Easter Vigil celebration. After blessing the new fire and greeting the Paschal candle, the story of salvation as told in the Hebrew Scriptures is proclaimed. The elect are baptized, confirmed, and invited to receive their First Eucharist. As the Gospel of the Resurrection is proclaimed, joyful Alleluias ring out for the first time since Ash Wednesday.

From Maryknoll

The Easter Season

Easter

This great, central feast commemorates the Resurrection of Jesus Christ and begins the seven-week Easter season. The name *Easter* comes from an Old English word for springtime feast, because Easter is always celebrated in the season of new life. Easter is a moveable feast; it does not fall on the same date every year but is calculated according to the natural calendars of the seasons and the cycle of the moon. Easter falls on the first Sunday after the first full moon after the spring equinox—generally falling within the month-long period between late March and late April. (Orthodox Christians use a slightly different formula for calculating the date of Easter, so it may not always coincide with Western celebrations.) This calendar echoes the timing of the Jewish feast of Passover, with which Easter is linked both historically and symbolically. In many European languages, the name for the Feast of the Resurrection echoes this connection (in French, *Pasque,* in Spanish, *Pascua*).

The Mass of Easter Sunday is the pattern for every Sunday Eucharist, because every Sunday is a "little Easter." Catholics are required to receive Holy Communion at least once a year, during the season of Easter.

The Feast of the Ascension

This feast recalling Jesus' return to his Father in heaven is traditionally celebrated forty days after Easter. (Remember that forty days is a symbolic length of time commonly used in Scripture to describe periods of intense encounter with God, such as Jesus' forty days in the wilderness.) Because this holy day of obligation falls on a Thursday, the obligation to attend Mass has been transferred to the previous or following Sunday in some parts of the world.

Pentecost

The Easter season concludes with the Feast of Pentecost, the seventh Sunday after Easter. This feast recalls the sending of the Holy Spirit to the Apostles and the beginning of their ministry of sharing the Good News. Pentecost is often celebrated as the "birthday of the Church." The red vestments and altar coverings recall the tongues of flame that symbolized the presence of the Holy Spirit. The name *Pentecost* is Greek for "fiftieth"; this same name was given to the Jewish feast (known in Hebrew as Shavuot) that celebrates the presentation of the first fruits of the spring harvest at the Temple. The crowds to whom the Apostles preached were gathered in Jerusalem for the Jewish feast of Pentecost.

The Sacraments

The sacraments are signs and sources of the relationship of grace between God and humans. The Church celebrates seven sacraments, each flowing from the ministry of Jesus and marking an important encounter with the divine in human life.

Through these sacraments, you become a full member of the Church, the Body of Christ.

Sacraments of Initiation

Sacrament	Sign	Minister	Effect
Baptism	Water, invocation of the Trinity	Ordained minister or (in an emergency) any baptized Christian	Celebrates belonging to the Christian community; cleanses original sin and all personal sin; makes a person a member of the Church
Confirmation	Hands over candidate's head, anointing with chrism	Bishop or priest	Celebrates the presence of the Holy Spirit; seals the candidate with the Gift of the Holy Spirit
Eucharist	Bread and wine	Priest	Celebrates Jesus' presence; invites the person to share in the Mass and receive Jesus in Holy Communion; forgives venial sin; increases grace.

Sacraments of Healing

Sacrament	Sign	Minister	Effect
Reconciliation (Penance)	Hands over penitent's head, prayer of absolution	Priest	Celebrates God's forgiving love; absolves penitent of all sin; restores sanctifying grace; strengthens person to live a better life
Anointing of the Sick	Anointing with oil	Priest	Celebrates Jesus' healing mission; offers spiritual and sometimes physical healing in time of illness or infirmity

Sacraments of Service to the Community

Sacrament	Sign	Minister	Effect
Marriage	Vows, ring	Spouses (witnessed by the priest and the community)	Celebrates human love; unites a man and a woman in a lifelong relationship of fidelity; begins a new family
Holy Orders	Laying on of hands, anointing with chrism	Bishop	Celebrates the call to ministry; ordains a man to the ministry of deacon, priest, or bishop

The Mass

The Eucharistic celebration is the center and source of Christian life. Instituted by Jesus at the Last Supper on the night before he died, the Eucharist is the chief way that Catholics gather to worship and give thanks to God, to share in the sacrificial actions of Jesus, and to receive Jesus in Holy Communion. The word *Mass* comes from the last action of the Eucharistic celebration, the dismissal, in which you are sent forth to live the Eucharist in your daily life.

Catholics are required by the commandments and by Church law to participate in the Mass on Sundays and on holy days of obligation. (The Sunday Mass obligation can be met by attendance at a Saturday evening Eucharist.) But obligation should be the last reason you need for choosing to go to Mass. From this investment of about an hour a week, given gladly and with full participation, you receive many blessings: the presence of Jesus in your life, the grace to overcome bad habits and make good moral choices, and the strength and support of belonging to a community of faith.

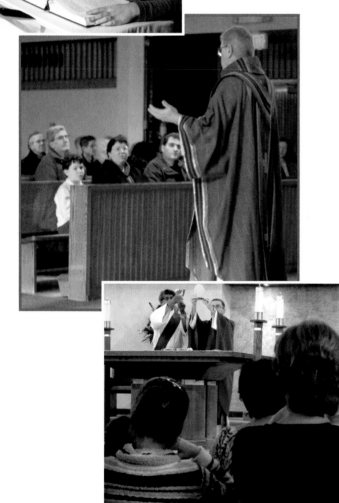

Words for Life

You are called not only to know about your faith and to love God, but also to put your knowledge and love into action by serving others and witnessing to God's kingdom of justice, love, and peace.

The teachings of Jesus should be on the tip of your tongue. Here are some of the things Jesus said about being a person of service and Christian witness.

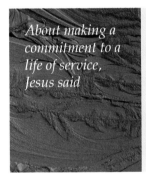

About making a commitment to a life of service, Jesus said

Whoever wishes to come after me must deny himself, take up his cross, and follow me. For whoever wishes to save his life will lose it, but whoever loses his life for my sake and that of the gospel will save it. What profit is there for one to gain the whole world and forfeit his life? *(Mark 8:34–36)*

About serving with generosity and willingness, Jesus said

Should anyone press you into service for one mile, go with him for two miles. Give to the one who asks of you, and do not turn your back on one who wants to borrow. *(Matthew 5:42–43)*

About including those that others leave out, Jesus said

When you hold a banquet, invite the poor, the crippled, the lame, the blind; blessed indeed will you be because of their inability to repay you. For you will be repaid at the resurrection of the righteous. *(Luke 14:13–14)*

About eliminating grudges and feuds, Jesus said

Be merciful, just as your Father is merciful. Stop judging and you will not be judged. Stop condemning and you will not be condemned. Forgive and you will be forgiven. *(Luke 6:36–37)*

About putting love of God and the needs of people before material possessions, Jesus said

Take care to guard against all greed, for though one may be rich, one's life does not consist of possessions. *(Luke 12:15)*

About having a balanced self-image, Jesus said

For everyone who exalts himself will be humbled, but the one who humbles himself will be exalted. *(Luke 14:11)*

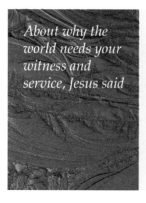 **From Maryknoll**

About not considering yourself too good to serve others, Jesus said

If I, therefore, the master and teacher, have washed your feet, you ought to wash one another's feet. I have given you a model to follow, so that as I have done for you, you should also do. *(John 13:14–15)*

About why the world needs your witness and service, Jesus said

You are the light of the world. A city set on a mountain cannot be hidden. Nor do they light a lamp and then put it under a bushel basket; it is set on a lampstand, where it gives light to all in the house. Just so, your light must shine before others, that they may see your good deeds and glorify your heavenly Father. *(Matthew 5:14–16)*

Seven Principles of Justice

Christian service and witness are rooted in the Church's teachings on personal and social justice. These teachings have been summarized by the U. S. Catholic Bishops in the form of seven principles, which you can use to guide your actions and choices.

1. **Justice is respect for the life and dignity of the human person.** The Catholic Church proclaims that life is sacred. The dignity of the human person, created in God's image, is the foundation of law and morality. Any direct attack on innocent human life, such as abortion or euthanasia, is seriously wrong.

2. **Justice is a call to active participation in family and community.** The family is the heart of society, and every person has the right and the duty to participate in society. Excessive individualism is contrary to the Gospel.

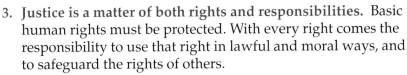
From Maryknoll

3. **Justice is a matter of both rights and responsibilities.** Basic human rights must be protected. With every right comes the responsibility to use that right in lawful and moral ways, and to safeguard the rights of others.

4. **Justice is exercising a "preferential option" for the poor and vulnerable.** When resources are scarce, justice requires that those in the greatest need be served first. The needs of those deprived of power by poverty or made vulnerable by age, illness, disability, or any other condition must take precedence.

5. **Justice is respect for the dignity of work and the rights of workers.** Concern for the economic bottom line can never outweigh the need to protect the rights of workers to organize, to receive just wages, and to labor in safety.

6. **Justice is acting in solidarity with the whole human family.** The human community is not limited by local or national boundaries. Catholics are called to work for the common good of all people and the peace of the world.

7. **Justice is caring for God's creation.** God made humans stewards of creation. Earth's fragile and limited resources must be protected, cared for, and shared justly.

Listening to the Shepherds

The pope and the bishops, the teaching authority of the Church, often speak to current issues and the need for service, guiding you in your mission to serve. This page contains a sampling of thought-provoking reflections.

The Pope Speaks

These reflections are drawn from various encyclicals and pastoral statements of Pope John Paul II.

On home as the place where all service begins:
To maintain a joyful family requires much from both parents and children. Each member of the family has to become, in a special way, the servant of the others.

On the special mission of Americans:
Radical changes in world politics leave America with a heightened responsibility to be, for the world, an example of a genuinely free, democratic, just, and humane society.

On the best means to peace:
Humanity should question itself, once more, about the absurd and always unfair phenomenon of war, on whose stage of death and pain nothing remains standing but the negotiating table that could and should have prevented it.

The Bishops Speak

These reflections are drawn from various pastoral letters and policy statements issued by the U. S. Catholic Bishops.

On the just use of material resources:
While the poor often have too little, others of us can be easily caught up in a frenzy of wanting more and more—a bigger home, a larger car, and so on. We need to ask about ways we can conserve energy, prevent pollution, and live more simply.

On seeking alternatives to violence in society:
We oppose capital punishment, not just for what it does to those guilty of horrible crimes, but for how it affects society; moreover, we have alternative means today to protect society from violent people.

On embracing diversity in the Church and the world:
The Church of the twenty-first century will be, as it has always been, a Church of many cultures, languages, and traditions, yet simultaneously one, as God is one—Father, Son, and Holy Spirit—unity in diversity.

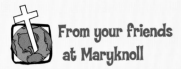

From your friends at Maryknoll

Faith in a Factory Town

When Jesús Manuel Aldaba Soto was just starting his teen years, life for him and his family changed dramatically. In search of a better life, the family moved from a small town in the Mexican state of Durango to Ciudad Juárez, a city of more than two million residents that lies on the Texas border with the United States. Looking back, fifteen-year-old Jesús acknowledges that it's been a difficult adjustment for everyone—his parents, Ascensión and Candelaria, and his two younger sisters, fourteen-year-old Lucia and eight-year-old Guadalupe, as well as Jesús himself. The whole family misses its small farm in the countryside and the close-knit community of its old village. "We couldn't have made it through all these changes," Jesús insists, "if it weren't for our faith and the help of the Virgin."

Jesús is referring to the Virgin of Guadalupe, a title under which Mary is especially known and loved by the Mexican people. A copy of her miraculous image hangs over the family dinner table here in Ciudad Juárez. When their parents are away at work, Jesús and his sisters don't feel alone, because the Virgin of Guadalupe is with them, a part of the family.

Still, Jesús admits, "We don't see our parents enough." They both work at one of the four hundred assembly plants, known as *maquiladoras*, that have sprouted up in the area in recent years. The factory where Jesús' parents work has 250,000 employees—a workforce many times larger than the population of the family's home village. His parents work from 3:30 in the afternoon to midnight, and they each make $3.50 an hour.

That may not sound like much, but to families like Jesús', it is the difference between devastating poverty and a good, if modest, life. Through hard work, the family now lives in a house with running water and electricity. Jesús says that his parents, like other *maquiladora* workers, are grateful for the work, though they are well aware that U.S. companies opened the factories so they could boost their profits by paying Mexican workers less than they would have to pay in the U.S. labor market.

Faith helps sustain Jesús and his family as they struggle with the changes that the move has brought, including these questions of economic justice. Faith has helped the family build new bonds of community in the big, anonymous city. Jesús will benefit from these new ties; he is one of fifty-seven students who will receive a college scholarship from a fund established by the faith community in Ciudad Juárez. "Faith and the Virgin" have taken Jesús' family far, and the journey continues.

We saw his glory, the glory as of the Father's only Son, full of grace and truth.

John 1:14b

Bangladesh From Maryknoll

Jesus the Christ

Chapter

WHO IS Jesus?

Who Are You, Really?

You are at a time in your life when you are experiencing many changes. These changes are bringing you closer to the adult person you soon will be. Right now, your identity is often tied to your parents, other members of your family, teachers, and your friends. On the chart, write one way each group of people might describe you. In the last box, identify yourself as you think you really are.

Who do your parents or family members say you are?

Who do your teachers say you are?

Who do your friends say you are?

Who do _you_ say you are?

Blessed be the Lord, the God of Israel, for he has visited and brought redemption to his people.

Luke 1:68

Do You Know?

◆ Who is Jesus Christ, and why is knowing about Jesus so important for Catholic Christians?

Peter's Answer

When Jesus was on earth, he often gave a very simple invitation to those he met. "Follow me," he said. People dropped everything and followed him. Those who followed Jesus were called his **disciples.**

Jesus and his disciples were traveling about in a region of Palestine known as Caesarea Philippi. The disciples had just seen Jesus take five loaves of bread and a few fish and feed about four thousand people. They had been talking among themselves about Jesus and the wonders of his teaching and of his actions. All at once, Jesus turned and asked them a very curious question.

"Who do people say that the Son of Man is?"

They replied, "Some say John the Baptist, others Elijah, still others Jeremiah or one of the prophets."

He said to them, "But who do you say that I am?"

Simon Peter said in reply, "You are the Messiah, the Son of the living God."

Jesus said to him in reply, "Blessed are you, Simon son of Jonah. For flesh and blood has not revealed this to you, but my heavenly Father. And so I say to you, you are Peter, and upon this rock I will build my church and the gates of the netherworld shall not prevail against it."

Matthew 16: 13–18

Dialog Box

◆ How would you have answered Jesus if you had been traveling with the disciples? Why?

◆ What does Peter's answer mean to you?

Meeting Jesus

While Jesus of Nazareth was on earth, he came into contact with many people. The people came to know Jesus through his actions, his teaching, and the way he related to people. Those who came in contact with Jesus were changed in one way or another. This year you will be coming in contact with Jesus and learning more and more about him. You are old enough to be making decisions about what you do, about who you are, and about who you will become. You are invited to be an active and faithful follower of Jesus.

WORD OF GOD

I am the way and the truth and the life.

John 14:6

? What questions about Jesus would you like to have answered this year?

VIRTUE

Compassion means showing your love for others by being aware of their needs, understanding their feelings, and trying to help.

†HIS WE BELIEVE!

Jesus is true God and true man.

Who Is This Jesus?

Every Sunday at Mass, the whole faith community recites the **Nicene Creed.** In that creed, you profess that you believe some very specific things about Jesus. The words are very familiar, but it can take a whole lifetime to learn their meaning. This year, you will get very serious about learning more and more about Jesus, about his teaching, and about the ways that you can show that you are his disciple.

ACTIVITY

Read through the Creed. Circle everything that tells you something about Jesus. On a separate piece of paper, using your own words, make a list of everything you know about Jesus from the Creed.

The Nicene Creed

We believe in one God, the Father, the Almighty, maker of heaven and earth, of all that is seen and unseen.

We believe in one Lord, Jesus Christ, the only Son of God, eternally begotten of the Father. God from God, Light from Light, true God from true God, begotten, not made, one in Being with the Father. Through him all things were made.

For us and for our salvation he came down from heaven; by the power of the Holy Spirit he was born of the Virgin Mary, and became man.

For our sake he was crucified under Pontius Pilate; he suffered, died, and was buried. On the third day he rose again in fulfillment of the Scriptures; he ascended into heaven and is seated at the right hand of the Father. He will come again to judge the living and the dead, and his kingdom will have no end.

We believe in the Holy Spirit, the Lord, the giver of life, who proceeds from the Father and the Son. With the Father and the Son he is worshiped and glorified. He has spoken through the Prophets.

We believe in one, holy, catholic, and apostolic Church. We acknowledge one baptism for the forgiveness of sins. We look for the resurrection of the dead, and the life of the world to come.

Amen.

Live and Learn

You already know a lot about Jesus. During the course of this year, you will be learning that following Jesus is something you do every day.

How can you get to know Jesus better? Look at the list below. How can the following help you? Write down some ideas for each suggestion.

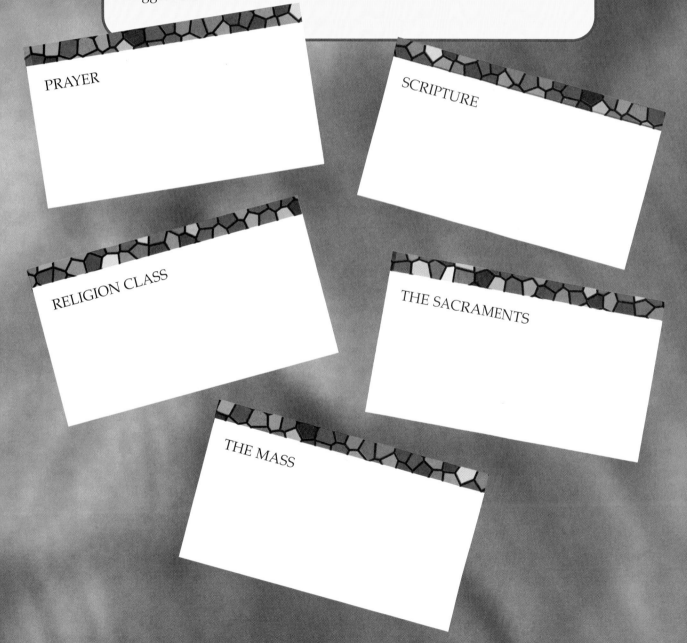

PRAYER

SCRIPTURE

RELIGION CLASS

THE SACRAMENTS

THE MASS

Meeting Jesus

Leader: Let us begin in the name of the Father, and of the Son, and of the Holy Spirit.

All: Amen.

Leader: Jesus, coming to know you is a lifelong journey. Our faith is built on meeting you and in responding to your call to follow you. Show us the way.

All: Amen.

Reader: A reading from the Gospel of Matthew.

All: Praise to you Lord Jesus Christ.

Reader 1: (Read Matthew 4:18–22. All pause for quiet reflection.)

Leader: Jesus, you call each of us by name and say, "Come, after me." We pray for the courage and faith to do so.

Reader 2: Jesus, sometimes it's hardest to see you in the people who are closest to us. Help us to meet you in the good and bad times of our family life.

All: Jesus, you are our friend and brother.

Reader 3: Jesus, your family was loyal to its Jewish beliefs and traditions. Help our lives to be grounded in Scripture so that we come to know your will.

All: Jesus, you are our teacher.

Reader 4: Jesus, we know who you are by the things you said and did while on Earth. We pray that others come to know you through our words and actions.

All: Jesus, you are the Way.

Reader 5: Jesus, we come to know you through the sacraments, the signs of your love. May we see the sacraments as ways to welcome you into our lives.

All: Jesus, you are our life.

Leader: Let us now reflect on the specific ways you can get to know Jesus better during this year. Write your pledge to Jesus.

The exercises and activities on this page will help you know, love, and serve God better.

Know

Learning About Jesus

Forms you

As a person | As a Catholic | As a Christian

Love

What have you done this week to learn more about Jesus? Write three examples.

1. _____

_____

2. _____

_____

3. _____

_____

Serve

What have you done this week to show others that you know Jesus? Write two examples.

1. _____

_____

2. _____

_____

Heroes of Faith

Hans and Sophie Scholl

In 1942, leaflets signed *The White Rose*, encouraging people to oppose Hitler and his regime, began to appear all over Munich. Hans and Sophie Scholl, a brother and a sister, were members of *The White Rose*. They were also devout Christians. They believed that the struggle against Hitler was the duty of all Christians. Eventually, Hans and Sophie were arrested and sentenced to death. They met their fate with bravery and faith that they would enjoy eternal life.

These projects and activities will help you keep this lesson alive all week long.

On your own

Test what you already know about Jesus. Write one thing Jesus said about love, and name one story Jesus told about forgiveness.

_____

_____

_____

_____

_____

_____

With others

With a friend, talk about the lessons you have learned through Jesus' teachings. Explain how those lessons have helped the two of you be better friends.

_____

_____

_____

With your family

Talk about how knowing Jesus has shaped your family. How does knowing Jesus help you in making family decisions? How does knowing Jesus help your family through difficult times?

_____

_____

_____

_____

_____

Jesus, help me to give my very best this year as I learn more about you.

GO ONLINE!
www.mhbenziger.com

The Son

> And Jesus advanced in wisdom and age and favor before God and man.
>
> *Luke 2:52*

Passing It On

Lily Clare is named for her two grandmothers. Everyone says she looks just like her grandmother Lily and acts just like her grandmother Clare. Lily Clare's cousin Jessie doesn't look like anyone in her family because she was adopted. But Jessie and Lily Clare spend so much time together that everyone says they could be sisters. They both love running cross-country, and they tell the same jokes.

Family members pass along many traits and characteristics to new generations. Some of these gifts are transmitted genetically. Others—like attitudes, traditions, faith, and values—are passed on by influence and example. Some traits—like a talent for basketball in a family full of readers—can only be traced to God's generosity.

Think of the gifts that have been passed on to you—genetically or by influence—from family members, and those that have come from God to make you uniquely who you are. Write about one trait or gift in each of the gift boxes below. If you know the source of the family traits, fill in the family members' names on the blank lines.

Do You Know?

◆ How do family members help shape your life?

◆ How did Jesus' family help shape his life?

From _____, genetically

From _____, by influence

From God

Family Values

Like you, Jesus grew up in a family. He had grandparents and great-grandparents. He had a human mother and a human adoptive father. The stories that Jesus heard about his family history and the values of the family's Jewish faith shaped Jesus.

His immediate family had a great influence on Jesus. Mary was only a young teen when God chose her to be the mother of Jesus. By saying a wholehearted "Yes" to the angel's good news, even though it must have been confusing and frightening, Mary allowed God's saving plan to be fulfilled.

Little is known of Joseph, the man who loved and supported Mary and her child. Jesus was known as "the carpenter's son," so Joseph was probably a skilled craftsman who worked with wood. What we do know is that he cared for his family and protected them through troubled times.

The Bible does not share many details about the daily life of this **Holy Family,** but it seems clear that Mary's strong faith and Joseph's compassionate care rubbed off on their son. You can see these qualities at work in Jesus' healing and forgiving actions, the way he reached out to the needy, and his own deep faith and trust in God his Father.

Dialog Box

◆ Why do you think the Gospels include stories about Jesus' human family, Mary and Joseph?

◆ What qualities did Mary and Joseph possess that made them the right people to shape young Jesus' life? How do you know that Mary and Joseph had these qualities?

Growing Pains

Family members can have a positive influence on one another, even in times of conflict. Luke's Gospel tells us a story from Jesus' adolescence—a time when misunderstandings can crop up in the best of families.

At twelve, Jesus was old enough to travel for the first time from Nazareth to Jerusalem, to celebrate the Jewish feast of Passover. He must have been excited about the journey, eager to take this first step into adulthood and the life to which God was calling him. To Mary and Joseph, however, Jesus was still their little boy.

WORD OF GOD

"Where did this man get such wisdom and mighty deeds? Is he not the carpenter's son? Is not his mother named Mary?"

Matthew 13:54–55

As they were returning, the boy Jesus remained behind in Jerusalem, but his parents did not know it. Thinking that he was in the caravan, they journeyed for a day and looked for him among their relatives and acquaintances, but not finding him, they returned to Jerusalem to look for him. After three days they found him in the temple, sitting in the midst of the teachers, listening to them and asking them questions, and all who heard him were astounded at his understanding and his answers. When his parents saw him, they were astonished, and his mother said to him, "Son, why have you done this to us? Your father and I have been looking for you with great anxiety." And he said to them, "Why were you looking for me? Did you not know that I must be in my Father's house?" But they did not understand what he said to them. He went down with them and came to Nazareth, and was obedient to them.

Luke 2:43–51

What did Jesus and his family learn about each other through this experience?

THIS WE BELIEVE!

Jesus grew up in a human family. His life was shaped by his family's Jewish heritage.

Jesus' Family Tree

The Gospels of Matthew and Luke contain **genealogies**—family trees that trace Jesus' ancestry to the great men and women of the Hebrew Scriptures. Jesus grew up hearing the stories of these heroic relatives.

As a Catholic Christian, you share this family tree with Jesus. How much do you know about these ancestors in faith?

God made a covenant, or sacred promise of relationship, with Abraham and his wife Sarah. They became parents very late in life, and their descendants became God's Chosen People of Israel.

Ruth was an outsider. When her husband died, she could have stayed in her own country, Moab. But Ruth loved her Israelite mother-in-law, Naomi, and honored Naomi's God. In Israel, Ruth found a new love and became the great-grandmother of Israel's greatest king.

David, the great-grandson of Ruth, united the twelve tribes of Israel into a strong nation. David juggled many opposites in his life—he was a shepherd and a king, a musician and a military leader, a great sinner and a man consumed with love for God. Jesus' family traced its roots to "the house of David."

ACTIVITY

Use your Bible to find out about one of these ancestors in faith. Tell what characteristics you think this ancestor passed on to Jesus.

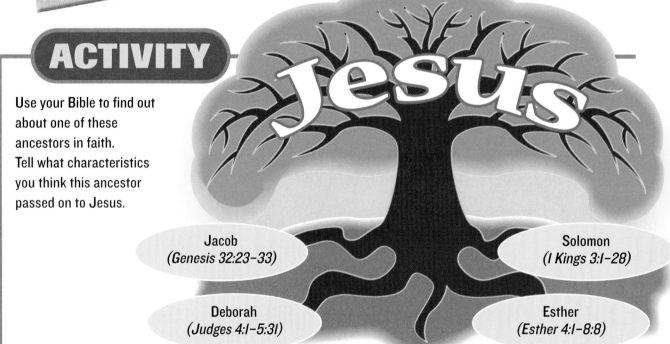

Jacob
(Genesis 32:23–33)

Solomon
(I Kings 3:1–28)

Deborah
(Judges 4:1–5:31)

Esther
(Esther 4:1–8:8)

Tradition!

The word **tradition** means "something that is handed down." For Jesus and his family, tradition was a way to touch the living faith of those who had gone before. The young Jesus learned important values by practicing the traditions of his family and his faith.

Jewish Tradition	How It Was Practiced in Jesus' Family	Values Jesus Learned
Go out of your way to help others (Leviticus 19:18, 34)	Mary cared for her aging cousin during Elizabeth's pregnancy (Luke 1:39–56); Joseph adopted Mary's child and protected the family during their years as refugees in Egypt (Matthew 1:24–25, 2:13–15)	love, compassion, respect for the elderly and for unborn children, self-sacrifice, courage
Make offerings to God at the birth of a first child (Numbers 18:15, 17)	Joseph and Mary offered the best they could afford (Luke 2:22–24)	thanksgiving, generosity, obedience to God's law
Celebrate the Passover in remembrance of Israel's deliverance from bondage in Egypt (Exodus 23:14–15)	Mary and Joseph took Jesus to Jerusalem for the Passover (Luke 2:41–51)	honoring the memory of the past, valuing freedom, prayerfulness, community

Write about a faith tradition your family has handed on to you.

Faith tradition	
How your family practices it	
Values you are learning	

Grounded in Love

This prayer is based on Saint Paul's blessing of the Christian community at Ephesus. When you pray, remember that all followers of Jesus, in every time and place, are part of your family.

All: We bow before God our Father, from whom every family in heaven and on earth takes its name. And we pray . . .

Reader 1: That our inner selves may be strengthened with power through God's Holy Spirit,

Reader 2: And that Christ may dwell in our hearts through faith, as we are being rooted and grounded in love.

Reader 3: May we have the strength to comprehend, with all the holy ones, the breadth and length and height and depth of Christ's love, which surpasses all knowledge,

Reader 4: So that we may be filled with the fullness of God.

All: To God, whose power working in us can do infinitely more than we can ask or imagine, may there be glory in the Church and in Christ Jesus to all generations, forever and ever. Amen!

Based on *Ephesians 3:14–21*

The exercises and activities on this page will help you know, love, and serve God better.

Know

Jesus' Family	My Family

• passes on traits and gifts
• shares family stories
• teaches faith and values
• celebrates traditions

Love

What have you learned about love, respect, or obedience from your family this week? Write two examples.

1. _____

   _____

2. _____

   _____

Serve

How can you help family members who are in need, as Mary and Joseph taught Jesus to do? Write three examples.

1. _____

   _____

2. _____

   _____

3. _____

   _____

Heroes of Faith

Maria and Luigi Quattrocchi

Imagine standing in St. Peter's Square as the pope declares your parents "Blessed"! That's what happened on October 21, 2001, to the three surviving children of an Italian married couple whom Pope John II recognized for "living their ordinary lives in an extraordinary way." Luigi and Maria raised four children through the turmoil of two world wars, sharing with those in need and opening their home to countless refugees. To honor this first married couple to be beatified together, the pope chose Maria and Luigi's wedding anniversary as their shared feast day.

These projects and activities will help you keep this lesson alive all week long.

On your own

Write (and illustrate, if you want) one family story or tradition you would like to pass on to the next generation.

_____

_____

_____

_____

_____

_____

With others

Talk with a friend about the best nonmaterial gifts your families have given you. How do these gifts help make you better followers of Jesus?

_____

_____

_____

With your family

Share with your family the story of the Holy Family's visit to Jerusalem when Jesus was twelve. With whom do family members identify? How does your family deal with similar "growing pains"?

_____

_____

_____

_____

_____

Jesus, Mary, and Joseph, bless my family with wisdom and grace.

GO ONLINE!
www.mhbenziger.com

The Messiah

> ### You are the Messiah, the Son of the living God.
> *Matthew 16:16*

Do You Know?

◆ How did people recognize Jesus as the Messiah, or "anointed one"? What does it mean to be anointed?

I Can Hardly Wait!

Do you remember what it was like when you were a young child waiting through the long December days for Christmas to come? Have you ever marked off the days on a calendar, wishing for the time to pass quickly and a long-awaited event to take place?

Patience is difficult for most people, regardless of their age. Just watch adults standing in line at a supermarket or waiting while the drive-through line snakes toward the pickup window at a fast food restaurant.

Write about a time when you found it difficult to wait for something you really wanted. Use descriptive language to tell how you felt while you waited, and how you felt when the wait was over.

The One Who Is to Come

✝ THIS WE BELIEVE!

Jesus is the Messiah, the Promised One sent by God to save all people from sin and death and to announce God's reign of justice and peace.

Jesus was born into a society that longed for deliverance. The Judea of his time was a poor, backwater colony of the powerful Roman Empire, not the proud kingdom Israel had been under King David. For centuries the Jewish people had been waiting for a Messiah to save them. The title *Messiah* means **anointed one,** a person chosen by God and consecrated to do God's work. As the prophet Samuel had anointed King David with oil, God anointed the promised Messiah with God's own Spirit.

But how would the Jewish people recognize the Messiah? Would he be a military leader, like Joshua and David, who would lead the people in a revolt against the tyranny of Rome? Or would he be a spiritual leader, like Moses and the prophets, calling for a change of heart, a return to the covenant and its justice?

Prepare the Way

When Jesus was about 30 years old, his cousin John caused quite a stir in Judea. John dressed in rough clothing made from camel's hide. He wore his hair and beard long and shaggy. He lived in the wilderness by the Jordan River, existing on meals of dried locusts and wild honey.

John began to preach a fiery message of repentance and justice, and he directed the crowds who gathered to wash themselves in the Jordan River as a sign of purification. People started to whisper. "Maybe he's the one!" they said. "Maybe this is the Messiah at last!"

John had an answer for them.

"I am baptizing you with water, but one mightier than I is coming. I am not worthy to loosen the thongs of his sandals. He will baptize you with the holy Spirit and fire."

Luke 3:16

JUDEAN · TIMES·

Imagine that you were in the crowd when John spoke these words. Write a headline and the first paragraph of a news report telling about John and his message about the Messiah.

In Fulfillment of the Scriptures

Jesus himself came to the Jordan River to be baptized by John. Recognizing who Jesus was, John at first refused to go through with the ritual. He knew that Jesus was no sinner in need of purification, but the one who had come to free others from sin. Jesus insisted on wading into the water, however, and the Gospels describe a moment when Jesus' identity and mission were confirmed in sight and sound.

> *After Jesus was baptized, he came up from the water and behold, the heavens were opened for him, and he saw the Spirit of God descending like a dove and coming upon him. And a voice came from the heavens, saying, "This is my beloved Son, with whom I am well pleased."*
>
> *Matthew 3:16–17*

After this amazing revelation, the Gospels tell us that Jesus went into the desert to spend time in prayer and fasting. When he emerged from the desert to begin his public ministry, Jesus found a powerful way to make it clear to his listeners what kind of Messiah he was.

> *He came to Nazareth, where he had grown up, and went according to his custom into the synagogue on the sabbath day. He stood up to read and was handed a scroll of the prophet Isaiah. He unrolled the scroll and found the passage where it was written:*
>
> *"The Spirit of the Lord is upon me,*
> *   because he has anointed me,*
> *   to bring glad tidings to the poor.*
>
> *He has sent me to proclaim liberty to captives*
> *   and recovery of sight to the blind,*
> *   to let the oppressed go free,*
> *and to proclaim a year acceptable to the Lord."*
>
> *Rolling up the scroll, he handed it back to the attendant and sat down, and the eyes of all in the synagogue looked intently at him. He said to them, "Today this scripture passage is fulfilled in your hearing."*
>
> *Luke 4:16–21*

Dialog Box

◆ What kind of Messiah is described in the passage from Isaiah that Jesus read?

◆ What did Jesus mean when he said that "this scripture passage is fulfilled in your hearing"?

◆ How do you think these words affected Jesus' listeners?

Virtue

Justice is working to make sure that all people receive those things to which they are entitled as humans made in God's image—dignity, respect, and a rightful share in the resources of creation.

How to Recognize the Messiah

John the Baptist's stern call for a return to morality and justice did not make him any friends among the rulers of Judea. King Herod had John jailed for disturbing the peace. But Herod could not silence the good news John had received on the banks of the Jordan. From prison, John sent his followers to Jesus. They asked Jesus for a sign confirming that he was the Messiah. Jesus responded:

"Go and tell John what you hear and see: the blind regain their sight, the lame walk, lepers are cleansed, the deaf hear, the dead are raised, and the poor have the good news proclaimed to them."

Matthew 11:4–5

Jesus reminded John's followers that they would recognize the Messiah by his actions. In everything he said and did, Jesus revealed that he was the Messiah. His healing, forgiving, life-changing actions showed that **God's reign,** or kingdom, of justice and peace is truly present in everyday life. Jesus' mission went far beyond a limited political dimension. He was sent by God, his Father, to save people not from the power of the Romans, but from the power of sin and death. Jesus came to bring not temporary political freedom, but everlasting life and joy.

ACTIVITY

Look for signs that God's reign is actively present in your world today. Find a newspaper or newsmagazine article that describes one of the signs by which Jesus told John's followers they would recognize the Messiah. (These signs do not have to be literally miraculous; God works through human ingenuity and care.) Copy the headline and briefly state what the article is about.

Anointed Ones

The Spirit of the Lord is upon you, too. In Baptism you were anointed as a sign that you are sent to share in the mission of Jesus Christ. **Christ** is the Greek word for Messiah, or "anointed one." As a *Christ*-ian, you are called to bring Isaiah's words to fulfillment in your life.

Think about each of the things that Isaiah said the Messiah would do. Give at least one example of how you can do these things in your daily life.

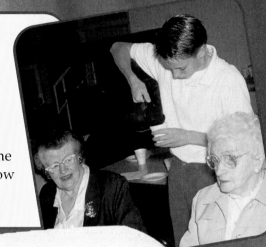

The Mission of the Messiah

Bring glad tidings to the poor

Proclaim liberty to the captives

Proclaim recovery of sight to the blind

Let the oppressed go free

Proclaim a year acceptable to the Lord

My Mission

Planting the Seeds

Jesus gave his followers a vision of God's reign in the sayings known as the **Beatitudes.** Pray these words as a reminder of how you can help plant the seeds of God's love, justice, and peace.

Group 1: Blessed are the poor in spirit,
Group 2: for theirs is the kingdom of heaven.
Group 1: Blessed are they who mourn,
Group 2: for they will be comforted.
Group 1: Blessed are the meek,
Group 2: for they will inherit the land.
Group 1: Blessed are they who hunger and thirst for righteousness,
Group 2: for they will be satisfied.
Blessed are the merciful,
Group 1: for they will be shown mercy.
Group 2: Blessed are the clean of heart,
Group 1: for they will see God.
Group 2: Blessed are the peacemakers,
Group 1: for they will be called children of God.
Group 2: Blessed are they who are persecuted for the sake of righteousness,
Group 1: for theirs is the kingdom of heaven.

Matthew 5:3–10

The exercises and activities on this page will help you know, love, and serve God better.

Know

Hebrew prophets described the Messiah as one who would bring God's reign of justice and peace.

↓

Jesus, anointed with God's Holy Spirit, announced the presence of God's reign of justice and peace.

↓

Christians, anointed in Baptism, carry on Jesus' mission of justice and peace.

Love

How did the prophet Isaiah say that the Messiah would show God's love? Write three examples.

1. _____

_____

2. _____

_____

3. _____

_____

Serve

How can you show people God's reign of justice and peace? Write three examples.

1. _____

2. _____

3. _____

Heroes of Faith

Saint John the Baptist

This child of Mary's cousin Elizabeth is honored as the last in the long line of Hebrew prophets who prepared the way for the coming of the Messiah. John was a radical figure. He rejected social customs, championed the poor, challenged religious and political authority, and confronted the quiet majority with their own hypocrisy. John fulfilled the description of a prophetic person as one who "comforts the afflicted and afflicts the comfortable." John was eventually imprisoned and beheaded by the corrupt governing family of Herod, whose immorality he had denounced.

These projects and activities will help you keep this lesson alive all week long.

On your own

Read or listen closely to the Gospel reading for this Sunday's Mass. What does this passage tell you about Jesus as the Messiah? What does it tell you about your mission as a Christian?

_____

_____

_____

_____

_____

_____

With others

Talk with a friend about how you can increase your use of words and gestures that bring healing. Carry out one healing action this week.

_____

_____

_____

With your family

Perform one "secret" or unannounced act of kindness for each family member this week. How do your acts of kindness make God's reign present at home? How do these acts make you feel?

_____

_____

_____

_____

_____

Holy Spirit, anoint me with your presence as I work to share God's reign of justice and peace.

GO ONLINE!
www.mhbenziger.com

"I Call You Friends"

> I have called you friends, because I have told you everything I have heard from my Father.
>
> John 15:15

Friendship

Humans weren't created to go it alone. Everyone needs friends. Here are some passages you might find if you look up *Friendship* in a book of quotations.

Do You Know?

◆ Who were Jesus' friends? What role did Jesus' closest friends and followers play in his mission?

> What is a friend? A single soul in two bodies.
> ◆ Aristotle

> The impulse of love that leads us to the doorway of a friend is the voice of God within and we need not be afraid to follow it.
> ◆ Agnes Sanford

> Blessed are they who hunger for friends—for though they may not realize it, their souls are crying out for God.
> ◆ Habib Sahabib

> No medicine is more valuable than a friend.
> ◆ Saint Aelred of Rievaulx

How would you like to be quoted on friendship? Write a statement about the importance of friends. Be sure to include your name as the source.

_____
_____
_____
_____
◆ _____

Virtue

Loyalty means remaining faithful to family and friends through good times and bad. Loyal friends stand up for one another and keep each other honest.

This We Believe!

God created humans to be in relationships. Jesus had friends and chose twelve close companions—the Apostles—to help carry out his mission.

Sharing Bread

Jesus was not a loner. During his years of public ministry, he developed close relationships with friends and many followers. They called him **Lord**—a sign of respect. Jesus' disciples learned from him, and in turn they shared what they had learned with others. According to the Gospel of Luke, when Jesus sent 72 disciples out on a special teaching mission, he asked them to travel in pairs. Jesus knew that sharing the mission with a companion would more than double each disciple's powerful witness.

The word *companion* literally means "one who shares bread." Jesus had twelve special companions—friends and followers with whom he broke bread, traveled the dusty roads of Galilee, preached, prayed, sang, laughed, and wept. We know this group of friends as the **Twelve**, or the **Apostles.** (You might recall that the word *apostle* means "one who is sent.") The Twelve are named differently in various Gospels; Matthew lists them as Simon (later named Peter), Andrew, James (called the Greater), John, Philip, Bartholomew, Thomas, Matthew, James (the Lesser, or younger of the two with same name), Thaddeus, Simon the Cananean, and Judas Iscariot.

Jesus spoke quite candidly with these twelve friends on the night before his death.

This is my commandment: love one another as I love you. No one has greater love than this, to lay down one's life for one's friends. You are my friends if you do what I command you. It was not you who chose me, but I who chose you and appointed you to go and bear fruit that will remain, so that whatever you ask the Father in my name he may give you.

John 15:12–14, 16

Think about your closest companions. Then fill in the chart.

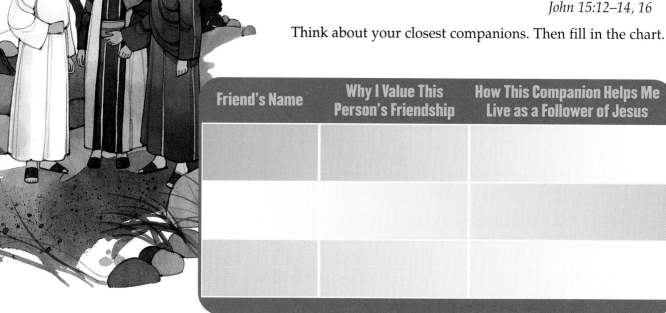

Friend's Name	Why I Value This Person's Friendship	How This Companion Helps Me Live as a Follower of Jesus

Follow Me

Jesus' first companions—James, John, Andrew, and Simon—were all fishermen. Here is how Matthew might have described his call to follow Jesus.

Dialog Box

◆ Why did Matthew have no friends? Why did he have a hard time imagining that God could forgive him?

◆ How did Jesus' invitation change Matthew's life? Has an invitation to friendship ever changed your life?

◆ Why do you think Jesus chose Matthew as his friend? What qualities did Matthew bring to the mission of the Twelve?

It's amazing how much your life can change in one short year. This time last year I was a tax collector in Capernaum. I took money from my neighbors to give to the Roman oppressors—and what's worse, I sometimes overcharged and pocketed the extra money for myself. I had no friends, as you can imagine, so I was very lonely. I hated what I was doing, but I loved the money.

I had heard about Jesus. I even went to hear him preach in the synagogue one day. He talked about God's love and forgiveness. How I longed for some of that love! But how could God forgive me?

Then came that morning I'll never forget. Jesus walked up to my tax collection table, smiled, and said, "Follow me." At first I thought he was talking to somebody else. Then I saw that he was looking right into my eyes. He knew all about me, but he wanted my friendship anyway! I was so overwhelmed with happiness that I jumped up, knocked over the table, and left the spilled coins behind as I walked away into my new life.

Now Jesus is sending me out with the others to bring the news of God's love and forgiveness. I'm a little afraid, but it helps to know that Jesus has faith in me. After all, who could be a better messenger of the Good News than I am? If God could forgive me, and Jesus could choose me for a friend, then love and hope are possible for everyone!

Based on *Matthew 9:9*

A Friendship Album

Jesus had many close friends whom the Gospels mention by name. Think about their stories. Then add your picture, your name, and a description of your friendship with Jesus to the blank space in this photo album.

Peter, James, and John were Jesus' closest friends among the Apostles. They accompanied him everywhere and were witnesses to his transfiguration on Mount Tabor.

Sisters Martha and Mary of Bethany and their brother Lazarus opened their home to Jesus and his followers. When Jesus heard that Lazarus had died, he wept. He restored life to Lazarus as a sign of God's never-ending love.

Mary of Magdala joined a group of women who supported the ministry of Jesus. She kept vigil at the foot of the cross and was one of the first to encounter the Risen Christ.

You Are My Friends

Jesus calls you to be his friend. He sends you to share the Good News. Read the advertisement below. Then write your own application for the job. Tell why you want to be a friend of Jesus. List your qualifications for discipleship.

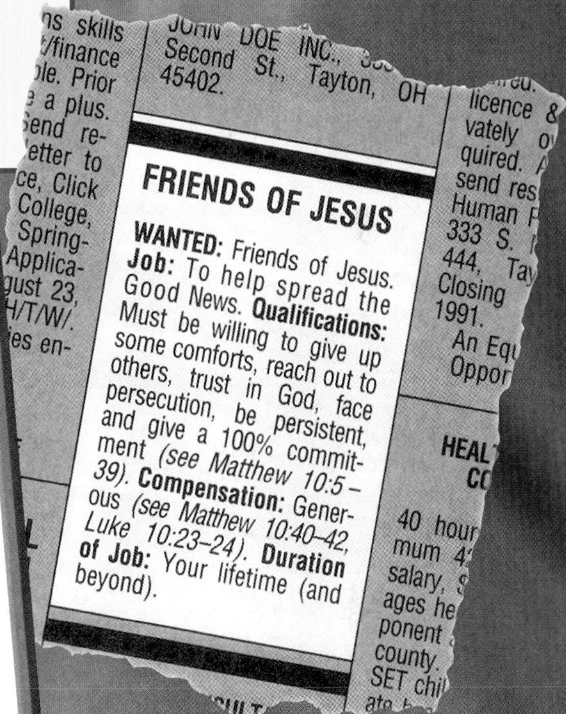

APPLICATION

FRIENDS OF JESUS

WANTED: Friends of Jesus. **Job:** To help spread the Good News. **Qualifications:** Must be willing to give up some comforts, reach out to others, trust in God, face persecution, be persistent, and give a 100% commitment *(see Matthew 10:5–39).* **Compensation:** Generous *(see Matthew 10:40–42, Luke 10:23–24).* **Duration of Job:** Your lifetime (and beyond).

The Lord's Prayer

Jesus taught his friends to pray as members of his own family, calling God "our Father." This remarkable prayer puts God first, leaving concerns for personal safety—the first thing most people pray for—in last place. Pray each line of this prayer thoughtfully, as though you were speaking these words for the first time.

Our Father, who art in heaven, hallowed be thy name.
Thy kingdom come;
Thy will be done on earth as it is in heaven.
Give us this day our daily bread,
and forgive us our trespasses
as we forgive those who trespass against us.
Lead us not into temptation,
but deliver us from evil.
Amen.

The exercises and activities on this page will help you know, love, and serve God better.

Know

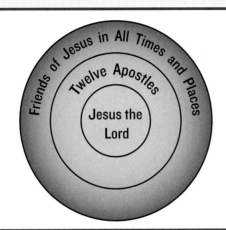

Friends of Jesus in All Times and Places
Twelve Apostles
Jesus the Lord

Love

What have you learned from your friends about love and forgiveness? Write two examples.

1. _____

_____

2. _____

_____

Serve

How can you reach out this week to people in need of friendship, forgiveness, and good news? Write three examples.

1. _____

2. _____

3. _____

Heroes of Faith

Saint Aelred of Rievaulx

Aelred was the abbot of an eleventh-century monastery in England. Cistercian monks were known for their austere life, which some interpreted as prohibiting even the luxury of friendship. Aelred had other ideas. He knew that the spiritual journey was meaningless without companions, and he encouraged the monks of his abbey to see their friendships with one another as a way of growing closer to Jesus. By promoting spiritual friendship, Aelred helped the monks overcome the petty bickering that can mar community life.

These projects and activities will help you keep this lesson alive all week long.

On your own

Learn more about one of the friends of Jesus named in the Gospels. What about this person interests you? What qualities do you share with him or her?

_____

_____

_____

_____

_____

_____

With others

Talk with your closest friends about the ways in which you encourage one another as followers of Jesus. Take turns naming strengths you want your friends to support and weaknesses you want your friends' help in overcoming.

_____

_____

With your family

Tell your family about your best friend. Ask family members to describe the qualities they value in their friendships.

_____

_____

_____

_____

_____

Jesus, Lord and Friend, help me to see in myself the good things your Father sees in me.

GO ONLINE!
www.mhbenziger.com

Make a Difference

"Enemies" become friends when young people from war-torn countries spend time together at the Seeds of Peace summer camp.

Friendship sometimes seems impossible when walls of prejudice and hate divide people. Someone has to take the first step toward making a difference. In 1993, an organization known as Seeds of Peace was established to help young people from the war-torn Middle East learn to take those first steps. That first year, several hundred teens representing the Arab and Israeli sides of the conflict were invited to spend time together at a summer camp in rural Maine. These "enemies" bunked together, shared leisure time, and worked with trained counselors to air their differences and get to know one another as people. The process has been repeated every year since then. Beginning in 1998, young people representing other conflicting nations and groups—such as Indians and Pakistanis, Greek and Turkish Cypriots, and Bosnian Serbs and Muslims—have also participated.

The goal of Seeds of Peace is to train the leaders of tomorrow in nonviolent methods of resolving conflicts. In this sense, the program is an investment in the future, and its success cannot yet be measured. In another way, however, Seeds of Peace is already bearing fruit, as walls break down and enemies become friends. These new friends are also apostles, sent to bring good news that transcends the divisions of religion or national origin. "We have to save the wisdom we learn here, and use it in our daily lives, and share it with the world so that they can learn, too," says Adar, an Israeli teen.

Tearing Down the Walls

Walls of division are not unique to distant war-torn lands. You can run into these obstacles to friendship right in your own neighborhood. Here are some things you can do to help tear down the walls. Choose one tip and take the first steps.

- Be honest about the cliques, "in-groups," and other patterns in your school that are used to exclude people from friendship. Don't support these walls. Find ways to reach out to people who are on the sidelines.
- Participate in a cooperative service project with teens from another neighborhood or church group. Get to know one another in person instead of relying on stereotypes and biased opinions.
- Learn more about Seeds of Peace at www.seedsofpeace.org. Explore opportunities for supporting this nonprofit, nondenominational group through a fundraising event or by inviting a Seeds of Peace spokesperson to address your school or parish.

Remember

1. **What does it mean to be a disciple? Who were the Apostles?**
Disciples (from a word that means "learners") are followers of Jesus. Jesus chose twelve of his disciples as special companions. These twelve are known as the Apostles (from a word meaning "one who is sent") because Jesus sent them to share his mission and his message with the world.

2. **Who are the members of Jesus' human family?**
Mary is the mother of Jesus. Her husband, Joseph, was the adoptive father of Jesus. Jesus, Mary, and Joseph are known as the Holy Family. Mary's cousin Elizabeth, Elizabeth's husband Zachariah, and their son John (later John the Baptist) were members of Jesus' extended family.

3. **Why is Jesus known by the titles Son, Messiah, and Lord?**
Jesus, who is God and human, is the Son of God (he is the Second Person of the Blessed Trinity) and the son of Mary. Christians believe that Jesus is the Messiah (the "anointed one") sent by God to save humanity from sin and death. Jesus is Lord (a title of honor given both to God and to human authorities) because of his divine mission and his powerful teaching authority.

4. **Why is King David considered an ancestor of Jesus?**
David was Israel's greatest king, a leader who saved the people and a prayerful man who spoke with God in the psalms. All of these qualities are later fulfilled in Jesus. Jesus' human family was descended from the house, or family tree, of David.

5. **Why is the Church called *apostolic*?**
The Church carries on the mission of the Apostles, led by the bishops and the pope, who are the successors of the Apostles.

Respond

Choose one of the following questions and write a response. If you wish, share what you have written.

1. What three big questions about Jesus would you like answered by the end of seventh grade?

2. The Hebrew prophets offered messages of hope to the people as they endured exile and suffered while waiting for the coming of the Messiah. How can you be a prophet offering the message of God's love to people today who have lost hope?

3. What can you do as a family member and a friend to have a positive influence on the people you care about? How do your family members and friends support your faith?

Act

Learn more about the Jewish religious heritage that shaped Jesus' prayer and teaching, and about Judaism today. Work with your teacher to arrange a visit to a Jewish synagogue or religious school, or ask a member of the local Jewish community to visit your class and answer your questions. Research opportunities for interfaith social action (such as outreach to homeless people) and education (such as Jewish-Catholic dialogue groups) that exist in your area, and participate if you can.

Share

The fish has several symbolic meanings for Christians: during the Church's early years of persecution the fish served as a secret sign of Christian identity (because the Greek word for *fish* is also an acronym, in Greek, for the phrase "Jesus Christ, Son of God, Savior"); it recalls Jesus' feeding of the crowd with only a few loaves of bread and a couple of fish; and it is a reminder of Jesus' call to the fishers Peter and Andrew. Cut a number of simple fish shapes out of colored paper. On one side, write these words of Saint Paul: "I give thanks to my God through Jesus Christ for all of you" *(Romans 1:8)*. Give the fish to family members and friends who support you in your growth in faith. (If you wish, write a short personal note on the back of each fish.) Explain the symbolism of the fish to each recipient.

For this is the will of my Father, that everyone who sees the Son and believes in him may have eternal life.

John 6:40a

Kenya  From Maryknoll

Jesus Gives Life

Chapter

Light of the World

> What came to be through him was life, and this life was the light of the human race.
>
> *John 1:3b–4*

A Powerful Sign

Of all the images in the world, the Statue of Liberty has the greatest impact on the Javovic family. After living many terrible years in a war torn country, the Javovic family arrived in New York City. The sight of the Statue of Liberty with her torch held high spoke to them of freedom and welcome to a country offering new opportunities.

The sight of the Statue of Liberty or a nation's flag calls forth an emotional response because of what it stands for or symbolizes.

Do You Know?

◆ Where do you experience signs of Jesus' presence?

What symbol evokes an emotional response in you? Write about a time when the sight of a particular object had a particular significance for you.

God's Love Made Visible

💬 Dialog Box

◆ How did Jesus' healing of the blind man "make God's love visible"? In what sense were the religious authorities "blind"?

◆ What do you think the narrator means by saying that you already see, hear, and feel the touch of Jesus?

You probably wish you could see Jesus, hear his voice, or feel the touch of his hand—just once. It would make all the difference to your faith, right? Would you be surprised if I told you that you already do all these things?

I would have been astonished if anybody had told me I would ever see the Light of the World with my own eyes. After all, I was born blind. In those days, people thought that my disability was a punishment for some sin my parents had committed. All I knew was that my world was very small and lonely until the day Jesus came into it. I was just sitting by the Temple as usual, begging for a few coins. Then I overheard someone ask, "Rabbi, who sinned, that this beggar is blind?" A voice of great kindness answered, "No one sinned. This man was born blind so that all could see God's love made visible. I am the light of the world."

Near me, I heard someone spit into his hand, mixing dust into the saliva. I felt warm fingers spread the soothing paste on my useless eyes. Then the same kind voice told me to go and wash in the Pool of Siloam. I didn't even argue. I just got up and stumbled to the pool, where I washed off the mud. And the world was suddenly wider than I could have imagined, full of light and color and hope. The religious authorities didn't understand. They didn't have any room in their thinking for this kind of miracle. In a way, they were the real blind ones. I didn't understand either, until I found my way back to thank the one who had healed me. I looked in his eyes, and I recognized what I had heard in his voice and felt in his touch—God's great, unlimited love.

Based on *John 9*

Sacramental Signs

You may have already guessed that one of the ways in which you encounter Jesus in your own life is through the **sacraments.** These powerful signs of God's love and sources of God's grace are the ways in which you can see Jesus, hear his voice, and feel his healing and forgiving touch. Through the Holy Spirit, in the Church, Jesus continues to be present and active in the sacraments, making God's love visible just as he did for the man born blind.

Baptism, Confirmation, Eucharist, Penance, the Anointing of the Sick, Marriage, and Holy Orders—these seven celebrations combine objects, words, and actions in symbolic fashion. Through the sacraments, you receive **sanctifying grace,** the gift of a deepened relationship with God that helps nourish your faith and gives you the means to live it.

The ceremonies in which the sacraments are celebrated are called **rites.** Each sacrament has a prescribed minister (the person who ordinarily celebrates the sacrament), words, and actions (the specific gestures that convey the meaning of the sacrament). Those who participate in or receive the sacraments must also meet certain conditions of readiness and eligibility. These regulations are not meant to reduce the sacraments to legalistic recipes, but to insure that the meaning of each sacrament remains clear and powerful.

Wonder is the gift of being open to signs of God's presence in creation and in the work of human hands. Through the eyes of wonder, such simple things as water, oil, bread, and wine become sacramental symbols.

WORD OF GOD

Just so, your light must shine before others, that they may see your good deeds and glorify your heavenly Father.

Matthew 5:16

? How are the sacraments ways in which you see Jesus, hear his voice, and feel his healing and forgiving touch? Give specific examples.

From Maryknoll

The Church as Sacrament

The Church, the Body of Christ, can also be seen as a sacrament. Jesus is present in the Church through the working of the Holy Spirit. Through the members of the Church—and this includes you!—Jesus' light is present to the whole world.

Read the following examples. Tell how Jesus is present in each encounter.

A young man who has not seen or spoken to his family in some time confesses his sins to a priest. The priest and the penitent share the Gospel story of the prodigal son. The priest listens compassionately to the young man's story, encourages him to change his life for the better, and grants him forgiveness in the name of Jesus. The young man leaves the reconciliation room and calls his family.

A homeless woman with young children asks for help. Your parish Christian Service volunteers find her a shelter, obtain food for the children from the emergency food bank, and line up several job interviews. The woman is told she can make use of the parish daycare center when she finds employment.

Once a week, teens from the parish meet with elderly residents of a local care center. The group members read the Scriptures together. They share the ups and downs of their everyday lives. They pray for one another and for the community.

Let Your Light Shine

As a member of the Church and a follower of Jesus, you are also the light of the world and a sign of God's loving presence. For each of the topics listed on the lamps, give an example of how people meet Jesus in you.

Offering forgiveness

Proclaiming the Good News

Reaching out to heal

Being a peacemaker

Being part of the community

Amazing Grace

One of the best loved Christian hymns was written by an English slave trader named John Newton. Aboard ship in a terrible storm, Newton prayed for deliverance. Not only was he saved, but he also had an experience of God's love that changed his whole life. Newton became a minister who worked for the abolition of slavery. He described his enlightenment in the hymn "Amazing Grace."

Sing or pray this hymn together, remembering that God's grace has the power to change lives.

Amazing grace! how sweet the sound
That saved a wretch like me
I once was lost and now am found
Was blind but now I see

'Twas grace that taught my heart to fear
And grace my fears relieved
How precious did that grace appear
The hour I first believed

The Lord has promised good to me
His word my hope secures
He will my shield and portion be
As long as life endures

Through many dangers, toils, and snares
I have already come
'Twas grace that brought me safe thus far
And grace will lead me home

When we've been there 10,000 years
Bright shining as the sun
We've no less days to sing God's praise
Than when we first begun

The exercises and activities on this page will help you know, love, and serve God better.

Know

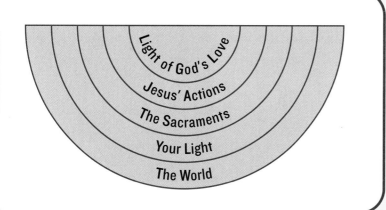

Light of God's Love
Jesus' Actions
The Sacraments
Your Light
The World

Love

What signs of love (God's love, family love, friendship) have you seen in your life this week? Write three examples.

_____

_____

_____

_____

_____

_____

_____

Serve

What areas of your world would be improved if you let your light shine there? Write three examples of how you could make Jesus' presence known by your actions.

_____

_____

_____

_____

Heroes of Faith

Saint Mechtild of Hackeborn

In thirteenth-century Germany, three remarkable women shared religious life in the same community. Mechtild of Hackeborn, Mechtild of Magdeburg, and Gertrude the Great were known as mystics who were open to signs of God's presence in creation. Mechtild of Hackeborn, who was like a mother to the two younger women, was especially devoted to the humanity of Jesus, which she saw as a sacrament. Through the "door" of the Incarnation, Mechtild wrote, we can see the light of God's love shining. Mechtild let her own light shine in poetry, teaching, and counseling.

CHAPTER 5
HOME and FAMILY

Thee projects and activities will help you keep this lesson alive all week long.

On your own

Keep a journal listing all the signs of "God's love made visible" that you encounter this week.

_____

_____

_____

_____

_____

_____

With others

Talk with your closest friends about how you can let your light shine every day. Agree to point out to one another times when you are "hiding your light," and find ways to encourage one another to be signs of Jesus' presence.

With your family

Find out how many of the seven sacraments have been celebrated by your immediate or extended family members. (Remember that you celebrate Eucharist at every Sunday Mass.) Ask family members to share their memories of special sacramental celebrations.

_____

_____

_____

_____

_____

Lord Jesus, help me to see you more clearly, love you more dearly, and follow you more nearly, day by day.

GO ONLINE!
www.mhbenziger.com

WATER AND SPIRIT

For in one Spirit we were all baptized into one body and we were all given to drink of one Spirit.

From *1 Corinthians 12:13*

Do You Know?

◆ How are Catholic Christians initiated into the Body of Christ?

Taking the Plunge

My name is Sara and I'm a junior lifeguard. I'm proud to wear my lifeguard badge because it shows how hard I worked to reach this point. For two months I got up at 5:30 every morning to be at the pool by seven o'clock. With the other junior lifeguard trainees, I did warm-up drills and swam for hours. When I got home at night I was so tired I usually fell into bed right after dinner.

The funny thing is, I've never put this much effort into anything. My family and friends thought I would give up the training after a couple of days—and I almost did. But Coach Hayes and the other trainees encouraged me to stick with it.

The night of the awards banquet, when we received our certificates, badges, and lifeguard uniforms, I knew it was all worth it. I didn't even complain when the coach and the older lifeguards gave the trainees the traditional initiation, drenching us with buckets of water as we emerged from the changing rooms in our new uniforms. "Congratulations!" Coach Hayes said as we stood there dripping. "You've passed the last test!" I'm so glad I took the plunge.

Tell about a time when you worked hard for something important. Who encouraged you? What tests did you face along the way?

Dialog Box

◆ How did Nicodemus interpret Jesus' words about the need to be born again? Why was this message such a problem for Nicodemus?

◆ What do you think Jesus really meant by saying that his followers needed to be "born of water and Spirit"?

◆ Have you ever had an experience that made you feel you had been "born again"? Why is this such a good image for initiation?

Born from Above

Initiation—the process of becoming part of a group—is in some ways like a second birth. The person who is initiated has a new life, a new identity as a group member.

Jesus used the image of being born again to explain what it meant to become his follower. A Jewish leader named Nicodemus came to Jesus secretly, at night, to learn more about the kingdom of God that Jesus had been preaching. Jesus' words about initiation took Nicodemus by surprise.

Jesus answered and said to him, "Amen, amen, I say to you, no one can see the kingdom of God without being born from above." Nicodemus said to him, "How can a person once grown old be born again? Surely he cannot reenter his mother's womb and be born again, can he?" Jesus answered, "Amen, amen, I say to you, no one can enter the kingdom of God without being born of water and Spirit."

John 3:3–5

WORD OF GOD

For all of you who were baptized into Christ have clothed yourselves with Christ.

Galatians 3:27

Sacraments of Initiation

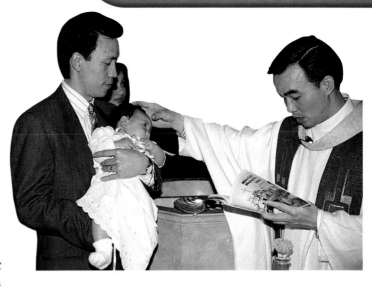

In Jesus' puzzling words to Nicodemus, you may have seen a connection to your own initiation into the Body of Christ. The phrase "born of water and Spirit" calls up images of the sacraments of Baptism and Confirmation, two of the three sacramental celebrations by which Catholic Christians are "born again" into full membership in the Church. The three **sacraments of initiation**—Baptism, Confirmation, and Eucharist—give Catholic Christians their new identity in Christ Jesus.

In Baptism, you take on Christ's redeeming journey through death to new life. You die to sin and are reborn—through water and the Holy Spirit—into new life. Confirmation seals the covenant of Baptism.

Through Baptism and Confirmation you receive a share in the ministry of Jesus. You share in the gifts of the Holy Spirit. Born of water and the Spirit, you are marked as Christ's own forever.

Participation in the Eucharist, the central liturgical celebration of the Church, completes your incorporation into the Body of Christ. Each time you participate in the celebration of Mass and receive Jesus in Holy Communion, you are reaffirming your identity as a follower of Jesus and a member of his Church.

Which of the sacraments of initiation have you celebrated? In the chart below, write how each sacrament identifies you as a Catholic Christian.

THIS WE BELIEVE!

The sacraments of initiation—Baptism, Confirmation, and Eucharist—make us followers of Jesus and members of the Church.

Sacrament of Initiation	How It Identifies Me As a Catholic Christian
Baptism	
Confirmation	
Eucharist	

Conversion is the willingness to keep turning toward God and away from sin. Conversion is not a once-in-a-lifetime event, but an ongoing commitment.

The Rite of Christian Initiation

Baptism is always the first sacrament, but the order in which Catholics celebrate the other sacraments of initiation can vary. Catholics are generally baptized as infants, receive their First Communion at about the age of seven, and are confirmed somewhere between the ages of twelve and eighteen. Adults and older children who decide to join the Church follow the ancient process of initiation known as the **catechumenate.** Following the Rite of Christian Initiation of Adults (RCIA), they move through several stages of preparation. They have the support of individual sponsors and the whole parish community at each step along the way. Catechumens celebrate Baptism, Confirmation, and Eucharist all at once during the Easter Vigil. This diagram shows the stages of the RCIA:

1. During the *pre-catechumenate, inquirers* share the Gospel and ask questions about the faith.

2. The *catechumenate* is a time of study and prayer for those who have made an initial decision to follow Jesus. It is celebrated in the rite of *acceptance or welcome.*

3. Once the catechumens and the community are sure of their commitment, they join the ranks of the *elect.* The period of *election,* coinciding with Lent, includes prayer, fasting, and self-examination.

4. The new members of the Church, known as *neophytes* ("newly born"), enter a 50-day period of additional learning and growth in faith called *mystagogia.*

Why do you think the Church offers new members an additional 50 days of learning and growth after celebrating the sacraments of initiation?

The candidates celebrate the sacraments of initiation at the Easter Vigil.

Priest, Prophet, and King

In Baptism you receive a share in the ministry of Jesus. The prayer of anointing with chrism (oil consecrated by the Bishop) from the Rite of Baptism puts it this way:

As Christ was anointed Priest, Prophet, and King, so may you live always as members of his body, sharing everlasting life.

Read the descriptions of each aspect of the ministry to which you are called. Then write two specific ways you can carry out each of these roles.

Priesthood of the Faithful
Participating in the Eucharist, sharing the Good News, inviting others to prayer

_____

_____

Prophecy
Standing up for what is right, working for justice, reaching out to help those who are in need

_____

_____

Kingship
Being a good role model, exercising leadership skills, using your gifts to promote the reign of God

_____

_____

From Maryknoll

By Water, Made Holy

Gather around a bowl of water to pray this prayer based on a blessing from the Easter Vigil. Conclude your prayer by making the Sign of the Cross with the water, in remembrance of your baptism.

Lord our God,
be with us as we recall the wonder of our creation
and the greater wonder of our redemption.
Your gift of water makes seeds grow;
it refreshes us and makes us clean.
Through water you set your people free,
and quenched their thirst in the desert.
With water the prophets announced a new covenant
that you would make with humanity.
By water, made holy by Christ in the Jordan,
you made our sinful nature new
in the bath that gives rebirth.
Let this water remind us of our baptism,
as we keep in our prayers all those preparing
to celebrate the sacraments of initiation.
In the name of the Father, and of the Son,
and of the Holy Spirit. Amen.

The exercises and activities on this page will help you know, love, and serve God better.

Know

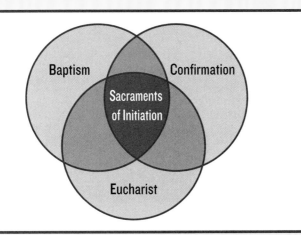

Baptism   Confirmation

Sacraments
of Initiation

Eucharist

Love

Who are the people who have made you feel most welcome as a member of the Church? List their names and pray for them this week.

_____

_____

_____

_____

_____

_____

Serve

How can you help others feel welcome as members of the Body of Christ? Write three examples.

_____

_____

_____

_____

_____

Heroes of Faith

Saint Joan Delanou

Joan Delanou was a long shot for sainthood. This 18th-century shopkeeper was a miser who chased beggars from her door and shocked everyone by keeping her store open on holy days. Then Joan met Madame Frances Souchet, an old woman everyone thought was crazy. Madame Souchet rented a room from Joan Delanou, telling her she was a messenger sent from God. Over the course of time, Madame Souchet's gentle, prayerful ways transformed Joan Delanou. The converted miser took in homeless families, turned her shop into a hospice and an orphanage, and founded a community of religious women.

These projects and activities will help you keep this lesson alive all week long.

On your own

Find out the name of a person preparing to celebrate the sacraments of initiation in your parish or diocese. Write the person a note promising to remember him or her in your prayers.

_____

_____

_____

_____

_____

_____

With others

Remember that your mystagogia—the time of learning and growing in faith—isn't limited to 50 days after baptism. Think of three aspects of your faith about which you would like to learn more. Share your questions with your teacher or a parish minister.

With your family

Take time to look through memorabilia from family members' baptisms. Look at photos or videos. Light your baptismal candles (or decorate a large white candle to serve as a family baptismal candle). Develop a family ceremony to celebrate baptismal anniversaries.

Holy Spirit, give me the grace to follow the path of conversion all the days of my life.

GO ONLINE!
www.mhbenziger.com

Bread of Life

He was made
known to them
in the breaking
of the bread.

Luke 24:35b

Do You Know?

◆ How is Jesus present
in the Eucharist?

A Memorable Meal

Meals make memories. Whether it's a quick bite from the drive-through shared with friends, the luxury of a weekend family meal lovingly prepared and lingered over, or the glitter of a year-end school awards banquet, every meal has the potential to make memories and change lives.

Every meal can bring people together. Shared meals can break down walls of suspicion and shatter old family feuds. (The word *companionship*, after all, literally means "breaking bread together.") A meal is not only a sharing of food; it is a sharing of one's own life. The table is a place to celebrate joys, mourn losses, tell stories of the past, and dream a better future. Share an example from your own experience of a memorable meal that brings people together.

THIS WE BELIEVE!

We meet Jesus Christ truly present in the Eucharist, the sacred meal and life-giving sacrifice, and we are sent to be his presence in the world.

WORD OF GOD

I am the living bread that came down from heaven; whoever eats this bread will live forever; and the bread that I will give is my flesh for the life of the world.

John 6:51

Meeting Jesus at the Table

Jesus knew and used the power of meals to bring people together, to offer healing and forgiveness, to share good news, to give thanks for God's gifts, to provide occasions for loving self-sacrifice, and to inspire people to action. The Gospels are full of examples of memorable meals.

Jesus used shared meals as opportunities to break down walls of difference and build community. Over supper in his friends' house in Bethany, he settled a long-standing disagreement between Martha and Mary by praising both of their gifts. He welcomed a woman with a bad reputation to the house of the virtuous religious leader Levi. Those who shared the table with Jesus during his travels were as likely to be sinners and social outcasts as they were to be the *good people.*

Jesus never let pass a chance to use meals as occasions for healing and forgiveness. Once, when Peter brought Jesus home for dinner, Jesus healed Peter's mother-in-law of a fever. Reaching out to the despised tax collector Zacchaeus, Jesus invited himself over for dinner to celebrate Zacchaeus's repentance. Peter must have been terrified meeting the risen Jesus on a beach, remembering how he had betrayed his friend. Imagine Peter's relief when Jesus' first words to him were not a rebuke but an invitation: "Come, have breakfast." *(John 21:12)*

Jesus often taught while he ate, so every meal with Jesus was an occasion to share the Good News. No one knew that more clearly than the disciples on the road to Emmaus who did not recognize the risen Jesus but invited the "stranger" to eat with them. They listened with hearts on fire with hope as their guest explained the Scriptures, and recognized him at last in the breaking of the bread.

A Powerful Message

Jesus reminded those who broke bread with him that all nourishment is a gift from God. He always gave thanks to his Father for the food and prayed a blessing over it before sharing it. The power of this gratitude was so great that on several occasions it enabled Jesus to stretch meager resources to feed multitudes.

Jesus knew that all meals represent sacrifice of some kind. The wheat is ground to make bread, the grapes crushed to make wine. Someone works hard to prepare the meal and to clean up afterward. Someone makes sure the guests are welcomed and cared for, as Jesus washed the feet of his disciples at their most memorable meal together. At that Last Supper with his friends, Jesus made the most profound connection of all between meal and sacrifice: he offered himself to them in the bread and wine of the Eucharist.

And finally, Jesus knew that his life-changing actions didn't end with the meal, or with him. He always sent those with whom he broke bread away from the table with a mission of their own: to be for others what he had been for them.

Gratitude is an attitude of thankfulness for all God's gifts, especially the gift of salvation in Jesus. The word *Eucharist* comes from the Greek for "giving thanks."

ACTIVITY

Look up each of the following passages to see the message Jesus gave to those who shared meals with him. Write Jesus' words of mission.

Mark 16:14–15

Luke 22:19

John 13:14–15

John 21:15

Meeting Jesus in the Eucharist

The presence of Jesus in the Eucharist—in the Word proclaimed, in Holy Communion, in the person of the priest, and in the gathered assembly—nourishes, heals, forgives, and brings new life.

Review the parts of the Mass and how Jesus is present in them. For each part, write one way in which it has helped you meet and recognize Jesus.

1 Introductory Rites

Jesus invites us to the table and offers us forgiveness and healing.
I recognized Jesus in the Introductory Rites when

_____

_____.

2 The Liturgy of the Word

Jesus speaks Good News to us in the words of the Scriptures and in the homily of the priest or deacon.
I recognized Jesus in the Liturgy of he Word when

_____

_____.

3 The Liturgy of the Eucharist

Jesus gathers us at the table to give thanks for God's gifts, to offer ourselves with him in sacrifice, and to receive him in the Bread and Wine of Holy Communion.
I recognized Jesus in the Liturgy of the Eucharist when

_____

_____.

4 Concluding Rites

Jesus sends us out into the world to be his loving, healing, forgiving, life-giving presence.
I recognized Jesus in the Concluding Rites when

_____

_____.

Living the Eucharist

When you celebrate the Eucharist and receive Jesus in Holy Communion, you are given the grace to *be* Eucharist for the world. Complete the chart with examples of how you can live each of the Eucharistic actions in your daily life.

Eucharistic Actions	How I Live the Eucharist
Building Community	
Healing and Forgiving	
Sharing Good News	
Giving Thanks for God's Gifts	
Making Sacrifices for the Good of Others	
Making Jesus Present	

Jesus Shares Himself With Us

Leader: Jesus gives himself to us.

All: Let us give thanks and praise.

Leader: Blessed are you Lord our God, who brings forth bread from the earth.

All: Amen.

Leader: Let us join together in prayer and thanksgiving.

All: Jesus, throughout your life, you shared many meals with all sorts of people. We ask that you be present with us whenever we share a meal. May we always remember that you are the bread which has come down from heaven to be food for the life of our spirit. Help us cherish your presence in the breaking of the bread and in the Blessed Sacrament. We make this prayer in your name, who live and reign with God the Father and the Holy Spirit, now and forever. Amen.

The exercises and activities on this page will help you know, love, and serve God better.

Know

| Jesus is present in the Eucharist: in the Word, in the Bread and Wine, in the priest, in the assembly. | → | We meet and receive Jesus in the Eucharist. | → | We are sent to be Eucharist to the world in our daily lives. |

Love

Write one sign of Christ's love you have received this week and one sign of Christ's love you have given.

_____

_____

_____

_____

_____

_____

Serve

How can you offer yourself and your gifts to others this week in thanksgiving for the Eucharist? Write three examples.

_____

_____

_____

Heroes of Faith

Pierre Teilhard de Chardin

A Jesuit priest, anthropologist, and 20th-century mystic, Pierre Teilhard de Chardin spent his life working to reconcile the worlds of science and faith. Teilhard found inspiration for this work in his great devotion to the Eucharist, the sacrament of Christ's incarnate presence in the material world. Teilhard spent many years at archaeological digs in remote parts of China. Far from a parish community, Teilhard wrote this prayer: "Lord, I have neither bread nor wine nor altar. I will make the whole earth my altar and on it will offer you all the labors and suffering of the world."

HOME and FAMILY

These projects and activities will help you keep this lesson alive all week long.

On your own

As you celebrate the Eucharist at Mass this week, pay special attention to the ways in which Jesus is present to you and is sending you to be Eucharist.

With others

Talk with your friends about the people, places, and situations in your world that could really use Christ's healing and loving presence. Think of two practical ways that you can be that presence.

With your family

Plan and share a special meal of thanksgiving for the gifts God has given your family. Work together to choose a menu, decorate the table, prepare foods, and clean up. Ask the youngest family member to pray a blessing before the meal.

This is the Lamb of God. Happy are we who are called to his supper.

GO ONLINE!
www.mhbenziger.com

THE VINE AND THE BRANCHES

This is my commandment: love one another as I love you.

John 15:12

Do You Know?

◆ How do you show that you are a member of the Body of Christ?

Outside Looking In

(A Screenplay)

Scene One

Fade in. Exterior. Wide shot. City street. Night.
A very cold night. Snow swirls along the pavement. The wind howls. The street of brownstone homes looks deserted.

Exterior. City street. New angle.
A solitary figure, wearing jeans, a T-shirt, and a jacket too thin to keep out the cold, appears at the end of the street. He walks slowly toward camera, approaching the only lighted window on the block.

Exterior. Close up. At the window.
As the figure reaches the light of the window, we see he is a teenager. He stands at the window, looking in, with a mixed expression of fear and longing.

Interior. Dining room, seen through window from boy's point of view.
A well-dressed group of family members and friends sit around a dining table full of food. A fire burns in a fireplace, and the room is lit with candles. The people talk and laugh.

Exterior. Front door.
The stranger staggers from the window to the front door. After a moment of hesitation, he knocks. Footsteps are heard, and the boy draws back from the door in panic. As he is about to run away, the door opens. Light spills into the street.

Scene Two

With a small group, brainstorm and act out what happens next.

◆ In your own words, explain what you think Jesus meant when he said that he is the vine and his followers are the branches.

◆ What does Jesus mean when he says, "remain in me"?

◆ What does it mean to love others the way Jesus loves us?

An Unbreakable Connection

Those who are initiated into the Body of Christ are like the family members sharing a meal, gathered around a common table, warm even on the coldest night. They are a **community**—a word that means *a unified body of individuals.* This community is so strong that it extends to those on Earth and to those who have died. This is the **Communion of Saints** that Christians profess in the Creed.

But what about the stranger outside in the cold—hungry, lonely, afraid? Who cares for his or her joys and sorrows? To whom is he or she connected?

Jesus had a surprising message for his friends about the meaning of community. On the night before he died, as they shared their most memorable meal, Jesus reminded his friends that they were joined to him in the closest possible way, in an unbreakable connection that not even death could sever.

Remain in me, as I remain in you. Just as a branch cannot bear fruit on its own unless it remains on the vine, so neither can you unless you remain in me. I am the vine, you are the branches. As the Father loves me, so I also love you. Remain in my love.

John 15:4–5, 9

Jesus' friends already sensed, to their sorrow, that they could not live without him. What he was trying to tell them was that he would always be with them in the love they shared. And he went on to explain something even more astounding: that love meant they could not live without each other, either. "This is my commandment: love one another as I love you," Jesus said *(John 15:12)*. In other words, being connected to Jesus means being connected, in that same unbreakable love, to others, whether friend or stranger—welcoming them in, celebrating their joys, sharing their burdens. In the Body of Christ, there are no outsiders.

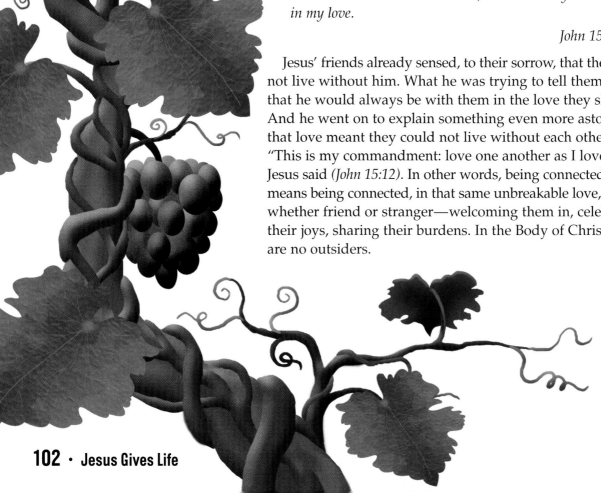

Opening Doors

Jesus knew that communities can become too involved with themselves, forgetting the needs of those outside the circle. So in everything he did, Jesus pushed the boundaries of the circle. He showed by example that the kingdom of God is a community with wide-open doors.

At a time and in a culture where women were not always seen as persons in their own right, Jesus welcomed women among his disciples. Mary of Magdala, Joanna, and Susanna traveled with him during his ministry *(Luke 8:2–3)*. He encouraged Mary of Bethany to discuss the Scriptures with him in her home as men did in the synagogue *(Luke 10:38–42)*.

When parents brought their children to be blessed by Jesus, the disciples tried to send them away, thinking the children were a nuisance. But Jesus welcomed them, and told his followers that they would do well to lighten up and view the world as children do *(Mark 10:13–15)*.

Jesus also refused to discriminate against Samaritans, a group excluded from Jewish life for religious reasons. He shared the Good News with a Samaritan woman *(John 4:4–29)* and surprised his listeners by holding up a Samaritan as a model of moral goodness *(Luke 10:29–37)*.

People with certain disabilities were shunned by society in Jesus' time, but he reached out to lepers and the mentally ill. By healing them, Jesus showed the world that these people were not excluded from God's love, and he helped restore them to the community *(Matthew 8:1–4; Luke 8:40–56)*.

This We Believe!

Christians are united in one body with Jesus and with one another, and are called to reach out in love to all people.

Virtue

Hospitality is reaching out to make people feel welcome. Hospitality opens the doors of community to others, breaking down the walls of fear and discrimination that keep people apart.

? Which groups of people are likely to be excluded from your community or society today? How can members of the Body of Christ open doors to these excluded ones?

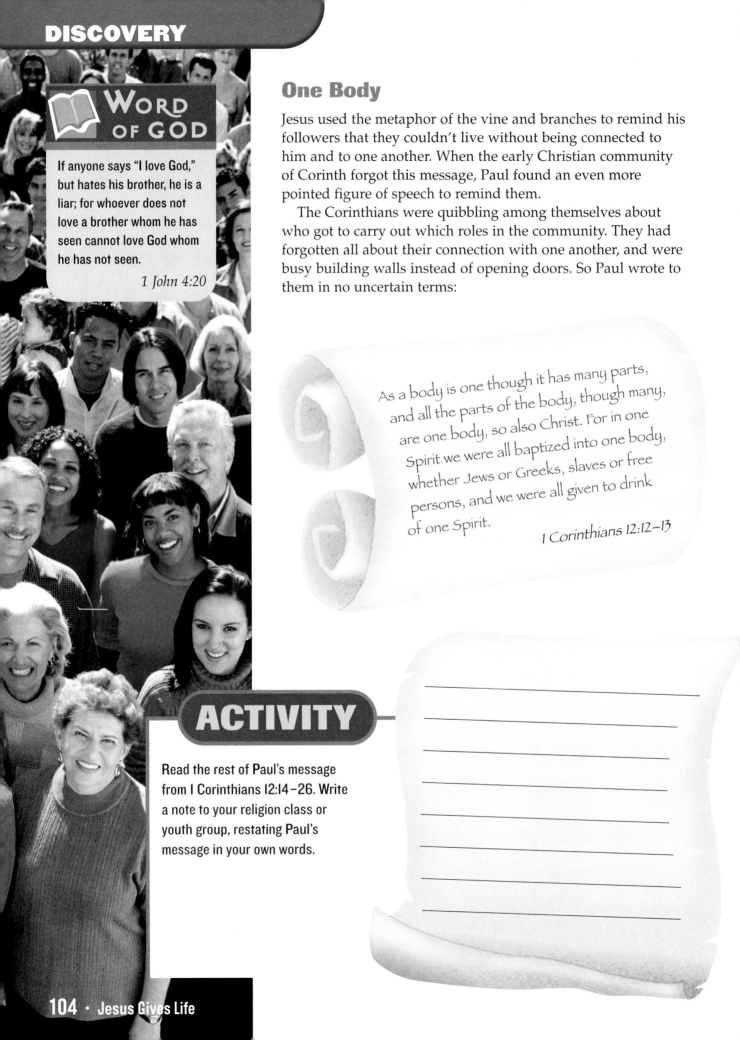

WORD OF GOD

If anyone says "I love God," but hates his brother, he is a liar; for whoever does not love a brother whom he has seen cannot love God whom he has not seen.

1 John 4:20

One Body

Jesus used the metaphor of the vine and branches to remind his followers that they couldn't live without being connected to him and to one another. When the early Christian community of Corinth forgot this message, Paul found an even more pointed figure of speech to remind them.

The Corinthians were quibbling among themselves about who got to carry out which roles in the community. They had forgotten all about their connection with one another, and were busy building walls instead of opening doors. So Paul wrote to them in no uncertain terms:

As a body is one though it has many parts, and all the parts of the body, though many, are one body, so also Christ. For in one Spirit we were all baptized into one body, whether Jews or Greeks, slaves or free persons, and we were all given to drink of one Spirit.

1 Corinthians 12:12–13

ACTIVITY

Read the rest of Paul's message from 1 Corinthians 12:14–26. Write a note to your religion class or youth group, restating Paul's message in your own words.

The Gifts You Bring

The Body of Christ needs the gifts of each of its members. Like a green vine, the community of the Church grows and flourishes when each branch and leaf is nourished and fed.

Think about what you have to offer the community that no one else can. On the leaves of the vine, write three gifts that you bring to the Body of Christ.

Never Alone

As members of the Body of Christ, branches of the vine, you are part of the **Communion of Saints**—the community of all followers of Jesus throughout the ages. The Litany of the Saints is a prayerful reminder that you are never alone on your journey of faith.

Take turns leading sections of this shortened litany. At each star **(*)**, all respond "Pray for us."

Reader 1: Holy Mary, Mother of God, most honored of virgins,* Michael, Gabriel, and Raphael,* Angels of God,*

Reader 2: Abraham, Moses, and Elijah,* Saint John the Baptist,* Saint Joseph,* Holy patriarchs and prophets,*

Reader 3: Saint Peter and Saint Paul,* Saint Andrew,* Saint John and Saint James,* Saint Thomas,* Saint Matthew,* All holy Apostles,*

Reader 4: Saint Luke,* Saint Mark,* Saint Barnabas,* Saint Mary Magdalene,* All disciples of the Lord,*

Reader 5: Saint Stephen,* Saint Paul Miki,* Saint Charles Lwanga,* Saint Perpetua and Saint Felicity,* Saint Agnes,* Saint Maria Goretti,* All holy martyrs for Christ,*

Reader 6: Saint Francis and Saint Dominic,* Saint Thomas Aquinas,* Saint Vincent de Paul,* Saint Catherine,* Saint Teresa,* Saint Elizabeth Ann Seton,* All holy men and women, saints of God,*

All: Amen.

The exercises and activities on this page will help you know, love, and serve God better.

Know

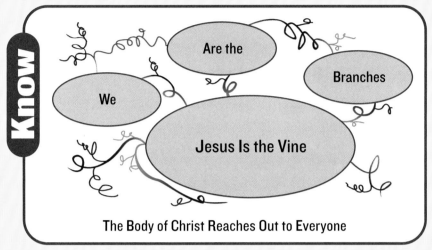

We | Are the | Branches

Jesus Is the Vine

The Body of Christ Reaches Out to Everyone

Love

Write three ways you can show love for God, whom you can't see, by showing love for those around you this week.

_____

_____

_____

Serve

What can you do to break down the walls of exclusion and discrimination that keep people out? Write two practical examples.

_____

_____

Heroes of Faith

The Syrophoenician Woman

We don't know her name, but the Gospels record that this anonymous woman, a non-Jew, asked Jesus to heal her daughter. Jesus answered her: "It is not right to take the food from the children and throw it to the dogs." He meant that his mission was to his own people, not to foreigners. The woman must have been stung, but her faith in Jesus and her love for her child gave her the courage to answer back. "Lord, even the dogs under the table eat the children's scraps." All people, she reminded Jesus, have a place at God's table (see *Mark 7:24–30*).

HOME and FAMILY

These projects and activities will help you keep this lesson alive all week long.

On your own

Make a poster showing a vine and branches, with Jesus' words from John 15:5. Hang your poster at home to remind you of the lesson of this chapter.

With others

Talk with your friends about the ways in which you knowingly or carelessly exclude others. Plan three things you can do to be more welcoming.

_____

_____

_____

With your family

At a family meal or prayer time, talk about ways that family members can extend hospitality to one another as well as to those outside the family who may be in need of community.

Jesus,
help me love others
as you love me.

GO ONLINE!
www.mhbenziger.com

Make a Difference

Imagine that you and your family have known nothing but the terror of war all your lives. You may never have had the chance to go to school, to sleep in safety, or to worship according to your beliefs. Suddenly you find yourselves stumbling off a plane, after hours or even days of traveling, in a new land. You were able to bring only a few possessions. You left behind your friends and everything that was familiar to you. This new place looks and sounds confusingly different; you don't even recognize the weather, never mind the language that people are speaking.

American parishes practice hospitality when they welcome refugee families and help them settle into new lives.

This experience is shared by thousands of refugees every year. Forced to flee their homelands by war, persecution, or natural disaster, refugee families may be resettled in the United States through programs coordinated by the U.S. Catholic Bishops' Office of Migration and Refugee Services. These families are lucky to escape the terrible conditions in their former homes, but they face a whole new set of obstacles in their new land. Unfamiliarity with English, the difficulty of finding employment, and attitudes of racial or ethnic prejudice can make life less than welcoming for refugees.

Putting Out the Welcome Mat

In 2002 the United States Catholic Bishops released a pastoral letter, *Welcoming the Strangers in Our Midst: Unity in Diversity,* to enlist all members of the Body of Christ in the ministry of hospitality toward refugees and immigrants (people who come to a new land by choice). The bishops asked parishes to become centers of welcome for refugee families resettled in their area. They suggested several ways in which young people might become involved in this outreach.

- Contact your diocesan Catholic Charities office to find out about programs to resettle refugees in your area. Learn more about the countries and cultures from which these refugees come. Learn to say "Hello" or "Welcome" in the languages spoken by newcomers to your community.

- Invite young immigrants, resettled refugees, or exchange students to visit your class. Talk about the things you have in common as young people. Ask what you can do to make people more welcome.

- Include prayers for immigrants, refugees, and migrants (workers who travel back and forth across national borders) in the intercessions when you plan prayer services or liturgies.

Make a plan and take the first steps.

Remember

1. **In what way can the Church be understood to be a sacrament?**

   The Church is the Body of Christ. Jesus is present in the Church through the working of the Holy Spirit. Through the members of the Church Jesus becomes present to the whole world.

2. **How do followers of Jesus become members of the Body of Christ?**

   Christians are initiated into the Body of Christ through the sacraments of initiation: Baptism, Confirmation, and Eucharist. These sacraments take away sin, fill people with sanctifying grace, and make people members of the Church.

3. **What actions does Jesus accomplish in the Eucharist and, through us, in the world?**

   Through the Eucharist Jesus builds community, heals and forgives, shares Good News, gives thanks to his Father, offers himself in sacrifice for the good of others, and becomes truly present in the lives of his people. We are sent forth to live these Eucharistic actions in the world.

4. **In what ways did Jesus reach out to those who were excluded from his society?**

   Jesus included women among his disciples; welcomed and blessed young children; shared the Good News with and praised the moral behavior of the Samaritans; and healed and forgave outcasts such as those with leprosy and mental illness and those with sinful reputations.

Respond

Choose one of the following questions. Write a response. If you wish, share what you have written.

1. How has sanctifying grace—the life-giving relationship with God that strengthens you through the sacraments—made a difference in your life?

2. Which saint, scriptural personality, or role model whom you have learned about in this unit made the biggest impression on you? If you could have dinner with this person, what would you talk about with him or her?

3. How important is community in your life? How do the communities to which you belong support you? What do you contribute to the communities to which you belong? How can you make the communities to which you belong more open and welcoming?

Act

Learn more about the ways in which your parish community reaches out to meet the needs of others. As a class, volunteer to help one of these outreach ministries. Remember that there are ways to become involved even when you are too young to carry out actual ministries. You can help with soup kitchen meals, for example, or wash cars to raise funds for the resettlement of a refugee family.

Share

Choose one of the following images and titles associated with Jesus or his followers:

• Light of the World
• Bread of Life
• Vine and Branches
• Body of Christ
• Communion of Saints

Using a creative medium—music, poetry, drama, dance, photography, painting, sculpture—develop a presentation on the meaning of this image for you. Present or display your finished work to the whole group.

And behold, I am with you always, until the end of the age.

Matthew 28:20b

Burma   From Maryknoll

With You Always

Chapter

I Lay Down My Life

> He humbled himself, becoming obedient to death, even death on a cross.
>
> *Philippians 2:8*

Do You Know?

◆ Why did Jesus sacrifice himself for others?

Heroes Make News

Since September 11, 2001, Americans have had an increased appreciation for ordinary heroes—people who carry out extraordinary rescues, risking their lives for others, and who refuse to take any special credit for it. "It's just my job," the police officer shrugs. "What choice did I have?" asks the firefighter who runs into a burning building to save a trapped child.

On almost any day of the week, you will find stories of ordinary heroes in the newspaper or on the evening news. Sometimes the heroes are young people, as in this example.

The Flood

A severe thunderstorm dropped nine inches of rain in East Texas, flooding roads and turning creek beds into raging rivers. When Allison Carter's car spun out on a wet road, she slid helplessly into a flooded ditch. Within seconds the car was filling with water.

Fifteen-year-old Eric Loya was walking home from his school bus stop when he saw the accident. Without a second thought, Eric dived into the ditch, opened the door, and unfastened the tangled seatbelt. He pulled Mrs. Carter from behind the car's inflated air bag, and helped her to safety. If he had hesitated, Mrs. Carter would have drowned. Asked to explain why he had acted so bravely, Eric said, "I saw someone in trouble. I couldn't just walk away."

Heroic Actions

Tell a story of someone risking his or her life to help others.

LOCAL HERO

THIS WE BELIEVE!

Jesus freely offered his life in sacrifice for the salvation of the world. By his death on the cross, Jesus freed us from sin and death.

WORD OF GOD

For God so loved the world that he gave his only Son, so that everyone who believes in him might not perish but might have eternal life.

John 3:16

A Hero's Death

Zachary was exhausted when he reached home. When he saw his friend Joshua waiting at the gate, Zachary could barely get out the terrible news.

"He's dead." Zachary choked on the words. "Jesus of Nazareth was crucified."

Joshua's usually cheerful face crumpled in sorrow and disbelief. "No!" he cried. "It's not possible! You saw what happened last week when he entered Jerusalem. We were all waving palm branches, and cheering, and hailing him as the Messiah. You were there!"

Zachary sighed wearily. "And I was there today, too, when he died a miserable death. The same crowds who cheered him last week were calling for his death last night, saying he was putting himself in God's place. Of course the Romans jumped on this excuse to get rid of the man they thought of as a rabble-rouser. I hear the soldiers tortured him—they beat him, and whipped him, and mocked him by crowning him with a circle of thorns. He was already half-dead when they nailed him to the cross at Golgotha. That's where our hero died—between two common thieves."

Joshua shuddered. "I can't bear it," he muttered. "Did Jesus say anything?"

"He said, 'Father, forgive them.' Can you believe it? The man was in agony, and still he preached forgiveness."

"What faith!" marveled Joshua.

"What foolishness!" responded Zachary bitterly.

"No," Joshua protested, as the light returned to his eyes. "Don't you remember? He said this day would come. He told us the Messiah would have to suffer, but that he would come back to save us."

Zachary shook his head. "Ah, friend," he sighed. "You hold on to hope if you can. I am too old. I have seen too many heroes come and go. Now let us honor the Sabbath, and then let me sleep."

 Zachary and Joshua have their own ideas about the meaning of Jesus' death. What about you? What do you think Jesus accomplished by his dying on the cross?

A Hero's Trust

Joshua was right. Jesus had spoken very clearly about the road of suffering he had to walk. Both during his life on Earth and after the resurrection, Jesus startled his listeners by reminding them that what was demanded of the Son of Man was not winning glorious victories but losing everything.

Nobody wanted to hear it. When Jesus told the Apostles that the road he was on passed through suffering and death, Peter picked a fight with him. Having just been praised for recognizing Jesus as the Messiah, Peter didn't want to think about what that meant. "Get behind me, Satan," Jesus said to Peter. "You are thinking not as God does, but as human beings do" *(Mark 8:31–33).*

How *did* Jesus know what was ahead? Jesus had a deep insight into human nature. He knew that crowds are fickle, and that popularity could shift to hatred at the blink of an eye. He knew how threatened many people might be by his message of universal love and forgiveness.

Jesus also knew the Hebrew Scriptures. Jesus understood his call and service as a prophet and it was his self-understanding as a prophet that helped Jesus recognize the inevitability of his own death. Jesus reminded his followers that the prophets had been rejected; some were even stoned to death.

But most of all, Jesus had enormous faith. That faith kept him in constant relationship with his Father, and moved him to complete obedience to his Father's will. Jesus' human consciousness, like that of his followers, had absolutely no guarantee that eternal life lay on the other side of the tomb. The difference between Jesus and his followers, however, was that he trusted and loved his Father enough to go into the future without question.

Dialog Box

◆ How did Jesus, the Messiah, win by "losing"?

◆ Why do you think Peter tried to stop Jesus from talking about the suffering ahead?

◆ How did Jesus' insight into human nature help prepare him for what was ahead?

◆ Jesus' trust in his Father was rooted in love. Why do trust and love go hand in hand?

Compassion is the ability to share in another person's sufferings. The virtue of compassion moves you to sacrifice your self in order to end the suffering of others.

A Hero's Gift

At any point along the road of his life, Jesus could have given in to Peter's temptation. He could have stepped off the way of the cross. He could have given in to the very human fear and pain we know he experienced. He could have said to his Father, "No, it's too much. Let somebody else be the hero."

It was Jesus' mission to bring **salvation**—freedom from sin and death—to all humanity by offering up his life on the cross. No one, not even his Father, forced Jesus to carry out this mission. It was always his choice. As he said,

I lay down my life in order to take it up again. No one takes it from me, but I lay it down on my own.

John 10:17b–18a

That's what makes a **sacrifice** heroic: that it is a gift freely given, out of love.

What makes Jesus' sacrifice so remarkable is that he willingly gave up his life for strangers. You can easily imagine a mother risking death to save her child, or a friend donating a kidney to save a friend. The bonds of love make sacrifice easier to understand. But Jesus' love had no boundaries. He saved everyone.

Another gift of Jesus' sacrifice is the knowledge that such self-giving is possible for each person. Jesus' **Passion** (from the Latin for "endurance of suffering") set an example. Because Jesus entered fully and completely into the most painful experiences of human life for the sake of others, you know it is possible for you to do likewise. You can be assured that any time you reach out in love to others—no matter how costly the choice may be—you share in Jesus' heroism and its eternal rewards.

ACTIVITY

On the banner, write about someone who made a sacrifice for you.

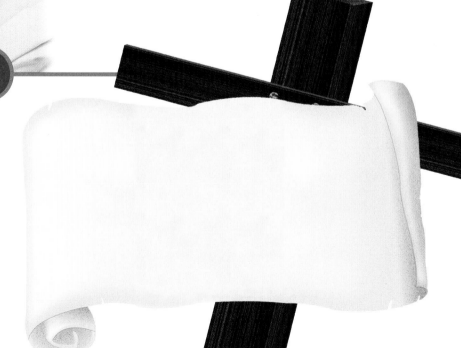

Showing Compassion

Imagine yourself approached by each of the people shown below. Write how you could show compassion to each person. In the center blank space, draw a situation of need that you see in your community, and tell how you could respond compassionately to it.

_____

_____

_____

_____

_____

_____

**Someone with a
death in the family**

**A friend whose parents
are separating**

_____

_____

_____

_____

A child with a serious illness

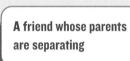

Someone who feels left out

_____

_____

Humbled and Exalted

The New Testament Letter to the Philippians contains an early Christian hymn in honor of Jesus' sacrifice. Pray this hymn together. Then write your own short hymn of praise and thanksgiving.

Christ Jesus, though he was in the form of God, did not regard equality with God something to be grasped.

Rather, he emptied himself, taking the form of a slave, coming in human likeness; and found human in appearance, he humbled himself, becoming obedient to death, even death on a cross.

Because of this, God greatly exalted him and bestowed on him the name that is above every name, that at the name of Jesus every knee should bend, of those in heaven and on earth and under the earth, and every tongue confess that Jesus Christ is Lord, to the glory of the Father.

Philippians 2:5b–11

My Hymn

The exercises and activities on this page will help you know, love, and serve God better.

Know

God the Father gave up his only Son.

Salvation

Jesus gave up his life for us.

We give ourselves for others.

Love

How can you show love for the people in your life through self-sacrifice? Write three practical examples.

_____

_____

_____

Serve

Who are the people who serve you by meeting your needs on a regular basis? List their names, and think of one thing you can do to show your gratitude to each person on the list this week.

_____

_____

_____

_____

Heroes of Faith

Christian de Chergé

In a world marked by tensions between Christians and Muslims, Father Christian de Chergé gave up his life to break down the walls of distrust and hatred. Christian began his life as a soldier. Saved from a bullet wound when a Muslim friend shielded him with his own body, Christian turned to religion. He became a devout Catholic and joined a Trappist monastery in Algeria. When Islamic fundamentalists threatened all foreigners with death, Christian refused to desert his adopted country, writing to his family: "Now all that is left to us is to follow Christ to the end."

These projects and activities will help you keep this lesson alive all week long.

On your own

Prepare a list of all the reasons you use to avoid making sacrifices for others. Next to each excuse, write what you think Jesus would say to you to help you be more generous with yourself and your gifts.

_____

_____

_____

_____

_____

_____

With others

Make a pact with your friends that you will offer one another a safe space to share troubles and sorrows without being teased or dismissed. Think of three ways you can treat one another more compassionately.

_____

_____

_____

With your family

Talk with family members about the sacrifices you make for one another. Decide on a way to sacrifice some of your family's time, talent, money, or possessions to meet the needs of people in your community.

We adore you, O Christ, and we bless you, because by your holy cross you have redeemed the world.

GO ONLINE!
www.mhbenziger.com

JESUS RISEN

Why do you seek the living one among the dead? He is not here, but he has been raised.

Luke 24:5–6

Do You Know?

◆ What difference does the resurrection make in the life of Christians?

Remembering Aunt Rose

"Come straight home after school today, okay, George?"

"Sure, Mom. What's up?"

"Your father's Aunt Rose died last night. The funeral will be on Thursday. Family members will be coming into town, and I'll need you to help me do some extra laundry and run errands," George's mother explained.

"Is Dad all right?" George asked.

"He's sad, honey, because it's always hard to lose someone you're close to. But Aunt Rose was very old, so we've all known this was coming—even Aunt Rose herself. She died peacefully at home, the way she wanted."

"Is there anything else I can do?" George asked.

His mother smiled. "Well, it turns out Aunt Rose left some instructions about her funeral service. She hoped that you and your cousin Ruth Anne would agree to serve at the Mass of Christian Burial. What do you think?"

George thought of his great-aunt, who had come to every one of his Little League games. "I'd be honored," he answered.

Rest in Peace

Funerals are times of both grief and hope for Christians, who mourn the loss of a loved one while trusting that he or she has entered into new life with God. Think of the way funerals are celebrated in your community. In the space below, list signs of grief and signs of hope that you might see at a funeral.

Rest In Peace

_____

_____

_____

_____

_____

Not the End

Mary of Magdala could not stop weeping. She had hardly slept since the soldiers had taken Jesus away. Mary thought that the hours she spent at the foot of the cross, holding Jesus' mother's hand tightly as both women watched Jesus' life slip away in agony, were the worst pain anyone could experience. But now, three days later, Mary had encountered something even worse.

She had come at dawn to anoint Jesus' body with the burial spices, a task postponed by the Sabbath. But when she got to the tomb, it was empty. Mary couldn't even perform this one last ritual for her beloved teacher.

"Woman, why are you weeping?"

Through her tears, in the gray dawn light, Mary saw a man approaching from the shadows of the trees. She thought he must be a gardener, and out of her pain she spoke sharply to him. "Please, sir," she begged. "If you carried him away, tell me where you laid his body."

The stranger spoke only one word in reply: "Mary."

Mary's heart jumped. She knew that voice. She rubbed the tears from her eyes with her veil, and rose to her feet. Could it be? "Teacher!" she cried (based on *John 20:1–18*).

✝ THIS WE BELIEVE!

God raised Jesus from death to new life. We are called to live the message of Easter every day, and to look forward with hope to new life with God after death.

ACTIVITY

Read the following accounts of meetings between the Risen Jesus and his followers. Then choose one account and retell it or act it out from the point of view of the person or persons encountering Jesus after his resurrection. Try to capture the emotions of the meeting.

• Luke 24:13–35
• Luke 24:36–43
• John 21:1–14

Doubt and Faith

Imagine that someone you love very much, someone you honor as a great teacher and perhaps even the promised redeemer sent by God, suddenly dies. Think about how your world would change, catastrophically. The grief and the confusion might cause you to question everything in which you believed. And if someone told you that the person was suddenly alive again, you might doubt the evidence of their senses.

That's what happened to Thomas, the follower of Jesus who imitated his teacher so closely that he earned the nickname *Twin*. Thomas was absent when the Risen Jesus first appeared to his disciples, and he just couldn't bring himself to believe that such impossibly good news could be true. Instead, Thomas made a shocking proposal, perhaps intended to jolt his friends out of what he thought was a delusion:

> Unless I see the mark of the nails in his hands and put my finger into the nailmarks and put my hand into his side, I will not believe." Now a week later his disciples were again inside and Thomas was with them. Jesus came, although the doors were locked, and stood in their midst and said, "Peace be with you." Then he said to Thomas, "Put your finger here and see my hands, and bring your hand and put it into my side, and do not be unbelieving, but believe." Thomas answered and said to him, "My Lord and my God!"
>
> John 20:25b–28

Today we know Thomas by another nickname, *Doubting Thomas*. But Thomas's response to the unbelievably good news of the resurrection isn't sinful doubt. It's the natural reaction each one of us would have to such a life-changing miracle. In the end, Thomas didn't need the proof he demanded. One look at the Risen Jesus stirred to life the deep faith that lay buried under Thomas's grief, and he responded with one of the shortest yet most heartfelt hymns of praise ever sung.

? How would you react if a beloved person whom you thought was gone forever suddenly came back into your life?

WORD OF GOD

For if we believe that Jesus died and rose, so too will God, through Jesus, bring with him those who have fallen asleep.

1 Thessalonians 4:14

VIRTUE

Hope is an Easter virtue. The eyes of hope see beyond the passing experiences of grief, loss, and death to the eternal realities of love and new life.

A Changed People

From the distance of 2,000 years, it can be easy to take the **resurrection** for granted. If you grew up as a Catholic Christian, celebrating years of Easter Alleluias, you might not be able to identify with the emotions of those friends of Jesus who encountered him alive after they knew, with every logical part of themselves, that he was dead. The resurrection is so much a part of your life that it can become just one more item in the Creed you recite every Sunday.

But the powerful emotions experienced by those who met the Risen Jesus changed their lives in remarkable ways, shaping the Church to this day. The story of the Body of Christ really begins not in the stable in Bethlehem but in the garden outside Jerusalem. The Gospel stories of Jesus' birth, life, and death are told in flashback from the standpoint of the empty tomb. The earliest Christian communities took their life from the message of the resurrection. As Paul wrote:

If Christ has not been raised, then empty too is our preaching; empty, too, your faith.

1 Corinthians 15:14

In honor of the resurrection, Christians moved their celebration of the Sabbath to Sunday, the **Lord's Day.** In Christian understanding, every Sunday is a little Easter. Every Sunday Eucharist commemorates the saving, life-transforming events of Jesus' death and resurrection.

Easter itself—the Feast of the Resurrection—is the first and greatest feast day of the Church. At the Easter Vigil on the night before the feast, new Christians are welcomed into the community through the sacraments of initiation. The newly-lighted **Paschal candle** proclaims the presence of "Christ, our Light!"

The great song of Easter is **"Alleluia!"**—from the joyful Hebrew shout, "Praise the Lord!" Saint Augustine wrote that every Christian should be "a walking Alleluia," a living sign of the joy of the Risen Christ alive in our hearts, impossible to take for granted.

Dialog Box

◆ What factors might lead Christians to take the remarkable event of the resurrection for granted?

◆ How did the resurrection shape the life of the early Church?

◆ What signs would identify a "walking Alleluia"—someone who took the message of the resurrection seriously, and lived it out every day?

Easter People

Saint Augustine wrote, "We are Easter people, and Alleluia is our song." Complete the activity below with observations and ideas about what it means to be an Easter person.

✤Alleluia✤Alleluia✤Alleluia✤Alleluia✤

How would you recognize an Easter person? List the qualities such a person might demonstrate, or the actions he or she might carry out.

_____

_____

_____

Write one example of how you have seen your parish community acting as Easter people.

_____

_____

Write three ways you can be an Easter person this week.

_____

_____

_____

Sing His Resurrection

This joyful Easter prayer is based on the Byzantine liturgy of Saint John Chrysostom, used by Orthodox Christians and Eastern Rite Catholics.

All: Christ is risen from the dead, trampling down death by death and upon those in the tombs bestowing new life.

Group 1: Where is your sting, O death? Where is your victory?

Group 2: Christ is risen, and death is overthrown.

Group 3: For Christ, having risen from the dead, became the first fruits of those who sleep in death.

Group 4: For by the cross, great joy is come into the world. Ever praising the Lord, let us sing his resurrection.

All: Christ is risen from the dead, trampling down death by death and upon those in the tombs bestowing new life.

The exercises and activities on this page will help you know, love, and serve God better.

Know

God raised Jesus from the dead.	We are called to be Easter people.	God will raise us to new life.
↓	↓	↓
We celebrate Easter.	We celebrate and live the Eucharist.	We look for the resurrection of the dead.

Love

What can you do this week to show that the power of love is stronger than anything, even death? Write two examples.

1.

2.

Serve

How can you be a messenger of hope to people who are dealing with grief and loss? Write three examples.

1.

2.

3.

Heroes of Faith

Saint Martha

Saint Martha lived with her sister Mary in Bethany. The sisters and their brother Lazarus were great friends of Jesus. Lazarus became ill and the sisters sent for Jesus. When Jesus arrived, Lazarus was already dead. Martha ran to meet Jesus saying, "Lord, if you had been here, my brother would not have died." Jesus asked her to believe that he was the resurrection and had power to give eternal life to all who believe in him. Martha trusted in Jesus and went on to profess, "I believe that you are the Messiah, the Son of God, the one who is coming into the world" (based on *John* 11:24–27).

These projects and activities will help you keep this lesson alive all week long.

On your own

Make a banner decorated with the word *Alleluia!* and images of new life. Display your banner at home as a reminder that you are called to be an Easter person.

With others

Tell a friend some of the ways that he or she has been an Easter person for you. Ask how you can be an Easter person for your friend.

With your family

Make a list of family members, friends, neighbors, and parishioners who have died during the past year. Once a week, at a Sunday family meal, choose a name from the list and pray a prayer of thanksgiving for that person's life.

_____

_____

_____

_____

_____

_____

_____

May the souls of the faithful departed through the mercy of God rest in peace. Amen.

GO ONLINE!
www.mhbenziger.com

THE HOLY SPIRIT

Do you not know
that the Spirit of
God dwells in you?

1 Corinthians 3:16

◆

Do You Know?

◆ How do you experience
the Holy Spirit's
presence in your life?

So Alive

Ben looked forward to his family's camping trips every year.
He enjoyed everything about being in the woods: hikes, hot
chocolate, the silly songs his dad made everyone sing—even
sleeping on the ground. What Ben liked best, though, was
staring into the campfire at night. The deep red embers and
shifting light made him feel safe and warm.

Erica was nervous about the school's whale-watching trip.
She had never been on a boat before. What if she got sick?
What if she fell overboard? But as the boat moved through the
blue Pacific Ocean, Erica forgot her fears. The fog lifted, and
she saw seagulls soaring overhead. The wind and the salt spray
were invigorating. When a gray whale surfaced majestically
right before her eyes, Erica gasped. She had never felt so alive!

Feeling Alive

Draw or describe an experience that made you feel really alive.
Include as many details as possible.

Do not quench the Spirit.

1 Thessalonians 5:19

◆ What qualities and emotions do you associate with wind? with water? with fire?

◆ Can you name any other examples from the Hebrew Scriptures of wind, water, or fire being used to symbolize the presence of God's life-giving Spirit?

Giver of Life

In Jewish and Christian tradition, the fullness of life is not possible outside of the presence of the Spirit of God. God's Spirit gives life, grace, power, freedom, joy, and peace—all the qualities that make us know we are fully alive.

The Hebrew Scriptures use a variety of natural symbols to indicate the presence of God's life-giving Spirit. In Hebrew, the word for *breath,* the word for *wind,* and the word for *spirit* are one and the same: *rûah.* At creation, the Spirit of God hovers over the abyss like a mighty wind *(Genesis 1:2).* God breathes the breath of life, and an immortal soul, into the first human *(Genesis 2:7).* And when the prophet Ezekiel sees the disheartened and exiled house of Israel as a heap of dry bones in a wasteland, he is told to call upon the wind of the Spirit to breathe new life into the people *(Ezekiel 37:1–14).*

Water is a sign of God's Spirit, too, especially to a desert people for whom even a little rain can mean the difference between deadly drought and abundant life. Though water can be destructive, as it was for the armies of Egypt, it can be the passageway from death to life, as it was for the Israelites crossing the Red Sea and the Jordan River *(Exodus 14:10–31, Joshua 3:1–17).* The prophets describe the coming of the longed-for Messiah, upon whom God's Spirit rests, as a time when deserts bloom *(Isaiah 35:1–10)* and justice surges like a mighty river *(Amos 5:24).*

Fire, too, has potential to bring both destruction and regeneration. God speaks to Moses out of a burning bush *(Exodus 3:12–22)* and gives him the covenant of life on Mount Sinai amid thunder, fire, and wind *(Exodus 19:16–19).* The prophet Elijah calls down fire from heaven to prove God's power against idol worshipers *(1 Kings 18:1–46),* and is taken up to heaven in a chariot of fire *(2 Kings 2:9–12).*

The Promise of the Holy Spirit

Jesus announced his public ministry with the words, "The Spirit of the Lord is upon me." His announcement was remarkable not only because of who Jesus was—the son of a carpenter from an undistinguished town—but also because of what it signified. With the coming of the Messiah, God's life-giving Spirit would never again be withdrawn from the world.

Jesus' friends were familiar with the history of God's People. They knew that in the past, when a great prophet died, God's Spirit seemed to retreat, too. Although God never left them, the people felt abandoned without the presence of the prophet to remind them. Jesus' friends must have recalled this history as they gathered on the night before his death. They must have felt that they were about to be abandoned. But Jesus had another surprising announcement for them.

If you love me, you will keep my commandments. And I will ask the Father, and he will give you another Advocate to be with you always, the Spirit of truth.

I will not leave you orphans. I have told you this while I am with you. The Advocate, the holy Spirit that the Father will send in my name— he will teach you everything and remind you of all that I told you. Peace I leave with you; my peace I give to you. Do not let your hearts be troubled or afraid.

John 14:15–17a, 18a, 25–27a, 27c

Jesus promised his disciples that the Spirit of God would never leave them. He described the Spirit as an **Advocate**—someone who speaks for or defends another—and as a **Paraclete**—a *consoler* who would sustain the disciples through their grief and fear. The Spirit would be a Teacher of Truth, one who would inspire (literally, "fill with breath, life, energy") the disciples to share the Good News.

VIRTUE

Joy is much more than temporary happiness. People who practice joyfulness have a deep sense of the Spirit's grace-filled presence that sustains them—and those around them—through difficult times.

 How do you think Jesus' friends reacted to his promise of the Holy Spirit? When did that promise come true?

The Spirit in Christian Imagery

The New Testament picks up on and adds to the images used by the Hebrew Scriptures to describe the presence of the Holy Spirit.

Fire. John the Baptist prophesied that Jesus would baptize the world with fire *(Luke 3:16–17)*, a sign of the transforming energy of the Holy Spirit.

Anointing. Jesus, the Messiah, was anointed with the Spirit of God *(Luke 4:18–19)*. In Baptism and Confirmation, Christians are anointed in the Holy Spirit.

Dove. At Jesus' baptism, the Spirit appeared in the form of a dove *(Matthew 3:16)*. Recalling the bird that returned to Noah's ark bearing an olive branch, doves are signs of peace and hope, and this symbol is often used to depict the Holy Spirit in Christian art.

Cloud and Light. During the Exodus, God's Spirit led the Israelites as a pillar of cloud and a pillar of light. The New Testament says that the Holy Spirit "overshadowed" Mary at the Annunciation *(Luke 1:35)*. The same cloud overshadows Jesus at the transfiguration *(Luke 9:34–36)*. The Risen Jesus ascended to heaven in a cloud *(Acts 1:9–11)*.

Water. The Holy Spirit empowers the waters of Baptism *(Mark 1:8, John 3:5–8)*. Jesus told the Samaritan woman that the Spirit wells up like water to give eternal life *(John 4:13–14)*.

ACTIVITY

Spirit Signs

What image would you use to symbolize the presence of the Holy Spirit?

Fruit of the Spirit

In his letter to the Galatians, Paul listed nine qualities that mark the Spirit-filled person or community (Galatians 5:22–23). These effects of the gifts of the Spirit, traditionally called the "fruit of the Spirit," are as easily recognized today as they were in the early days of the Church.

Think about what each fruit of the Spirit means to you. Note one way you can express each quality in your life.

Peace

_____

_____

_____

Patience

_____

_____

_____

Kindness

_____

_____

_____

Generosity

_____

_____

_____

Faithfulness

_____

_____

_____

Love

_____

_____

_____

Gentleness

_____

_____

_____

Self-Control

_____

_____

_____

Joy

_____

_____

_____

Love Creates a Place

Pray or sing this nineteenth-century English hymn, based on a medieval poem, to invite the Holy Spirit into your life.

Come down, O Love divine,
Seek thou this soul of mine,
And visit it with thine own ardor glowing;
O Comforter, draw near,
Within my heart appear,
And kindle it, thy holy flame bestowing.

O let it freely burn,
Till earthly passions turn
To dust and ashes in its heat consuming;
And let thy glorious light
Shine ever on my sight,
And clothe me 'round, the while my path illuming.

And so the yearning strong
With which the soul will long
Shall far outpass the power of human telling;
For none can guess its grace,
Till Love create a place
Wherein the Holy Spirit makes a dwelling.

The exercises and activities on this page will help you know, love, and serve God better.

Know

Signs of the Holy Spirit

In the Hebrew Scriptures	In the New Testament	In the Church Today
• Natural signs • God's actions on behalf of the people • The words and example of the prophets	• Jesus' life and teachings • The mission of the Apostles • The fruit of the Spirit in the early Church	• The sacraments • The mission of the Church • The fruit of the Spirit in you

Love

The kind of love that is a fruit of the Spirit is generous and joyful. Write three examples of how you have experienced this love.

_____

_____

_____

Serve

The Spirit energizes people to reach out to those in need. Who could use some inspiration from you this week? Write three ways you can share the Spirit.

_____

_____

_____

Heroes of Faith

Saint Ephraim of Syria

When his homeland was overrun by the Persian army, Ephraim, a Christian monk, escaped to a wilderness area in present-day Iraq. He took shelter in a cave, which he left only once for the rest of his life. While there, Ephraim opened himself up to the deep joy of the Holy Spirit, and composed beautiful hymns that made complex theology understandable to ordinary people. His songs were so moving that later generations called Ephraim "the Harp of the Holy Spirit."

CHAPTER 11
HOME and FAMILY

These projects and activities will help you keep this lesson alive all week long.

On your own

Write your own prayer to the Holy Spirit, asking for courage to live the Good News.

_____

_____

_____

_____

_____

_____

With others

Talk with your friends about how you can be advocates and consolers for one another and for others in your community who need defense and comfort. Put one of your ideas into action this week.

With your family

Work together to make wind chimes, a kite, a candleholder, or some other object that will remind you of the natural signs of the Holy Spirit while adding beauty and enjoyment to your family's life.

Come, Holy Spirit!

GO ONLINE!
www.mhbenziger.com

Go Make Disciples

Growing Into Your Gifts

"It's no use!" Carmen sobbed, throwing the folder with her speech in it across the room. "I'm *terrible* at this! Who ever thought I could be a competitive speaker?"

Carmen's speech coach calmly picked up the folder, sorted the pages so they were in order, and handed them back to Carmen. "I did," Ms. Klein answered, "and I still do. Believe me, Carmen, you are just suffering from first-meet nerves. You've written a really good speech about something important to you. You have it mostly memorized, and next week you will represent our school at the speech competition."

"Sure," Carmen groaned. "I'll probably come in last!"

Ms. Klein smiled. "I don't think so," she said. "But if you do, you'll still come out ahead of me. At my first meet, I was so nervous I ended up placing sixth—out of only four competitors!"

Carmen couldn't help herself. She burst out laughing. "No way!" she said. "Didn't you just die?"

Ms. Klein shook her head, remembering. "Well, I thought I would, for a few minutes there. But then *my* speech coach told me I needed to lighten up and enjoy the process of growing into my gifts—which is exactly what I'm telling you to do now."

Carmen thought about that for a minute. Then she stood up, walked back to the podium, and opened the folder. When she started her speech again, her voice had a new confidence.

The Cheering Section

Tell about a time when someone gave you the inspiration to keep doing something important to you.

> Go, therefore, and make disciples of all nations, baptizing them in the name of the Father, and of the Son, and of the Holy Spirit.
>
> *Matthew 28:19*

Do You Know?

◆ Where do you get help to carry out your Christian mission?

Who—Us?

Imagine how the Apostles felt in the days after Jesus' resurrection, as they came to realize that everything he had predicted had come true. Gradually, they realized that this joyful period of reunion was not going to last forever. Jesus would be returning to his Father in heaven—and then what? Did Jesus really expect this little group of fishermen and reformed tax collectors to carry on the work he had begun? Surely Jesus remembered how slow they had been to understand his mission, how frightened they had been by his arrest and execution! Yes, Jesus had promised to send the Holy Spirit to help them, but the Apostles must have wondered whether even the Spirit of God could transform them into brave and eloquent messengers of the Good News.

Jesus left no room for misunderstanding the mission he had in mind for his friends. His last words to them, on the mountain of the **ascension,** made this clear:

All power in heaven and on earth has been given to me. Go, therefore, and make disciples of all nations, baptizing them in the name of the Father, and of the Son, and of the Holy Spirit, teaching them to observe all that I have commanded you.

Matthew 28:18b–20a

After Jesus was taken up into heaven, his friends stayed in Jerusalem, waiting for the coming of the promised Holy Spirit. Of course, they waited behind closed doors, because they were still fearful. Jesus' words must have echoed in their minds as they prayed and waited in that upper room. "Make disciples of all nations—who, *us?*"

WORD OF GOD

But you will receive power when the Holy Spirit comes upon you, and you will be my witnesses to the ends of the earth.

Acts 1:8

ACTIVITY

While We Wait

Imagine you are one of the Apostles, waiting in the upper room for the coming of the Spirit that Jesus promised. Write a letter to a friend, sharing your feelings when you think about what Jesus has sent you to do.

All Nations

The Apostles need not have worried. When the Spirit came to them on the morning of Pentecost, their doubts lessened. In an experience so powerful that they described it as being crowned with tongues of flames in the midst of a whirlwind, the Apostles were given the gifts they needed for the mission ahead.

They burst from their locked room into the crowded streets, so fearless and joyful that some people thought they had been drinking wine for breakfast. And if the Apostles had wondered about whether they would stumble over the message Jesus had entrusted to them, all questions were answered on Pentecost. Not only were the Apostles eloquent in their testimony about Jesus' life, death, and resurrection—they were understood even by people who didn't speak their language.

Peter preached so moving a sermon, according to the Acts of the Apostles, that about 3,000 people, from lands all over the Mediterranean, stepped forward to be baptized. It was a great start to the mission that was destined to reach "all nations."

Father, Son, and Holy Spirit

The friends and followers of Jesus did not think of their life-changing experience in theological terms. But what they had experienced in knowing Jesus and in the Pentecost event was the mystery of the **Blessed Trinity,** one God in Three Divine Persons.

- Through Jesus they had come to know God as Father, the loving Creator of the world whose will guides all things.

- In Jesus they recognized the Son of God, sent by the Father to save the world from sin and death.

- At Pentecost they were filled with the Holy Spirit, the giver of life who proceeds from the love of the Father and the Son.

- By baptizing in the name of the Father, and of the Son, and of the Holy Spirit, the Apostles passed on this life-changing encounter with the Blessed Trinity to everyone they welcomed into the Body of Christ.

 How have you experienced the work of the Blessed Trinity in your life?

VIRTUE

Courage is not the absence of all fear, but the determination to face difficult situations with trust in God. Courage makes it possible for Jesus' followers to carry on his mission.

THIS WE BELIEVE!

The Holy Spirit empowers the followers of Jesus to carry out his commission to make disciples of all nations.

Dialog Box

◆ Why did the Apostles need these gifts of the Holy Spirit? Why do you need them?

◆ Which of the seven gifts do you feel you already express well? Which of the gifts do you feel you still need to develop?

◆ Which of these gifts do you think the world needs most right now? Why?

Seven Gifts

The same gifts that the Apostles received at Pentecost are given to you in Baptism and Confirmation. And for good reason— you too are called to "make disciples of all nations." The work of bringing the Good News that Jesus began on earth was continued by his Apostles and, through the apostolic Church, continues today in every follower of Jesus.

The qualities known as the gifts of the Holy Spirit are given to you to assist you in your mission—which is not some career choice far in the future but something you do every day, everywhere, with everyone you encounter. Here are the gifts and the help they can give you.

- **Wisdom** is the gift of seeing all people and situations as God does. Wisdom gives you the big picture, and allows you to stay focused on what is right.

- **Understanding** is the gift of sharing others' feelings and seeing things from their point of view. With understanding you can overcome the boundaries that divide people.

- **Right judgment,** sometimes called *counsel,* is the gift of forming your conscience and seeking good advice. With right judgment you will be more likely to make good moral choices and avoid temptation.

- **Courage,** sometimes called *fortitude,* is the gift of standing up for what is right even when it is difficult or scary. Courage helps you get through hard times and come to the defense of people in need.

- **Knowledge** is the gift of openness to learning and growing. Knowledge enables you to see God reflected in the things of this world.

- **Reverence,** sometimes called *piety,* is the gift of a prayerful heart. With reverence you maintain a close relationship with God and treat all God's people with respect and dignity.

- **Wonder and awe,** sometimes called *fear of the Lord,* is the gift of seeing signs of God's awesome presence in all creation.

Living the Gifts

Tell what each of the Spirit's gifts means to you. Then tell one way you can use each gift of the Spirit to help you carry out the mission of Jesus.

Gift of the Spirit	What This Gift of the Spirit Means to Me	How I Can Use This Gift to Carry Out the Mission of Jesus
Wisdom		
Understanding		
Right judgment		
Courage		
Knowledge		
Reverence		
Wonder and awe		

On a Grand Scale

Leader: Let us pray to be filled with the Holy Spirit.

Reader 1: O Holy Spirit, Paraclete,
perfect in us the work begun by Jesus.

Reader 2: Nourish in every one of us a life of prayer.

Reader 3: Give energy to our mission so that it may reach all peoples.

Reader 4: Let nothing on Earth keep us from our mission.

Reader 5: Allow no cowardly hesitation to stand in the way of our fight for justice.

Reader 6: Protect the abundance of our charity from the narrowness of petty selfishness.

All: Let everything in us be on a grand scale:
our search for truth and our devotion to it,
our love and compassion,
our readiness to sacrifice ourselves in
carrying the cross.

Leader: May everything we do be done according to your will,
O Holy Spirit of love,
whom the Father and the Son poured out over the Church
and over each and every human soul.

All: Amen!

Adapted from *a prayer of Pope John XXIII*

The exercises and activities on this page will help you know, love, and serve God better.

Know

The Father and the Son send the Holy Spirit to the Apostles.

↓

The Apostles are sent to make disciples of all nations.

↓

You receive the Holy Spirit in Baptism and Confirmation, and are sent to continue Jesus' mission.

Love

How have you used the gifts of the Spirit to share God's love with others this week? Write two examples.

Serve

Who are the people to whom Jesus is sending you to bring Good News? How will you carry out this mission? Write three examples.

Heroes of Faith

Sister Thea Bowman

Bertha Bowman was an African American teenager from a Baptist family when God called her to become a Catholic sister. Bertha took the religious name Thea. As the only African American member of her community, Sister Thea considered it her mission to evangelize the whole Church about the gifts of African Americans. Filled with the Spirit, Sister Thea spoke, sang, told stories, shouted, and danced in praise of God. She refused to accept attitudes of racial prejudice or gender bias as she preached: "Testify! Teach! Act on the Word! Witness!"

HOME and FAMILY

These projects and activities will help you keep this lesson alive all week long.

On your own

Read Peter's Pentecost sermon (Acts 2:14–36). Think of two ways you could convey this same message in ways that people of today would understand.

With others

Make an agreement with your friends to support and nourish one another's gifts. When you start running yourselves or one another down, stop yourselves and say or do something positive.

With your family

Make cards for family members acknowledging their gifts and thanking them for supporting you as you grow in your mission as a follower of Jesus.

The grace of our Lord Jesus Christ and the love of God and the fellowship of the Holy Spirit be with us all.

GO ONLINE!
www.mhbenziger.com

Make a Difference

Jesus sent the Apostles to make disciples of all nations. Since 1986, young disciples from all nations have come together every two years to celebrate World Youth Day with Pope John Paul II. The first year, 50,000 young people participated and heard the pope's message of encouragement in their ministry. "Love is stronger than death," the pope told the gathered pilgrims.

At the center of the World Youth Day festivities is a large wooden cross that was entrusted to the youth of the world by Pope John Paul II in 1984. The cross is carried around the world during the two-year period between World Youth Day celebrations, passing from place to place much like the Olympic torch. The pope told young people to see the cross as a symbol of their ministry to bring the Good News to the whole world. "The cross walks with young people, and young people walk with the cross," John Paul said. Sebastien Lacroix, the young man who was in charge of supervising the cross during preparations for World Youth Day 2002 in Toronto, Canada, had this to say about the symbol's power:

> *This cross accompanies thousands of young people on their journey to Jesus Christ. The cross has stood in vigil throughout entire nights, and in parks close to young people who are wounded. It has stood silently in chapels allowing for quiet contemplation. The cross transforms. The cross heals. The cross touches hearts. Let us allow ourselves to be touched by the cross.*

The World Youth Day cross has been carried around the world and serves as a symbol for young people's faith.

All the Continents of the World

Participants in World Youth Day are older teens and young adults from every nation. They plan and save in order to afford the journey. In some cases, they are supported by scholarship donations. Students and teachers from a home mission parish in Ohio's Appalachian region, for example, were able to attend World Youth Day 2002 through a special donation made by other participants. A sixteen-year-old boy from the parish said he wanted to go to "get an overall perspective of the cultural diversity of the Catholic Church and see how youth like me are trying to spread the love of Christ on all the continents of the world."

You can find out more about the World Youth Day cross at www.worldyouthday.org. Contact your diocesan Office of Youth Ministry to learn about plans for future World Youth Day celebrations.

Remember

1. Why did Jesus die on the cross?

Jesus gave up his life in loving sacrifice to win for all people salvation from sin and death.

2. What central event of our Christian faith gives hope that death will be the beginning of new life with God? When do we celebrate this event?

Jesus' resurrection, celebrated solemnly at Easter and also at every Sunday Mass, teaches us that death is not the end. God has the power to offer us eternal life.

3. What gift did Jesus promise to his followers to help them continue his work?

Jesus promised that the Holy Spirit would come to be with the Apostles forever to protect, comfort, and teach them.

4. When did the Apostles receive the Holy Spirit?

The Apostles received the Holy Spirit on the morning of Pentecost, about ten days after Jesus had returned to his Father in heaven.

5. What gifts of the Holy Spirit help Christians carry out their mission to "make disciples of all nations"? When do Christians receive these gifts?

The gifts of the Holy Spirit are wisdom, understanding, right judgment, courage, knowledge, reverence, and wonder and awe. These gifts are given in the sacraments of Baptism and Confirmation.

Respond

Choose one of the following questions. Write a response. If you wish, share what you have written.

1. How do the Passion, death, and resurrection of Jesus influence the way Christians understand suffering and death? Based on your beliefs, what comfort could you give to someone who was afraid of illness, aging, or death?

2. How can someone your age answer Jesus' call to "make disciples of all nations"?

3. Some theologians describe the Blessed Trinity as a community of love. How would you describe the Blessed Trinity to someone who asked what this belief meant to you?

Act

List the gifts of the Holy Spirit on the board. Brainstorm three ways that you, as a group, can use each of these gifts to teach, serve, or care for others in your community. Choose the best ideas you come up with for each gift and put them into practice over the next few weeks.

Share

During the Eucharistic Prayer at Mass, you recall Jesus' saving actions when you pray or sing the Memorial Acclamation. Recall or read from a missalette the four forms used for the Memorial Acclamation. Note that each refers in some way to three events: Jesus' death, his resurrection, and his coming again at the end of time. Choose one form of the Memorial Acclamation and make a triptych—a three-panel folding screen—that illustrates it. You can use magazine photos, drawings, or an abstract collage to express the meaning of each event commemorated. Write the words of the acclamation across the bottom of the triptych. Display your finished artwork for the parish community.

Amen, amen, I say to you, whoever believes in me will do the works that I do, and will do greater ones than these, because I am going to the Father.

John 14:12

Russia  From Maryknoll

I Am the Way

Chapter

Jesus Remembered

We Remember

"This is a story I learned from my grandmother," Francine began in a strong, clear voice. "This is our story of freedom."

Livingston family members from all across the country had gathered at grandmother's house, as they did every year, for a reunion and a celebration. This year it was Francine's turn to tell the family story.

"Our ancestors were a free people in Africa," Francine continued. "They were farmers who tended the land, loved their families, and gave thanks to God.

"Then the slavers came and put our ancestors in chains. They carried our ancestors away across the sea, bound and stacked like lumber in the holds of ships. Our ancestors suffered humiliation and violence. They watched helplessly as their children were sold away. Some of them lost their lives trying to escape from bondage.

"Today we celebrate the ending of that terrible time," Francine went on, as her grandmother had taught her. "We remember the suffering of our ancestors, and we remember the struggles that won us back our freedom. And we make this promise: We will never be slaves again. This we remember, this we celebrate, this we believe!"

> What we have seen and heard we proclaim now to you, so that you too may have fellowship with us.
>
> *1 John 1:3a*

Do You Know?

◆ How does the Church keep alive the memory and teachings of Jesus?

Family Memories

How does your family remember special people, times, or events?

WORD OF GOD

We possess the prophetic message that is altogether reliable. You will do well to be attentive to it, as to a lamp shining in a dark place, until day dawns and the morning star rises in your hearts.

2 Peter 1:19

Remembering Jesus

The Apostles had no trouble remembering Jesus after he returned to his Father. Filled with the Holy Spirit, they shared their memories of Jesus and his message with everyone they met. But the Apostles did not live forever. So how did their message and their memories live on?

One of the most important ways was through words. As Christians know, Jesus is not only *in* the Word of God—he *is* the Word of God, made flesh. Words keep alive the memory of Jesus.

Today you can turn to the New Testament to find Jesus' teachings and the stories of his saving actions. But the earliest Christians had no written Scriptures of their own. Those who were familiar with the Hebrew Scriptures found in the words of the prophets many passages that reminded them of Jesus. They read and prayed these traditional Jewish writings with new eyes. They composed new prayers and hymns that celebrated their faith in Jesus. Missionaries and leaders of the new Christian communities wrote letters explaining the message of Jesus. And of course the people told stories, passing along from one generation to the next the memories the Apostles had passed on to them.

ACTIVITY

Memory Makers

Each of the passages below is an example of the ways the early Christians kept alive the memory of Jesus and his teachings. Read each passage and summarize in your own words what it tells you about Jesus and his teachings.

Colossians 1:15–20, an early Christian hymn

1 John 2:1–6, a letter

Mark 10:17–31, a story

Meeting Jesus in the Word

By the end of the first century, the **oral tradition**—the memories, stories, and prayers of the first Christians—had been set down in writing. Eventually these writings were collected into what Christians today know as the New Testament of the Bible. The New Testament is made up of the following books:

- **Gospels.** These four accounts of Jesus' life and teachings were collected by and for different early Christian communities. The Gospels of Matthew, Mark, and Luke are so similar in their structure that they are called **synoptic** Gospels, meaning "seen with the same eyes." John's Gospel has a tone and structure all its own.

- **Acts of the Apostles.** This account of the growth of the early Church and the spread of the Good News is a testament to the powerful presence of the Holy Spirit.

- **Letters (Epistles).** Most of the New Testament letters were written by or attributed to Paul, the Church's first great missionary. Other New Testament letters are attributed to James, Peter, John, and Jude.

- **Revelation.** This **apocalyptic** book provides a symbolic vision of Jesus' Second Coming, meant to provide hope to early Christians enduring persecution.

A Weekly Reunion

At every Sunday Mass, Catholic Christians gather to remember Jesus in the Eucharist. The Christian family story is shared in the **Liturgy of the Word,** the part of the Mass during which the Scriptures are proclaimed and opened up for understanding. The Liturgy of the Word contains examples of all the ways that the memory of Jesus is kept alive in the community. On most Sundays, the Liturgy of the Word consists of a reading from the Old Testament, followed by a psalm sung or recited in response. Next a passage from one of the New Testament letters is read. Then a portion of a Gospel is proclaimed. After the Scriptures are proclaimed, the priest or deacon preaches a **homily** that helps the assembly understand and apply the scriptural message to their lives.

VIRTUE

Fidelity is faithfulness to what is true and right. Fidelity to the Word of God in the Scriptures and to the teachings of the Church will help keep you on the right track as you follow Jesus.

ACTIVITY

Share the Word

In a small group, read the Scriptures for the coming Sunday. Then work together to compose a homily that would help young people understand the readings.

Dialog Box

◆ Why do you think Jesus gave the Apostles and their successors the authority to interpret and apply the message of the Scriptures?

◆ Why is it important to think of Scripture and Tradition as woven together?

◆ What are some issues or problems unique to today's society that have been addressed by the teaching authority of the Church?

A Living Tradition

For Catholic Christians, the memory of Jesus' life and teachings is very important. The **revelation**—or showing forth of the truth—contained in the Scriptures is kept continually fresh and alive by the inspiration of the Holy Spirit. Jesus gave his Apostles the authority to teach in his name, and sent the Spirit to keep the Church always faithful to the truth. Through apostolic succession, the bishops and the pope inherit this authority and duty to teach the truth, known as the Church's **magisterium.** The power of the Holy Spirit helps the Church interpret the Scriptures and apply their universal message to the needs of a particular time or place.

The body of wisdom produced over the centuries by the Church's faithful reflection on the Scriptures is known as sacred **Tradition.** This process began with the Apostles, as they tested their preaching against the memory of Jesus' words. It continued with the first *theologians,* or students of the Christian message—people like Saint Paul and the early bishops and teachers known as the Fathers of the Church. It continues today in the work of councils of bishops and in the encyclical letters of the pope. Scripture and Tradition are woven together like a beautiful tapestry to reveal an authentic portrait of Jesus and his teachings.

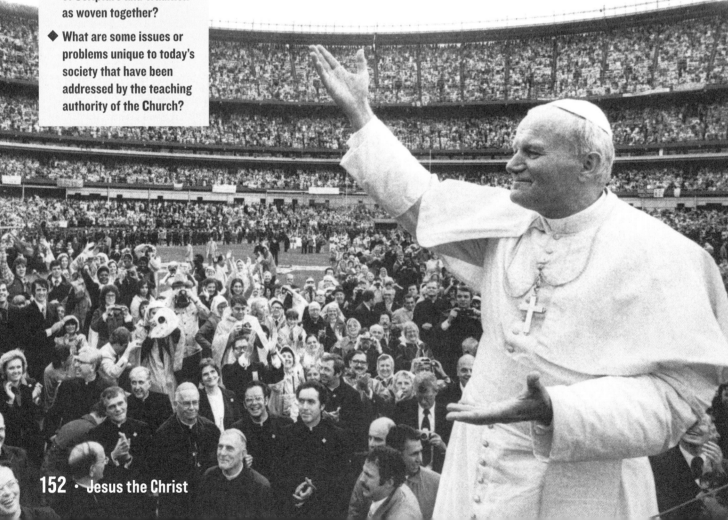

An Apostle's Scrapbook

Imagine that you are one of the Apostles. Draw pictures and write captions on this scrapbook page to show the four most important things you want people to remember about Jesus and his teachings.

The Seed on Good Ground

Prepare and celebrate your own Liturgy of the Word, based on the readings for the 15th Sunday in Ordinary Time, Year A. After sharing the readings and praying the responses together, talk about what the readings mean to you. Close with a favorite hymn.

First Reading *Isaiah 55:10–11*
The power of God's Word

Reader: The Word of the Lord.
All: Thanks be to God.

Responsorial
Antiphon: To you we owe our hymn of praise,
O God on Zion,
To you our vows must be fulfilled.

Psalms 65:2

Second Reading *Romans 8:18–23*
Creation awaits revelation

Reader: The Word of the Lord.
All: Thanks be to God.

Alleluia Verse
Leader: Alleluia.
All: Alleluia.
Leader: Blessed are your eyes, because they see, and your ears, because they hear.
All: Alleluia.

Gospel *Matthew 13:1–24*
The parable of the sower and the seed

Reader: The Gospel of the Lord.
All: Praise to you, Lord Jesus Christ.

The exercises and activities on this page will help you know, love, and serve God better.

Know

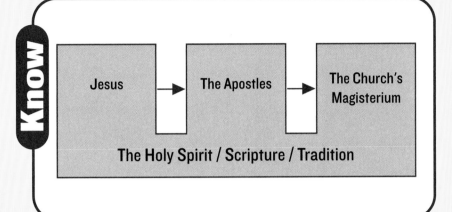

Jesus → The Apostles → The Church's Magisterium

The Holy Spirit / Scripture / Tradition

Love

Which stories about Jesus are most memorable to you? Write three examples.

Serve

How can you share the Word of God with others? Write three examples.

Heroes of Faith

Saint Paula

Paula was a wealthy young Roman woman, happily married and the mother of several children, when her husband died. Seeking consolation, Paula turned to Jerome, the monk who was the pope's spiritual advisor. Paula and Jerome became good friends. They inspired each other. When Jerome moved to the Holy Land to undertake the work of translating the Scriptures into Latin, Paula and her daughter accompanied him. Paula paid Jerome's expenses from her inheritance and used her knowledge of Greek and Hebrew to assist him in his research. Paula's devotion to her friend helped the Word of God reach a whole new audience.

These projects and activities will help you keep this lesson alive all week long.

On your own

Choose one of the New Testament letters and read it straight through, imagining that it is addressed directly to you. In your journal, write a brief response.

With others

Talk with friends about the readings you heard at Mass last Sunday. What did they mean to you? How helpful was the homily? What more would you like to know about these readings?

With your family

Ask family members to share with you their favorite New Testament stories or passages. Talk about what values these passages communicate to your family.

Glory to you, Word of God, Lord Jesus Christ!

GO ONLINE!
www.mhbenziger.com

THE GOOD SHEPHERD

I am the good shepherd. A good shepherd lays down his life for the sheep.

John 10:11

Do You Know?

◆ Where do you get the help you need to make good moral choices?

Is Anyone in Charge?

When Olivia walked into Mr. Scott's classroom to help with the school play she found the whole place in a panic.

"Where's Mr. Scott?" Olivia asked Ken.

"He had to leave. Some kind of emergency." Ken looked distracted. "I need you to start painting the backdrop."

"She can't do that!" Jan interrupted. "We don't have the paint yet. Olivia, go to the hardware store and pick up the paint."

"Wait a minute," Sam broke in. "She can't buy paint yet. We still don't know what colors we need."

"She could round up the cast and have them do a read-through," Gina suggested.

"No way!" called Trish from across the room. "Mr. Scott hasn't even assigned the parts!"

Olivia felt like a tennis ball in a wild match. Her head snapped back and forth as each person tried to find something for her to do. Finally she held up her hands in a gesture of surrender, and backed out of the room.

"Hey! Where are you going?" Ken called.

Olivia laughed. "I'll see you tomorrow," she answered, "when Mr. Scott's back."

Taking Charge

What happens to projects when no one is in charge? Act out an example for the class.

The Shepherd and the Sheep

If you have ever seen a flock of sheep being moved from one place to another, you will have some idea of how Olivia felt walking into the drama room. On their own, without the guidance of shepherds and sheepdogs, sheep wander aimlessly in any direction, making a lot of noise but not getting anywhere.

Jesus lived and taught in the midst of a herding culture. Sheep and shepherds were familiar sights in the hills of Galilee, and Jesus often used metaphors drawn from the herding life to communicate his message.

On one occasion, Jesus was overwhelmed by the size of the crowd that followed him, begging for healing, forgiveness, comfort, and advice on how to live their lives. According to Matthew's Gospel, Jesus was "moved with pity for them because they were troubled and abandoned, like sheep without a shepherd" (*Matthew 9:36*). Jesus knew that he had been sent to be the help, guidance, and moral authority that people needed in order to move in the right direction.

Jesus shared a parable about his role in leading people to new life:

> *Amen, amen, I say to you, whoever does not enter a sheepfold through the gate but climbs over elsewhere is a thief and a robber. But whoever enters through the gate is the shepherd of the sheep. The gatekeeper opens it for him, and the sheep hear his voice, as he calls his own sheep by name and leads them out. When he has driven out all his own, he walks ahead of them, and the sheep follow him, because they recognize his voice. I am the gate. Whoever enters through me will be saved, and will come in and go out and find pasture. I came so that they may have life and have it more abundantly. I am the good shepherd, and I know mine and mine know me, just as the Father knows me and I know the Father; and I will lay down my life for the sheep.*

From *John 10:1–4, 9, 10b, 14–15*

In the Right Direction

You might be thinking, *Wait a minute! I'm not a sheep! I don't need any shepherd bossing me around!* But think again.

Every day, you face choices—not only relatively simple ones, like what to have for lunch or what clothes to wear, but also important choices about moving your life in the right direction. Everybody needs help and guidance for these more important **moral** choices. Without moral direction—some sense of what's right and what's wrong—you would find yourself wandering around indecisively, mindlessly following the pack of your peers, or worse, making choices that endanger yourself and others. Not unlike sheep without a shepherd, right?

Jesus, in his role as the Good Shepherd, does not simply boss people around. You have been gifted by God with **free will,** the right and ability to make choices. If you were overpowered and forced to do the correct thing that would be a violation of God's gift. Instead, Jesus' moral authority *empowers* you, giving you what you need in order to make good choices. The Good Shepherd doesn't order his sheep around. He calls them lovingly by name, leads them safely out into the world, offers them the nourishment they need, and stands by to protect them from wolves and from the consequences of their own foolishness. Jesus the Good Shepherd has laid down his life for you, not so that your life would be boxed in or your real freedom limited, but so that you would "have life abundantly."

VIRTUE

Integrity is faithfulness to one's beliefs and moral values. When you choose and act with integrity, you stay on the right path.

WORD OF GOD

My sheep hear my voice; I know them, and they follow me. I give them eternal life, and they shall never perish.

John 10:27–28a

? When it comes to making moral decisions, how might giving in to peer pressure be like "mindlessly following the flock"? What are the dangers of letting peer pressure determine your choices and actions? Is there such a thing as *good* peer pressure?

Listening for the Shepherd's Voice

How do you hear the voice of the Good Shepherd, guiding you on the right path? When you face moral choices, where do you turn for advice?

God has given you an important tool to use in navigating your way through a world of choices. It's called your **conscience,** your inner moral compass that can help you stay on the right track or return to it when you have gone astray. But your conscience doesn't operate automatically. You have to keep it finely tuned so it can give you authentic moral guidance—not just the answers you want to hear.

Jesus recognized that you have many voices around you telling you what you should do. Your family, your friends, your teachers, the many voices of the popular media—you are bombarded with messages. Some of them, you may already have learned, are misleading or even deliberately false. "Beware of false prophets, who come to you in sheep's clothing, but underneath are ravenous wolves," Jesus told his disciples. Anyone or anything that seeks to convince you of the rightness of something you know to be wrong is a false prophet, a wolf in sheep's clothing.

Here are some ways you can help fine-tune your conscience:

- **Learn more about Jesus and his teachings.** The more you know, the better you can apply your knowledge.

- **Learn and follow the Church's teachings on moral issues.** Jesus gave the Apostles and their successors, the pope and the bishops, the authority to shepherd his followers. Through the Holy Spirit, the Church's teachings are kept faithful to the truth.

- **Keep good company.** The more time you spend with people who share your values and who give good moral example the stronger you will grow in your ability to stand firm in doing what you know is right.

- **Nurture your relationship with God through prayer and the sacraments.** It's easier to hear the voice of the Good Shepherd when you're in regular communication with him!

☦ THIS WE BELIEVE!

A well-formed conscience helps us hear and follow the authoritative moral teachings of Jesus. The pope and the bishops are shepherds, or teachers and moral leaders, of the Church.

ACTIVITY

Shepherds and Wolves

With a partner, make a list of qualities to look for in a *good shepherd* (someone who can help you grow in your ability to make good moral decisions) and qualities that identify a *wolf in sheep's clothing* (someone or something that seeks to lead you morally astray).

Good Shepherding

One way to be a good shepherd is to seek and to offer good moral advice, or counsel. Read each of the following letters. Respond to each questioner with good advice.

Dear Good Shepherd,

My friends all want to see the new slasher film. I don't like blood and gore, and I hate it when the audiences at those movies laugh or cheer at scenes of people being hurt or killed. But I don't want my friends to think I'm a wimp, either.

Any suggestions?

Signed,
Peer Pressured

Dear Peer Pressured,

Dear Good Shepherd,

My friend has a D average in Math. He asked me to help him cheat on a test "just this once" so he won't be cut from the basketball team. He's a really good guy otherwise; he just can't seem to pass a Math test. What would be so bad about giving him a little help?

Signed,
Math Whiz

Dear Math Whiz,

Imitating Jesus

The popular phrase "What would Jesus do?" is a new version of an old message: when it comes to making moral choices, the best course is to follow the Good Shepherd's lead. Pray for the grace to listen to the voice of Jesus.

Grant us, O Lord, the grace
to know what we ought to know,
to love what we ought to love,
to praise what delights you most,
to value what is precious in your sight,
and to turn from what offends you.
Do not let us be content
to judge only according to what we see,
or to make decisions
based only on what we hear from others.
Help us to make decisions with true judgment,
to choose between what is momentary
and what is lasting,
and above all to seek always
that which is pleasing to you.

(Adapted from *The Imitation of Christ,*
by Thomas à Kempis)

The exercises and activities on this page will help you know, love, and serve God better.

Moral Authority in the Church

Know

God the Father gives each person free will and conscience, and gives Jesus complete moral authority.

↓

Jesus, the Son of God, teaches with the authority of his Father and passes moral authority to his Apostles and to their successors, the pope and the bishops.

↓

The Holy Spirit keeps the Church faithful to the truth, guides its leaders, and bestows grace through the sacraments to all members of the Church so they can witness to their moral values.

Love

How can making a good moral choice, even when it means disappointing a friend, be a loving action? Write your thoughts on this question.

Serve

If a friend asked you for advice on making good moral choices, how would you respond? Write three steps for making good moral choices.

Heroes of Faith

Saint Thomas More

Thomas More was the second most powerful man in England, chancellor to his good friend King Henry VIII. When King Henry quarreled with the pope and declared himself the head of the Church in England, he was sure his friend Thomas would go along with him. After all, to defy the king's order was treason, a crime punishable by death. Thomas surprised Henry by choosing to follow the teachings of Jesus. He put his conscience before his position, his friendship, and his life. Just before he was executed, Thomas said, "I die the king's good servant—but I am God's servant first."

HOME and FAMILY

These projects and activities will help you keep this lesson alive all week long.

On your own

Review the list of ways to fine-tune your conscience from page 214. Decide on one way you can do each of these things this week.

With others

Talk with your friends about the "wolves in sheep's clothing" messages you receive from popular media. Express your disagreement with one of these messages by writing to those responsible: newspaper or magazine editors; companies whose ads promote false values; or TV, movie, video game, or music producers.

With your family

Ask family members who they consider their moral authority figures or good examples. If you are struggling with a moral choice or issue, ask for advice from an older family member whose values you respect.

Good Shepherd, lead me on the right path!

GO ONLINE!
www.mhbenziger.com

Jesus Forgives

Your faith has saved you; go in peace.

Luke 7:50

◆

Do You Know?

◆ How can you make things right when you do something wrong?

A Bad Choice

Jack sat dejected in the waiting area of the emergency room of the hospital. A few doors away, his friend Brendan was being examined by a doctor.

Jack hadn't really meant to hurt Brendan. He was just fooling around. When Jack saw Brendan standing on a high ladder, pulling leaves out of the storm gutters, he just couldn't resist. He grabbed the ladder and started shaking it. He thought he'd give Brendan a scare. But Brendan fell and hit his head on the porch steps. He was still unconscious when the ambulance arrived.

When Brendan's dad came out of the examining room, Jack lost it. He started crying. "I'm so sorry, Mr. Tully," Jack choked. "Brendan is my best friend. I did a really stupid thing."

Mr. Tully patted Jack on the shoulder. "It sure was a bad choice, Jack, but I know you regret it," he said. "Thank God, Brendan is going to be all right. He has a concussion, but the doctor says no real damage was done."

Jack still shivered when he thought about what could have happened. "I don't know about that," he said. "I think I did some damage. Can you ever forgive me?"

Mr. Tully smiled. "I already have," he answered. "And so has Brendan. He sent me out here to get you."

"Thanks, Mr. Tully," Jack said. He stood up, rubbed the tears from his face, and took a deep breath. "I'll see you in a minute. I've got some apologizing to do."

Damage Control

With a partner, act out the next scene of this story. What will Jack say to Brendan? What will Brendan's response be?

A Lost Lamb

I led a lonely life. Men and women alike turned their faces away when they saw me coming. The loneliest part of all was the emptiness I felt inside. I knew I hadn't made the best choices. I was a sinner, and I wanted to change my life. But I didn't know where to begin.

Then one day I stood on the edge of a crowd and heard Jesus of Nazareth preach. He said God loved everyone, even sinners like me. He compared God to a shepherd who leaves his flock of ninety-nine sheep to look for one lost lamb. I knew I was that lamb. How could I get the attention of the shepherd? Jesus said that it started with simply asking forgiveness and promising to do better.

Could it be that simple? I followed Jesus around the village that whole day listening to him preach. I knew in my heart that his words were true. I knew that I was forgiven. In the afternoon, I bought an alabaster jar of expensive perfumed oil from a street vendor. I wanted to offer Jesus a gift to show my love and gratitude.

That night, Jesus attended a dinner at the house of Simon the Pharisee. I waited until the servants left the door for a moment, and I slipped into the house. The men were at table, eating. They looked up when I came in—some puzzled, some irritated, some disgusted. I couldn't bear to look at Jesus. I approached him, carrying the jar of ointment. I knew I had only a minute before Simon's guards threw me out into the street again. But I couldn't seem to make my mouth form the words I longed to say, so I let my heart speak.

Read Luke 7:36–50, the passage that inspired this story, to see what happens next.

THIS WE BELIEVE!

Jesus forgave sinners and gave to the Church the power to absolve sin and to celebrate God's forgiveness through the sacrament of Reconciliation (Penance).

WORD OF GOD

I tell you, in just the same way there will be more joy in heaven over one sinner who repents than over ninety-nine righteous people who have no need of repentance.

Luke 15:7

? What did the woman do? What was Jesus' response to her? What did Jesus say to help Simon and his guests understand the significance of the woman's actions?

Turning Around

The Gospels are full of stories of people whose lives were changed by Jesus' offer of forgiveness and healing. Jesus' mission was all about gathering the lost and the sinners and returning them to the joyful embrace of the community.

You may never have sent a friend to the emergency room, and you probably do not live your life as a social outcast because of your wrong choices. But you do make wrong choices, sometimes sinful choices. You live in a world that includes the reality of evil, and you sin by deliberately choosing to do what you know is wrong. You know how sin can damage your relationships with others, and with God. But you also need to remember that Jesus overcame the power of sin. He made sure no lost sheep would be denied the chance to come home.

Jesus' message of forgiveness shouldn't be confused with the idea that anything goes, however. When Jesus offered forgiveness, he didn't say, "Forget it, no problem." Jesus confronted people with their responsibility for their own choices. He then left an opening for them to demonstrate that they wanted to start turning things around by asking forgiveness. That *turning around* is the process of **conversion,** a necessary path to being forgiven and welcomed back into the community.

Contrition is sorrow for sin and acknowledgment of the harm sin does to relationships. People who practice contrition have the humility to recognize when they have done wrong and to ask forgiveness.

ACTIVITY

The Path of Conversion

Study the steps on the path to conversion. Then tell how Jack and the woman with the alabaster jar followed these steps.

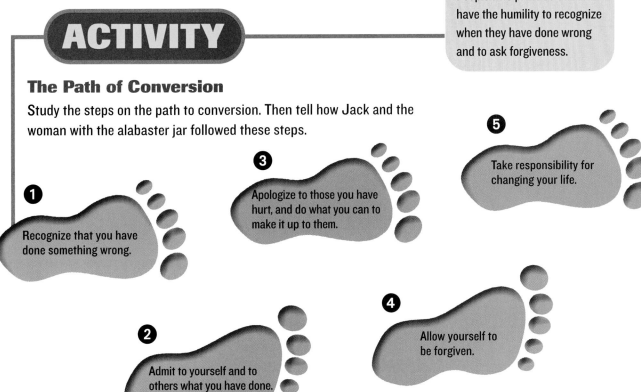

1 Recognize that you have done something wrong.

2 Admit to yourself and to others what you have done.

3 Apologize to those you have hurt, and do what you can to make it up to them.

4 Allow yourself to be forgiven.

5 Take responsibility for changing your life.

Reconciliation

Jesus offered forgiveness to those he met who had walked the path of conversion. He continues to offer that same forgiveness to you today, through the Church, in the sacrament of **Reconciliation,** which means "coming back together." This sacrament is also known as **Penance,** from the name of the actions a person undertakes in order to make amends for sin and practice living a better life.

In the sacrament of Reconciliation, the priest represents Jesus. He offers **absolution,** the sacramental sign of God's forgiveness. The word *absolve* means "to loosen" or "to set free." The grace of the sacrament of Reconciliation loosens the paralysis of sin and guilt and sets you free to begin again.

In order to receive absolution, you must sincerely walk the path of conversion. The first step on the path is an acknowledgment of sin. Pray to the Holy Spirit asking for guidance to know your sins and failings and to be sorry for them. Then continue the process of conversion by doing the following:

• **Confess your sins.** Admit that you made wrong choices, without making excuses.

• **Express *contrition*, or sorrow for having sinned.** Your prayer of contrition is a way of apologizing to God and to the community for your wrong choices. It is an acknowledgment of God's mercy.

• **Agree to do penance,** which can include both actions to make up for any harm you have caused and/or prayers for God's help in starting over.

• **Promise to do better.** The advice of the priest and the guidance of the Holy Spirit will help you turn away from bad habits and develop good ones.

The sacrament of Reconciliation celebrates God's loving forgiveness. The sacrament restores a person to God's grace and friendship and helps heal the sinner's broken relationships with others.

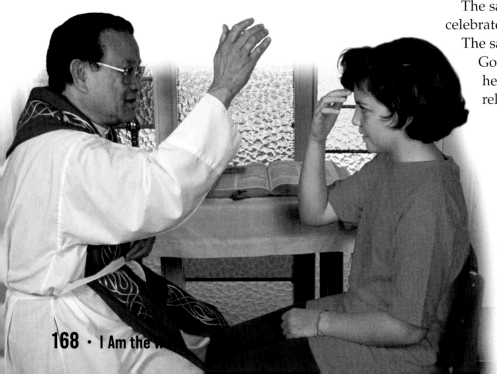

It Hurts

Sins do not have to be spectacular or uncommon to cause harm. The actions listed below are typical of the kinds of harmful patterns that anyone can fall into. Consider the action, and then tell how each action could be sinful and could damage relationships. Name other actions to add to the list and discuss how they can be harmful or sinful.

Actions:

Gossiping or hurtful words

Stealing or cheating

Lying

Fighting

Selfishness

Other

Merciful and Gracious

Pray antiphonally these verses from Psalm 103, which praises God's loving forgiveness.

Side A: Bless the Lord, my soul;
all my being, bless his holy name!

Side B: Bless the Lord, my soul;
do not forget all the gifts of God,

Side A: Who pardons all your sins,
heals all your ills,

Side B: Delivers your life from the pit,
surrounds you with love and compassion,

Side A: Fills your days with good things;
your youth is renewed like the eagle's.

Side B: Merciful and gracious is the Lord,
slow to anger, abounding in kindness.

Side A: God does not always rebuke,
nurses no lasting anger,

Side B: Has not dealt with us as our sins merit,
nor requited us as our deeds deserve.

Side A: As the heavens tower over the earth,
so God's love towers over the faithful.

Side B: As far as the east is from the west,
so far have our sins been removed from us.

Side A: Bless the Lord, all creatures,
everywhere in God's domain.

Side B: Bless the Lord, my soul!

Psalm 103:1–5, 8–12, 22

The exercises and activities on this page will help you know, love, and serve God better.

Know

The Path of Conversion

Recognize your wrongdoing.

Admit to yourself and others what you have done.

Apologize to those you have hurt.

Do what you can to make up for what you did wrong.

Allow yourself to be forgiven.

Take responsibility for changing your life.

The Sacrament of Reconciliation

Examine your conscience and be sorry for your sins.

Confess your sins to the priest.

Pray an Act of Contrition.

Accept the penance the priest gives you.

Receive absolution from the priest in the name of God and the Church.

Make a sincere promise to do better.

Love

How can asking for and offering forgiveness be signs of love? Write an example of each.

Serve

What can you do this week to become a more forgiving, less judgmental person? Write three examples.

Heroes of Faith

Saint Patrick

As a teenager, Patricius was kidnapped by Irish raiders who sold him into slavery. Patricius escaped and swore he would never again visit Ireland unless it was to get revenge. Patricius was studying for the priesthood when he began having dreams about the Irish people. He asked to be sent to Ireland—not for vengeance, but to carry the word of God's forgiving love. Patrick of Ireland, as he came to be known, spent the rest of his days in the land that had once been his prison. He is credited with the conversion of the Irish people to Christianity, but the first conversion happened in Patrick's own heart.

These projects and activities will help you keep this lesson alive all week long.

On your own

Plan to celebrate the sacrament of Reconciliation. In preparation, spend some time examining your conscience and thinking about how you can practice making better choices. Reflect on God's great love for you.

With others

Ask a friend to be your *conscience partner,* steering you away from bad habits and sinful choices and supporting you in good choices. Do the same for your friend.

With your family

Talk with family members about how your family can be more forgiving. Think of three good ways to break habits like refusing to apologize or holding a grudge.

Lord Jesus, Son of God, have mercy on me, a sinner.

GO ONLINE!
www.mhbenziger.com

Come, Follow Me

As the Father
has sent me,
so I send you.

John 20:21

Do You Know?

◆ How do Christians live their call to follow Jesus?

Called

Joe sat at the table, his notebook open in front of him. He was trying to outline an essay on his hopes and dreams—what he felt he might be called to do with his life. He had trouble getting started.

Joe remembered being at his grandmother's bedside when she died. Father Tom was right there in the hospital room with Joe's family, praying with Grandma Anna and consoling the family members at her death. Joe had been so impressed by Father Tom's kindness and care. Maybe God was calling Joe to be a priest like Father Tom.

Joe's uncle Steve was a Christian Brother. He had a degree in microbiology and divided his time between working to develop chemical-free ways to clean up water pollution and teaching biology in college. Joe knew Uncle Steve believed he had been called to his unique vocation as a young teen during the family camping trips he still loved to share. Joe thought it was great that Uncle Steve could find a way to use his gifts as a member of a religious community.

And then there were Joe's parents. Both worked, raised five children, and somehow found time to help with the parish food bank and other outreach efforts. Joe liked the way his parents always showed that they loved each other, and shared that love with everybody else.

Inspiration

What kind of person inspires you to follow in his or her footsteps? Write about someone you know who lives the kind of life you want to imitate.

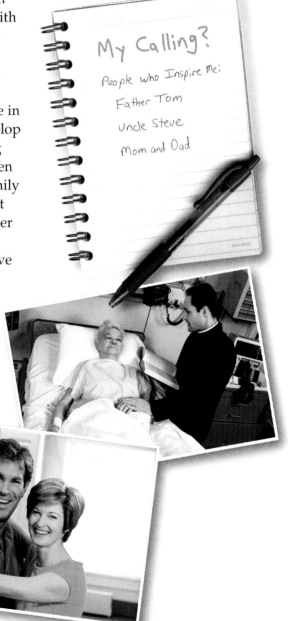

My Calling?

People who Inspire Me:
Father Tom
Uncle Steve
Mom and Dad

WORD OF GOD

To this end, we always pray for you, that our God may make you worthy of his calling and powerfully bring to fulfillment every good purpose and every effort of faith, that the name of our Lord Jesus may be glorified in you.

2 Thessalonians 1:11–12a

Vocation

The seventh graders were stumped. It was the youth group's turn to nominate people for the "Christian of the Week" award in the parish bulletin, and the teens had some questions for Jim, their advisor.

"How are we supposed to define *Christian* for this award?" Megan asked.

Jim answered her with another question. "Well, what does the word *Christian* mean?" he asked the group.

"A follower of Jesus," Megan answered.

"A baptized person," Nick added.

"Someone who is anointed, as Jesus was," Valerie responded.

"A person sent by Jesus to carry on his work," suggested Lee.

Jim smiled. "Good," he said. "Now put that all together. What kind of person are we looking for?"

The group agreed that they were looking for someone who lived out his or her baptismal call to serve others as Jesus did—someone with a **vocation.**

"But wait," Joe interrupted. "Doesn't that mean it would have to be a priest or a sister?"

"Not necessarily," Gina replied, thinking it through. "In Baptism, everyone gets the same vocation to serve, but we live it out in different ways. The Christian of the Week could be a married person, or a single person."

"It could even be—" Jim paused in suspense, "a seventh grader!"

ACTIVITY

∞ *Parish Bulletin* ∞

Christian of the Week

Come up with three nominations for Christian of the Week in your parish. Try to include a variety of ways to live out the vocation to serve.

THE NOMINATIONS FOR CHRISTIAN OF THE WEEK IN OUR PARISH ARE

Loving and Serving

Every Christian is called to a life of loving service, but not every Christian will answer that call in the same way. Some will be **laypeople**—single, married, or members of religious communities. Some will be **ordained** clergy—deacons, priests, and bishops.

Every vocation offers a rewarding and challenging way to follow Jesus and serve others. Two callings, however, are so important to the life of the Church—and require so much sacrifice of those who answer these calls—that they are blessed and supported by sacramental grace. The sacraments of Marriage and Holy Orders strengthen those who receive them for their mission to love and serve as Jesus did.

Marriage

If you think of the way the sacrament of Marriage is presented in movies and on TV, you may wonder what challenges this calling could present. To judge from the images of radiant brides and grooms dancing in their wedding finery, you'd think that marriage is all about "happily ever after." That's how all the fairy tales end, right?

But a wedding is not an ending. It is the beginning of a whole new life lived not as an individual, but as part of a community of two. The faithful intimacy of Marriage requires the willingness to **compromise**—to put someone else's needs first at times. That's a big sacrifice in a "me-first" society. The **vows,** or sacred promises, of Marriage bind the spouses to lifelong fidelity and mutual care. That loving service to each other, like every vocation, also carries the obligation to love and serve the wider world.

In most marriages, the community of two soon expands to include children, with all the joys and sacrifices that parenting involves. Put that together with the fact that many spouses today must take responsibility for the care of their own aging parents, and you can see why the grace of the sacrament of Marriage, and the support of the whole community that comes with it, is so welcome.

✝ THIS WE BELIEVE!

In Baptism, all are called to love and serve as Jesus did. The sacraments of Marriage and Holy Orders bless and support the important vocations of marriage and ordained ministry.

Virtue

Chastity is the right use of God's gift of sexuality. Married people practice chastity by expressing their love for each other and welcoming children in faithful married love. Single people, including ordained ministers who have taken a vow of celibacy, practice chastity by abstaining from sexual activity.

From Maryknoll

ACTIVITY

Christ Present

Study this chart to recall important information about the sacraments of Marriage and Holy Orders. Then tell one way each sacrament makes Christ present in the world.

Holy Orders

The vocation to ordained ministry, like the call to marriage, offers great rewards and requires great sacrifices. Those called to serve in the apostolic tradition receive grace and support through the sacrament of Holy Orders, which confers upon them the authority to carry out the mission of teaching, leading, and serving that Jesus gave to his Apostles.

Each of the three orders of ministry in the Church has its own special gifts and challenges. Those ordained to the **diaconate** as permanent deacons assist the bishop and the priests in serving the whole community, both liturgically and through social action. Permanent deacons usually combine their ministry with a full-time career outside of the Church and may be married at the time of ordination, so the demands on their time are great.

Those ordained to the **presbyterate** (priests) and to the **episcopate** (bishops) have the mission to teach and lead the Church, celebrate the sacraments, preach, and—in the case of bishops—guide the Church in its faithfulness to Church teaching. In the Roman Catholic tradition, priests and bishops are **celibate,** giving up the right to marry in order to serve all of God's people.

? What are some of the rewards of ordained ministry? What role do you think the community plays in the sacrament of Holy Orders?

Sacrament	Who Is Called?	Who Is the Minister?	How Is the Sacrament Conferred?	What Are the Visible Signs of the Sacrament?
Marriage	a man and a woman	the couple (witnessed by the priest)	The couple exchanges vows before the priest and other witnesses.	wedding rings
Holy Orders: Diaconate	a man	the bishop	The bishop lays hands on the head of the candidate, anoints him, and says a prayer of consecration.	deacon's stole
Presbyterate	a man	the bishop		priest's stole
Episcopate	a man	other bishops		pectoral cross, miter, crosier

Hearing the Call

God is calling you to a special vocation, although you may not yet be aware of what it is. Your ideas about your vocation may change often over the next few years. But you can listen for God's call by paying attention to the areas of life that really interest you. Complete the web to explore one area of life that is of interest to you now.

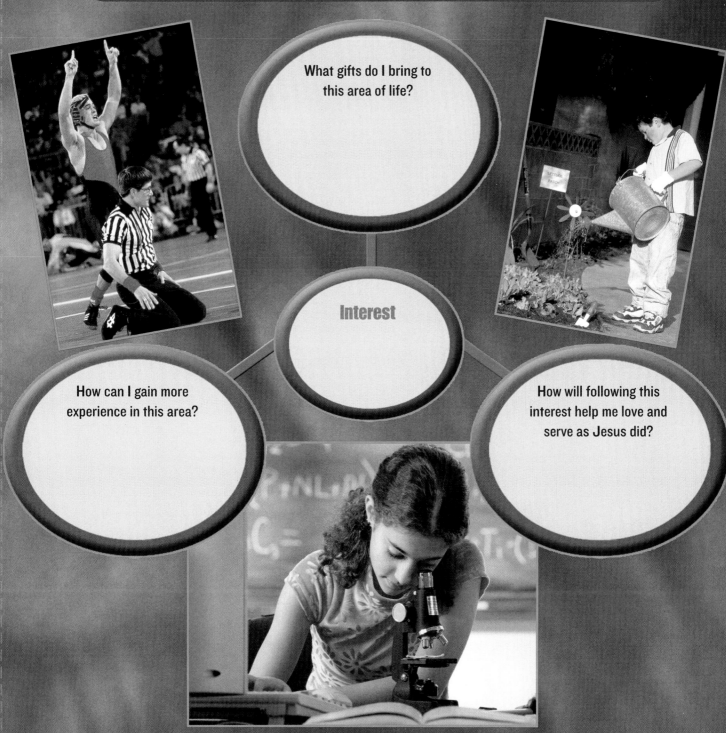

What gifts do I bring to this area of life?

Interest

How can I gain more experience in this area?

How will following this interest help me love and serve as Jesus did?

Into Your Harvest

Jesus compared the world to a field in need of harvesting and urged his followers to ask God to call more workers into the fields. Pray the following for vocations of all kinds.

All: Creator of the Universe, God of the Nations, your people are longing to hear your word. Send laborers into your harvest—women and men on fire with your love;

Reader 1: Dedicated single people—who incarnate your presence in their daily lives, whose availability enables them to respond to a diversity of needs;

Reader 2: Married couples—whose relationships serve as a sign of your fidelity to your people, whose love overflows to their children and neighbors;

Reader 3: Ordained ministers—who gather the prayers and longing of your people, who serve as a channel of your presence through the sacraments;

Reader 4: Religious sisters, brothers, and priests—whose life in community foreshadows our eternal unity in Christ, whose service brings your life to the world.

All: May each of us respond with courage and generosity to our particular vocations, and may the Church recognize the Spirit's call to men and women of good will, trusting in your abundance to answer all our needs.

Amen.

© National Conference of Catholic Bishops

The exercises and activities on this page will help you know, love, and serve God better.

Know

- Single Life
- Marriage
- Religious Life
- Lay Ministry
- Vocations
  To love and serve as Jesus did
- Ordained Ministry
- Diaconate
- Presbyterate
- Episcopate

Love

How can you demonstrate the kind of unselfish love that marriage calls for?

Serve

How can you demonstrate the qualities of leadership and service that ordained ministry calls for?

Heroes of Faith

Felix and Mary Barreda

The Barredas, a Nicaraguan couple, had been married for thirty years and had six children and fifteen grandchildren when they put their lives on the line. They volunteered to harvest coffee beans in a communal field, knowing that their actions might make them a target of contra rebels working to overthrow Nicaragua's socialist government. Mary wrote to her friends, "The opportunity to pick coffee will be converted into health, clothing, homes, roads, and food, so I will do it with love." For Felix and Mary, that loving harvest led to death at the hands of the contras, but their witness lives on.

These projects and activities will help you keep this lesson alive all week long.

On your own

Make a list of the ways you have been served by those who have celebrated the sacraments of Marriage and Holy Orders.

With others

Sometimes God calls with a friend's voice. With your friends, make a point of praising one another's gifts and talents. Try to think of at least one gift that each of your friends might bring to a future vocation.

With your family

Talk with your parents or other family members about the qualities they think are most important for marriage and family life. At family prayer, remember the married couples, parents, single adults, ordained ministers, and religious who are part of your family's life.

**Here I am, Lord!
Send me!**

GO ONLINE!
www.mhbenziger.com

Make a Difference

It takes a special kind of person to answer the call to serve others through leadership. Vocation directors—those charged with the responsibility of identifying tomorrow's priests, religious, and lay ministers—are always on the lookout for people who demonstrate the qualities of leadership necessary for ministry. They often find that the strongest recommendations come from a potential leader's friends and classmates, who are in a position to see how a young person answers God's call long before it becomes an official vocation.

From Maryknoll

Tomorrow's Church leaders may be sitting next to you!

Who Is Called

The following survey is often given to high school students by vocation directors. Students are asked to think about the people they interact with every day who demonstrate qualities of leadership and caring. Read through these questions and think about how you might answer them, but keep your answers private:

1. Who reaches out to you in friendship?
2. Who is very caring and compassionate?
3. Who always maintains trust and confidences?
4. If you had a personal problem, with whom would you like to discuss it?
5. Who always has a positive attitude and has a way of lifting people up?
6. Who is a leader who can make things happen?
7. Who has a close relationship with God?
8. Who has the courage to stand up for what he or she believes?
9. Who is respected most by his or her peers?
10. Whose actions remind you of Jesus?
11. Who has a strong desire to help others and make a difference in people's lives?
12. Who enjoys being around people and has a good sense of humor?

Then ask yourself, honestly, whether your name might have come to your classmates' minds as they read through these questions. If so, think about talking to your family or your pastor to further explore your vocation. If not, how could you work on developing some of these characteristics?

- As a class, discuss the survey but don't reveal your answers.
- Did you find it easy or difficult to think of people who fit these descriptions?
- Do you agree that these questions describe people who would make good Church leaders? Were there any qualities that surprised you? Were there any you would add?
- How might these questions also apply to those called to marriage and family life?

Remember

1. How does Jesus' teaching ministry continue?

Jesus continues to teach and guide the Church in the Scriptures, the Word of God, especially as they are shared in the Liturgy of the Word at Mass and explained in the homily. The magisterium, the Church's teaching authority, is guided by the Holy Spirit in interpreting the Word of God and applying it to the circumstances of today.

2. How do Christians live a moral life?

Every person has been given the gift of free will by God and can choose between right and wrong. These are moral choices. Christians are guided by their conscience, which is formed by studying the Scriptures and the teachings of the Church, in making moral choices. The Holy Spirit offers grace through the sacraments to grow in virtue.

3. What happens in the sacrament of Reconciliation?

In the sacrament of Reconciliation, or Penance, a person who is sorry for his or her sins confesses those sins to the priest, expresses contrition, accepts a penance, and is absolved of sin by the priest in the name of God and through the Church. The sacrament reconciles the sinner to God and to the community.

4. Which two sacraments celebrate special ways of living out one's baptismal call or vocation?

The sacraments of Marriage and Holy Orders celebrate vocations to married life and to ordained ministry. These vocations are particularly important to the life of the Church, although all people are called to love and serve as Jesus did.

Respond

Choose one of the following questions. Write a response. If you wish, share what you have written.

1. What moral issue of today most concerns you? From what you have learned, how do you think Jesus would respond to this moral issue? What does the Church teach about this issue?
2. How important is forgiveness in human relationships? How can you be a force for reconciliation in your family and community?
3. How do you see yourself ten years from now? How will you be using your gifts, talents, and interests to answer God's call to love and serve others?

Act

Search community newspapers for situations in your neighborhood or local area that could use the loving service of you and your classmates. Look for opportunities to serve that do not necessarily require a long-term commitment or a high degree of expertise. Is there a park, playground, or natural area that needs cleaning up? (Be sure you follow safety precautions and dispose of litter properly.) Could a local community center use volunteer child care workers or the profits from a bake sale or car wash? Don't limit your search to official calls for volunteers. If you see a problem that needs fixing, take the initiative.

Share

With your teacher's help, find out more about the rite, or specific order of prayers and actions, for one of the following sacraments:

- Reconciliation (communal or individual)
- Marriage
- Holy Orders (ordination of a priest)

On a display board, illustrate the parts of the celebration. Write your own prayer expressing contrition or asking God's blessing for married couples or priests and include your prayer on the display.

For this I was born and for this I came into the world, to testify to the truth. Everyone who belongs to the truth listens to my voice.

John 18:37b

Guatemala From Maryknoll

I Am the Truth

Chapter

Servant

> Take my yoke upon you and learn from me, for I am meek and humble of heart.
>
> *Matthew 11:29a*

Do You Know?

◆ How can you follow Jesus' example of service to others?

Service With a Smile?

In the twenty-first century, the United States is largely a service economy. That means that many industries revolve around offering services instead of products, and many jobs involve providing service to others. From the people at the counter in the fast-food restaurant to the health care workers in hospitals, from auto mechanics to teachers to firefighters, almost everyone is either serving or being served at any given minute of the day.

But how does our society feel about service? Do we support those who provide important services, or do we disregard them? Do we consider it an honor to serve others, or a humiliating burden? Think about these messages society sends:

- Service workers'—teachers, nurses, police officers, and firefighters—salaries are generally much lower than those paid in other sectors of the economy.

- Popular wisdom downplays the idea of service, with its undertones of humility, powerlessness, and putting others first. You've heard the slogans "Look out for Number 1," "You're not the boss of me," "I'm not your servant!"

Your Serve

How do you feel about service? List all the words and phrases that come into your head when you hear the word *serve*.

Guest Check 0000

A Different Perspective

You already know that Jesus had a way of looking at the world that differed greatly from most people. For example, his definition of happiness in the Beatitudes must have been as surprising to his listeners then as it is to people today. Material poverty, mourning, purity, and meekness don't sound much like the sources of happiness promoted in TV and magazine ads.

Jesus' ideas about power were similarly unsettling. In spite of the advice of well-meaning friends, Jesus persisted in spending most of his time among the least powerful people in his world: women, children, uneducated laborers, the mentally and physically ill, and the scorned social outcasts. He chose twelve of these humble friends to receive the full power of his ministry. And wherever he went, Jesus reminded people that God doesn't always see things the way we do.

Asked who the greatest being in the kingdom of heaven might be, Jesus did not point to a king or a religious leader but to a child *(Luke 9:46–48)*. When a rich, virtuous young man asked what good he must do to gain eternal life, Jesus responded, "If you wish to be perfect, go, sell what you have and give to the poor, and you will have treasure in heaven. Then come, follow me" *(Matthew 19:16–30)*. That is difficult to do if you are attached to your possessions. At dinner in the home of a wealthy and prominent Pharisee, Jesus did not search for a good seat as did the other guests. Instead, he gave this advice, the complete opposite of the usual social custom:

> *When you are invited by someone to a wedding banquet, do not recline at table in the place of honor. Rather, when you are invited, go and take the lowest place so that when the host comes to you he may say, 'My friend, move up to a higher position.' Then you will enjoy the esteem of your companions at the table. For everyone who exalts himself will be humbled, but the one who humbles himself will be exalted.*
>
> Luke 14:8a, 10–11

 How do you think the dinner guests responded to Jesus' advice? How would most people today respond to Jesus' call to be humble? How do you respond to this advice?

The Call to Serve

Jesus didn't just serve others or talk about the importance of humility. He also called every one of his followers to a life of service, too.

You may know people who volunteer their time in various service projects. You may be in a Confirmation preparation program or a parish youth group that requires a certain number of hours of Christian service. But this is only the beginning. Service is neither an option nor a short-term commitment for Christians. Service is asked of every baptized follower of Jesus. The question is not "Should I serve others?" but "How can I serve others today?" After all, Jesus taught that the People of God would ultimately be judged not on how wealthy, powerful, and important they had become, but, like that fast-food restaurant, on how many billions they had served.

You may be more familiar with the qualities associated with worldly power and success than you are with the characteristics of servant–leaders like Jesus. Here are the myths and realities about five qualities that mark "good and faithful servants."

Helpfulness is the practical skill that underlies all Christian service. People who are helpful recognize a need, offer assistance without having to be asked, and choose the most practical and respectful means of meeting the need.

The World Thinks . . .	Followers of Jesus Know . . .
Humility is groveling weakness.	Humility is the ability to see oneself and one's gifts honestly. Humble people know that stepping aside in favor of another is a real strength.
Respect is reserved for those with power and money.	Respect is owed to everyone, especially those overlooked by the world. Respectful people make everyone feel special.
Generosity is fine once you have given yourself everything you want, but charity begins at home.	Generosity is not about things but about an openness of spirit that loves to share. Generous people aren't satisfied until everyone has what he or she needs.
Kindness is for suckers; nice guys finish last.	Kindness costs nothing and opens every door. Kind people go out of their way to make sure everybody feels like a winner.
Compassion is a waste of energy. Needy people would be better off helping themselves instead of asking for help from "bleeding hearts."	Compassion is the ability to put oneself in another's place. Compassionate people recognize that "there but for the grace of God am I"—anyone can be in need at any time.

ACTIVITY

Service in Action

Choose one of the qualities of Christian service. With a partner, act out a situation in which this quality is put into action to serve another.

Dialog Box

◆ How difficult is it for you to believe Jesus' promise that real service can be a "light burden"? What attitudes in the world around you try to convince you otherwise?

◆ Would you rather be served by someone who is cheerful or someone who is grudging? How can attitude make a difference in the way you experience service, both as a giver and a receiver?

◆ Who are your role models when it comes to Christian service? What qualities do these people demonstrate? What is their attitude toward serving others?

WORD OF GOD

Do nothing out of selfishness or out of vainglory; rather, humbly regard others as more important than yourselves, each looking out not for his own interests but also everyone for those of others.

Philippians 2:3–4

The Easy Yoke

You may still feel that Jesus' call to service is a sentence of lifetime servitude. If you think of service as an uncomfortable obligation instead of as a gift, you're missing an important point Jesus made.

Speaking to the crowds of his day, who were convinced that real ministry had to be painfully difficult, Jesus used another one of his familiar agricultural metaphors. He compared his followers to oxen who were yoked, or joined together with a wooden bar, so they could pull a plow or a cart. Jesus told people not to be afraid to take up his call to service, because he would be right alongside them.

> *Come to me, all you who labor and are burdened, and I will give you rest. Take my yoke upon you and learn from me, for I am meek and humble of heart; and you will find rest for your selves. For my yoke is easy, and my burden light.*
>
> *Matthew 11:28–30*

The rest that Jesus promised is actually *shalom*, the Hebrew word that means deep peace and a sense of wholeness. Jesus wanted people to know what all those who serve with open hearts come to recognize—that true service is not a burden, but a joy. Those who give with generous hearts almost always find that they receive much more in return. Those who serve with gladness and cheer, instead of grudges and whining, hardly ever talk in terms of obligation or sacrifice. They speak of rewards and personal fulfillment.

Jesus also wanted his followers to know that they would never be alone in their service. You are yoked to Jesus in Baptism. Whenever and wherever you serve, Jesus is present— in you, and in "the least of these" whom you serve.

Distinguished Service

Many organizations or groups award medals and ribbons for "distinguished service" that is above and beyond the call of duty. On the *medals* and *ribbons*, write one way you can demonstrate each quality of distinguished service.

A Prayer of Service

Lord, you created us for yourself
and our hearts are restless until they rest in you.

Please show us how to love you with all our hearts
and our neighbor as ourselves.

Teach us to be practical about loving one another
in you and for you and as you desire.

Show us our immediate neighbor today;
call our attention to the needs of others.

Remind us that you count as done to you
what we do for one another,
and that our turning away from one another
is really turning our backs on you.

Make us know, love, and serve you in this life
and be happy forever in the next
in union with all our sisters and brothers,
children of a common Father.

To serve you is to reign.

Amen.

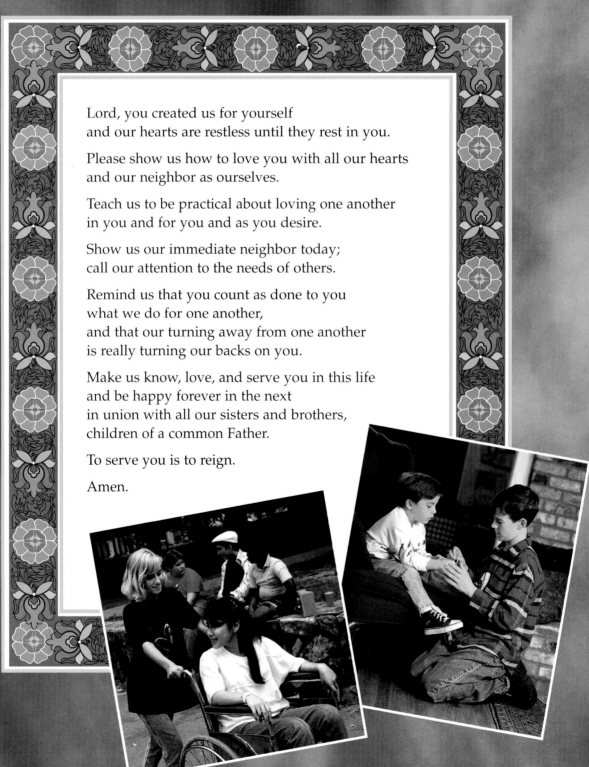

The exercises and activities on this page will help you know, love, and serve God better.

Know

Jesus served others and called his followers to serve.

Jesus is present in you when you serve.

Jesus is present in those you serve.

Love

Christian service does not have to mean working only with strangers in need. List some ways you can serve your family.

Serve

What people and situations in your world could benefit from your service? Write three examples.

Heroes of Faith

Saint Camillus de Lellis

Camillus de Lellis was a six-foot-tall, rowdy, bad-tempered ex-soldier with an incurable leg wound and an addiction to gambling. He got a job in a hospital but was soon fired because everyone feared his anger. He went to work as a builder at a Capuchin monastery, and there God spoke to his heart and Camillus was a changed man. He went back to the hospital, bringing kindness and loving service to all. He founded a religious order of male nurses called the Ministers to the Sick. Today, the Church recognizes Camillus as the patron of those who are ill and the nurses who serve them.

These projects and activities will help you keep this lesson alive all week long.

On your own

Think about the qualities of service: humility, respect, generosity, kindness, and compassion. Choose the quality you need to work on the most, and plan three ways to practice it this week.

With others

Watch and listen for media messages that counteract Jesus' call to serve others. Try rewording these messages to make them promote the values of Christian service.

With your family

Plan one service activity your whole family can share. After the activity, talk about your responses to the experience.

Lord, help me be a cheerful giver!

GO ONLINE!
www.mhbenziger.com

One in Christ

For through faith you are all children of God in Christ Jesus.

Galatians 3:26

Do You Know?

◆ How are the members of the Body of Christ united?

Unity in Diversity

"I can't believe it," Tina said, looking around the school gym. "Who'd have thought there were so many cultures and traditions represented in our little town?"

Rick stopped grazing from his plate piled high with Mexican tacos, African yams, and Chinese dumplings just long enough to answer. "Yeah. I never knew Charlie's family was Greek Orthodox, or that Lily's family escaped from a massacre in Cambodia. They're all just kids I grew up with."

Tina sighed. "It's too bad it took a few people's wrongdoing to bring us together, but I'm glad it did."

Tina and Rick's town was holding its first Unity in Diversity festival in response to an earlier incident when some kids had spray painted ethnic slurs on the walls of a local grocery that sold imported foods. The community had gotten together to show that it welcomed diversity and rejected the prejudice of a few misguided young people.

Rick shook his head. "How could anybody think all this great variety was *wrong?*" he asked. "So what if we all have different foods and customs and accents? We're all Americans, right?"

"Right!" Tina agreed. "You know, you're pretty philosophical sometimes."

But Rick had stopped listening. "Hey, look!" he interrupted. "They just put out a whole tray of pizzas!"

Laughing, Tina followed her friend through the maze of colorful booths and tables. Talking about diversity was fine, she thought, but there was nothing like food to bring people together!

Gifts of Diversity

Imagine your community was composed entirely of people just like you. What would you miss most if there was no variety of foods, customs, clothing, accents, music, and art in your world?

For where two or three are gathered together in my name, there am I in the midst of them.

Matthew 18:20

Virtue

Respect honors the God-given dignity of all people. The word *respect* literally means "look again." If you see with the eyes of respect, you can overlook superficial differences to recognize and work for unity.

One in Jesus

Jesus wanted his followers to be united. He knew that his chosen successors, the Apostles, would have differences of opinion among themselves, even though they came from essentially the same background. And Jesus foresaw the time when his message would reach far beyond Palestine, to be embraced by people of many languages and cultures. How could the Body of Christ be kept united in spite of the diversity of its members? Jesus knew that this great task would be impossible without God's help.

On the night before he died, Jesus turned to his Father in prayer. He asked protection for the Apostles in the difficult days ahead. And Jesus prayed, too, for all those in every time and place who would one day take their place in the Body of Christ:

I pray not only for them, but also for those who will believe in me through their word, so that they all may be one, as you, Father, are in me and I in you, that they also may be in us, that the world may believe that you sent me. Father, they are your gift to me. I wish that where I am they may also be with me, that they may see my glory that you gave me, because you loved me before the foundation of the world. Righteous Father, the world also does not know you, but I know you, and they know that you sent me. I made known to them your name and I will make it known, that the love with which you loved me may be in them and I in them.

John 17:20–21, 24–26

Jesus' prayer was for unity among all those who followed him. Through this unity, all people would recognize Jesus' living presence. He would be in his followers and they would be in him, united as closely, in spite of their superficial differences, as Jesus and his Father were united in love. The sign and defender of that loving unity would be the gift of the Holy Spirit, alive and at work in the Church around the world.

What signs of unity in diversity do you see in your parish? What signs of unity in diversity do you see in your city or town?

From East to West

One of the most important signs of the unity that Jesus prayed for is the Eucharist. Around the world and through the centuries, the Eucharistic **liturgy,** the Mass, has been celebrated in ways that differ somewhat according to the time and place but always contain the same basic elements. Today, you can visit a Catholic parish in any part of the world, and although you might not understand the language and some of the music and other customs might be unfamiliar, you would still participate in the same ritual of gathering, hearing the Word, receiving Communion, and being sent forth. This is true whether the liturgy is celebrated according to the **Roman Rite,** the order most familiar to American Catholics, or according to one of the several other ancient rites recognized by the Church. It is true whether the liturgy is celebrated in English, in some other **vernacular** (the common language of a country or a people), or in the traditional ritual languages of Latin, Greek, Slavonic, Aramaic, or Coptic.

From Maryknoll

The unity and **catholicity** of the Church extend beyond the Mass to include the same sacraments, the same teachings, and the same reliance on Scripture and Tradition. But the Church's unity does not mean sameness. The liturgy reflects the great diversity of the Body of Christ in its richness of languages, music, feasts, gestures, customs, and art.

This unity in diversity is what Jesus prayed for. It is what we celebrate in the words of Eucharistic Prayer III:

From Maryknoll

Father, you are holy indeed,
and all creation rightly gives you praise.
All life, all holiness comes from you
through your Son, Jesus Christ our Lord,
by the working of the Holy Spirit.
From age to age you gather a people to yourself,
so that from east to west
a perfect offering may be made
to the glory of your name.

✝ THIS WE BELIEVE!

Jesus is present in the Church in every age and place. Christians are called to work for the unity and interfaith understanding that Jesus desires for his followers.

ACTIVITY

The Mass Around the World

Use the Internet and other resources to research how the Mass is celebrated around the world. Share with the group any experiences you have of participating in the Eucharistic liturgy in a language, rite, or culture that is different from your own.

◆ Why are divisions between Christians a "sinful wound" in the Body of Christ?

◆ How much do you know about other Christian denominations and non-Christian religions? What would you like to know? Why is it important to learn about other denominations and faith traditions?

◆ How can young teens contribute to the movements for ecumenism and interfaith understanding? What first step in the direction of unity could you take right now?

Working for Unity

Jesus is present wherever his followers gather together. Sadly, however, the complete unity Jesus prayed for is not yet a reality. Over the centuries, the Body of Christ has been divided by differences and conflicts both theological and cultural. The Church is no longer united—Orthodox Christians and Protestant Christians of many denominations have significant differences with Roman Catholics. In some eras and parts of the world, these divisions have even given rise to hatred and violence.

Division in the Body of Christ is a sinful wound for which all Christians bear responsibility. Around the world, Christians of good will work together to overcome differences and move closer to the unity Jesus intends for his Church. This movement, which involves clergy and laypersons of all ages, is known as **ecumenism.**

Christian unity is only the first step in recognizing that all people are united as children of one God. Prejudice, hatred, and violent clashes between people of different faiths are a scandalous betrayal of God's good creation. That is why, in addition to working for unity among Christians, the followers of Jesus are called to work for mutual respect among people of all beliefs.

The Power to Unify

Every person has the power to help achieve unity where there is division. Read each situation below. Tell what you could do to help reach unity in each case.

Your parish includes older Irish and Italian Americans and a growing number of young families who have recently emigrated from Central America. The groups have very different ideas about language and music for liturgy. Tensions between parishioners are growing. You have been asked to be part of a committee that will suggest solutions.

Your parish youth group and the teens from a local Protestant church both want to reserve the recreation center for an activity on the same night. The young people from either group will be disappointed if they can't carry out their plans. The rec center staff asks you and a representative from the Protestant church to work out a compromise.

A classmate has been telling anti-Semitic jokes and using ethnic slurs. When you ask him to stop, he seems honestly surprised. He says, "I'm not hurting anybody—there aren't any of *them* around here." How do you answer?

A Visible Sign of Unity

The unity for which Jesus prayed needs your prayers, too. Pray together this confession and prayer developed by leaders in the ecumenical movement.

Reader 1: We confess that we are diminished by pride and separation.

Reader 2: We acknowledge the sinful divisions of our churches, which keep our ministries unreconciled.

Reader 3: We admit our failures in the mission of justice and love.

Reader 4: We confess that we support systems of racism and other oppression that mar your incarnate image and violate creation.

All: Merciful God, forgive us. In Jesus Christ, transform our hearts to obey your commandments, restore our love for one another, and proclaim your glory. Ever-living God, our Judge and Healer, have mercy on us.

All: Lord, show us your mercy.

Reader 5: By the power of your Spirit remove from us the divisions that separate Christians, so that your Church may be a visible sign of unity in a fragmented world.

Reader 6: Grant us a renewed love, a true wisdom, and a new impulse for that unity so that the eternal message of your Son may be received as Good News for all.

All: Rekindle our faith and our hope so that we may journey with joy toward your heavenly kingdom, trusting in your promise of eternal glory.

Amen.

The exercises and activities on this page will help you know, love, and serve God better.

Know

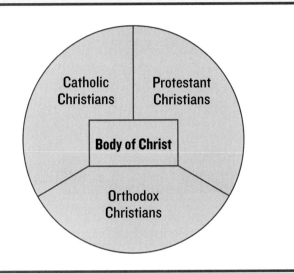

Catholic Christians

Protestant Christians

Body of Christ

Orthodox Christians

Love

What can you do to fight hatred and prejudice? Write your suggestions.

Serve

How can you learn more about people of other Christian denominations and faith traditions? Write some suggestions.

Heroes of Faith

Mollie Rogers (Mother Mary Joseph)

In 1905, Mollie Rogers volunteered to help the newly founded Maryknoll publish their magazine. Mary, however, wanted to have more of a role in mission work. Her persistence finally resulted in the formation of the Maryknoll Sisters of Saint Dominic, with Mollie Rogers—now Mother Mary Joseph—as their director. The first sisters worked in Japan, and eventually made their way to China. By the time Mollie died in 1950, she had seen her community grow to more than a thousand members who served in missions around the world.

HOME and FAMILY

These projects and activities will help you keep this lesson alive all week long.

On your own

Compose your own prayer for unity among the members of the Body of Christ and understanding among all God's children.

With others

Attend Mass in a parish that celebrates the Eucharist in a different language or according to a different rite than the one with which you are familiar. You could also arrange ahead of time to visit a Protestant or Orthodox Christian church, a Jewish synagogue, a Muslim mosque, or a Buddhist or Hindu temple as a group. Be sure to follow required customs and show respect.

With your family

Ask family members to share how they picture Jesus. Look at the images of Jesus displayed in your home, or choose or make a new image of Jesus that expresses your family's heritage.

Lord, make us one with one another as we are one in you.

GO ONLINE!
www.mhbenziger.com

Witness

For you will be his witness before all to what you have seen and heard.

Acts 22:15

Where Do You Stand?

The whole lunchroom was buzzing. Everybody knew something was up, but only the girls at Abby's table were in on the plan.

"This is going to be so great!" Lisa said. "I can't wait to see the look on those snobby cheerleaders' faces when they're covered in garbage!"

"Keep your voice down!" Jill hissed. "All we need now is for the dean to hear what we're up to!"

Abby twisted her hair, a sure sign that she was troubled. "I don't know," she said. "It still seems just way too mean."

"Are you kidding?" Megan whispered. "They're the ones who are mean. They rag us every day for being brainy geeks who can't play sports and don't wear the perfect clothes. I'm sick of it, and I know you are, too."

"So we get a little old-fashioned revenge," Lisa added. "When they come out of the locker room before today's game, someone accidentally knocks a bucket of garbage out a window. It's not like anybody's going to get hurt."

Abby swallowed. "It *will* hurt them," she said. "You know that. There has to be some other way to work this out. Maybe if we talk to Mrs. Berry."

Lisa, Megan, and Jill stared at their friend. "Just where do you stand, anyway?" Lisa snapped. "Abby, are you with us or against us?"

Your Witness

Imagine that Abby asks for your advice. What will you tell her to do?

Do You Know?

◆ How do people today give witness to Jesus?

Stephen Stands Up

Just like people today, the first Christians were called to take a stand by living their beliefs. Standing up for the message of Jesus is not always popular or easy, but those who take that message seriously do not feel they have a choice. Betraying their beliefs would mean denying the truth they have witnessed at work in their lives.

Stephen was a young man when he heard the preaching of the Apostles and was baptized. Stephen's commitment was so strong that he was chosen by the Apostles to help carry out the ministry of service in the Christian community. Stephen did this with energy and joy, and wherever he went he preached the Good News of the Messiah, Jesus.

Stephen's outspoken message upset some members of the Jewish community in Jerusalem, who sincerely believed that Jesus had been guilty of **blasphemy** by claiming such a close, personal relationship with God. After Jesus' crucifixion, Jewish leaders thought the whole problem would go away, but Stephen stirred it up again. They threatened to arrest Stephen for the crime of blasphemy—the punishment for which was death by stoning.

Stephen continued preaching and was eventually brought before the Sanhedrin to answer to the charge of blasphemy.

VIRTUE

Commitment means choosing to remain faithful to what you believe and to what you have promised, even when it is difficult. Christian witness requires commitment.

ACTIVITY

The Death of a Witness

The story of Stephen is told in the Acts of the Apostles. Read Acts 7:54–60 to find out what happened to Stephen. Then answer these questions:

• What vision did Stephen see before his death?

• Who was the young man who guarded the cloaks of those who executed Stephen? What would happen to this young man later?

• How did Stephen follow Jesus' example as he died?

Witnesses to Christ

Stephen is remembered as the Church's first **martyr**—a person who gives up his or her life for the faith. The word *martyr* is Greek for "witness."

Throughout the centuries, many more followers of Jesus have been called to give witness to their beliefs with their lives. When the message of the Gospel confronts the message of worldly power and institutional evil, the consequences may be persecution, imprisonment, and martyrdom for individual witnesses. But the power of the Gospel is greater than death. The example of witnesses willing to stand up for their beliefs even to the point of death makes a profound impression, often converting those responsible for the persecution. Whether officially recognized as saints or memorialized on the evening news, martyrs continue to testify to the power of faith.

✝ THIS WE BELIEVE!

Every Christian is called to witness—in living as well as in dying—to the truth that Jesus revealed. Christians give witness in both words and actions.

Saint Joan of Arc was only fourteen when she heard heavenly voices telling her to save France. Saint Joan led France to several victories before she was captured and tried for witchcraft. She was burned at the stake in 1431 for standing up for her beliefs.

Sister Ita Ford proclaimed the Gospel by serving the poor in El Salvador. Death squads were sent to expel Christian missionaries who worked to help the poor improve their lives. Sister Ita, along with two other nuns and a lay mission worker, was murdered in 1980 for preaching the Gospel.

Vilmos Apor was a Hungarian baron who became a priest and later a bishop. He condemned racist laws that were being introduced in Hungary and through his efforts, many Jews were spared from Nazi extermination camps. Soviet soldiers shot him in 1945 as he tried to protect about 100 women to whom he had given refuge.

Archbishop Joachim Ruhuna of Burudi, a nun, and two lay catechists were murdered by Hutu rebels in 1996. The bishop, a member of the Tutsi minority, condemned the violence on both sides. The bishop received death threats and was later killed because of his call for peace.

ACTIVITY

Witness to the Witnesses

The people pictured on this page have all witnessed to Jesus with their lives. Read about each of them and then answer the following questions:

1. What does it mean to be a martyr?
2. How does the example of martyrs help spread the message of Jesus?
3. How can you be a living witness to the Gospel?

WORD OF GOD

Therefore, since we are surrounded by so great a cloud of witnesses, let us persevere in running the race that lies before us, while keeping our eyes fixed on Jesus, the leader and perfecter of faith.

Hebrews 12:1–2a

Living Witness

You may be inspired by the example of the martyrs, but it is unlikely that you will ever be faced with the choice to die for your beliefs. Like the great majority of Christians through the centuries, you are called to be a living witness, giving testimony to the Gospel by the things you do and say in your everyday life.

That does not mean that being a living witness is always easy. Although you may not face torture or imprisonment for your faith, standing up for what you believe can cost you popularity or false friends. But there are rewards, too. As you grow in integrity—the wholeness that comes from acting according to what you know is right—you will attract friends who share your values. You may even convince others to follow your example.

How can you be a living witness? Here are four specific areas in which you can testify to your beliefs every day:

- **Professing your faith.** Be proud to identify yourself as a follower of Jesus. Be respectful of other people's religious traditions, but be comfortable about inviting others to attend Mass or a youth retreat with you. Be firm in your beliefs, and do not participate in or tolerate conversations that make fun of religious commitment.

- **Defending life.** In a culture that often devalues God's gift of life, standing up for the rights of unborn children, terminally ill people, people with HIV/AIDS, and those challenged mentally or physically is an important way to witness. You also witness to the value of life when you show respect for all people and care for animals and the environment as part of God's creation.

- **Seeking justice.** When you see injustice—whether in the lunchroom or around the world—do what you can to speak out against it. Stand up for other people, especially those who are too weak or who feel too powerless to defend themselves. Be just in all your actions and choices.

- **Speaking the truth.** There should never be a difference between what you say and what you believe. Don't go along with the group when you know it is wrong; speak up. Don't allow yourself to be drawn into gossiping and hurtful teasing. Let people know that you will not listen to so-called jokes that make fun of the way people talk or dress.

ACTIVITY

I Witness

Give an example of how you can witness in each of these ways in your daily life.

I can profess my faith by . . .

I can defend life by . . .

I can seek justice by . . .

I can speak the truth by . . .

Renewing Your Commitment

You were called to be a witness in Baptism. You (or your family in your name) made promises to reject evil and to live your belief in God—Father, Son, and Holy Spirit. Use the pledge form below to renew your commitment to witness to the message of Jesus every day. Ask a friend to "witness" your commitment by signing the pledge, too.

Pledge

I, _____ ,

do hereby renew my commitment to be a living witness to the Good News of Jesus Christ.

I will stand up for my beliefs by

_____

_____ .

Other people will meet Jesus in me when I

_____

_____ .

I will continue to grow in my faith by

_____

_____ .

I make this commitment in the name of the Father, and of the Son, and of the Holy Spirit.

Signed

Date

Witnessed by

BRAVE MUSIC

Pray together this prayer attributed to Saint Augustine, asking God's help as you live your Christian witness.

God of our lives,
there are days when the burdens we carry
chafe our shoulders and weigh us down;
when the road seems dreary and endless,
the skies gray and threatening;
when our lives have no music in them,
and our hearts are lonely,
and our souls have lost their courage.
Flood our path with light,
turn our eyes to where the skies are full of promise;
tune our hearts to brave music;
give us the sense of comradeship
with heroes and saints of every age;
and so quicken our spirits
that we may be able to encourage the souls
of all who journey with us on the road of life,
to your honor and glory.
Amen.

The exercises and activities on this page will help you know, love, and serve God better.

Know

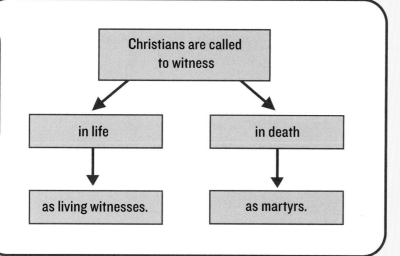

Christians are called to witness

→ in life → as living witnesses.

→ in death → as martyrs.

Love

How can the choice to accept martyrdom be seen as a loving action? Give an example from the life of a martyr you have studied.

Serve

How can standing up for what you believe be a service to others? Write three examples.

_____

_____

_____

Heroes of Faith

Sister Alicia Domon

Alicia Domon joined a French religious community as a young woman and traveled to Argentina to be a catechist. She loved working with children but eventually joined a small group of women, the mothers of the *disappeared*—those imprisoned, tortured, missing, and killed by the government-sanctioned death squads. These mothers held a silent protest vigil every day outside the government headquarters. In 1977, while planning a retreat for the mothers, Sister Alicia herself became one of the *disappeared*. She was taken away by soldiers and never seen again.

HOME and FAMILY

These projects and activities will help you keep this lesson alive all week long.

On your own

Make a list of three situations in your life right now that call for your witness as a Christian. For each situation, write one way you can witness to the message of Jesus.

With others

Look through newspapers or online resources for examples of people today who are witnessing to the message of Jesus by their lives or through their deaths.

With your family

Ask family members to share with you stories of people whose witness inspired them. Watch a video about someone who stands up for his or her beliefs, and talk about it afterward.

Holy Spirit, give me the courage to stand up for what I believe.

GO ONLINE!
www.mhbenziger.com

PEACEMAKER

> Peace I leave with you; my peace I give to you.
>
> *John 14:27*

Do You Know?

◆ What does it mean to be a peacemaker?

Peace!

Alex sat at the kitchen table, trying to do his homework. Outside the open window of the apartment, traffic roared five flights below. The construction workers' power drills seemed to rattle Alex's teeth. Horns honked, radios blared.

It wasn't much quieter inside. Alex could hear the Spanish soap operas his grandmother loved on the TV in the living room. His younger brothers were arguing over a toy, and his older sister was on the phone with her best friend while she tried to start dinner around the spot where Alex was perched. Their mom had already called to say she'd be late, because she had to work overtime.

Alex looked at his dad's latest letter home with a picture showing him in his uniform. The part of the world where Alex's dad was stationed was pretty dangerous, and the family couldn't wait for him to get back home.

Alex looked at his assignment book. "Write your definition of peace," he had written. Alex laughed out loud. "Peace! Yeah, right!" he said to himself sarcastically. It was hard to imagine peace in Alex's noisy world. But then his thoughts drifted to a summer day of fishing in a stream with his dad, just the two of them and the woods. No traffic, no arguments, no worries about money or war. "Yeah, right," he said again, this time longingly. "Peace!"

Remembering Peace

Share a memory of a peaceful day. Where were you? Who was with you? What made it so peaceful?

The Peace of Christ

The world Jesus lived in was not a peaceful one. His country, Palestine, was a colony of the powerful Roman Empire, and anyone who spoke up for freedom was quickly and violently silenced. Constant quarreling took place among various groups of Jewish leaders, each of whom believed he spoke for God. The streets of Jerusalem were filled with poor, homeless, sick, and mentally ill people who were forced to beg for a living. On the country roads between towns, gangs of thieves waited to ambush and rob wealthy travelers.

Just as in our time, everyone in Jesus' world had his or her own definition of peace. For the Romans, it was order, with no rioting or protests. For the Jews of Palestine, it was the freedom to worship God in the Temple as their ancestors had done, without the burden of paying taxes to Rome. For the poor and distressed, peace was a crust of bread, a warm corner to sleep in at night, and a smile instead of a curse. For travelers, it was freedom from fear.

How did Jesus define peace? He didn't—at least not directly. Jesus told his disciples to bless with peace the homes they visited—but added that it would do no good if those within the house were not already peaceful people *(Luke 10:5–6)*. To those who looked to him for easy solutions to life's problems, Jesus' surprising answer was, "Do not think that I have come to bring peace upon the earth. I have come to bring not peace but the sword" *(Matthew 10:34)*. And on the night before he died, Jesus tried to explain that the kind of peace he *had* come to bring—God's peace—was not going to follow the pattern most people had in mind:

Peace I leave with you; my peace I give to you. Not as the world gives do I give it to you. Do not let your hearts be troubled or afraid.

John 14:27

What do you think Jesus meant by saying he had not come to bring peace but a sword?

Making Peace

Even though Jesus did not define peace, and many of his statements about peace seem puzzling, he did give some hints about the kind of peace he had come to share. Those hints suggest that, for the followers of Jesus, peace is not a substance but a process, not a noun but a verb. "Blessed are the peace*makers*," Jesus said—you will be happy not to the degree that you are *at* peace, but to the degree that you make peace happen.

And how do you do that? Here, Jesus was very specific.

What is the secret to getting along peacefully? "Do to others whatever you would have them do to you. This is the law and the prophets" *(Matthew 7:12)*.

What's wrong with fights with family or friends? "You have heard that it was said to your ancestors, 'You shall not kill.' But I say to you, whoever is angry with his brother will be liable to judgment. If you recall that your brother has anything against you, go first and be reconciled with your brother. Settle with your opponent quickly while on the way to court with him." (from *Matthew 5:21–25*)

How do we stop violence from escalating? "You have heard that it was said, 'An eye for an eye and a tooth for a tooth.' But I say to you, when someone strikes you on your right cheek, turn the other one to him as well." (from *Matthew 5:38–39*)

How do we put an end to war? "Love your enemies, and pray for those who persecute you, that you may be children of your heavenly Father." (from *Matthew 5:44–45*)

What do people need in order to find peace? "I was hungry and you gave me food, I was thirsty and you gave me drink, a stranger and you welcomed me, naked and you clothed me, ill and you cared for me, in prison and you visited me" *(Matthew 25:35–36)*.

ACTIVITY

Blessed Are You

Give a specific example of how you can make peace in each of these ways:

- Follow the golden rule. (Matthew 7:12)
- Be reconciled with family members.
- Turn the other cheek.
- Love your enemy.
- Give people what they need.

Justice and Peace

The vision of God's reign that Jesus announced completely intertwines justice and peace. In fact, Christians believe that true peace is impossible without justice.

You can see why. When people are treated unjustly, they become frustrated and angry. That anger can easily turn to violence between family members, economic or ethnic groups, or nations. Real peace is not just the absence of war: it is a state of being in which all people are treated justly.

Injustice does not excuse violence, of course. Every person has a choice as to how he or she will react to the circumstances of life. But when the social environment, culture, and public institutions accept violence as a means of settling disagreements, it is difficult to see other options clearly. Part of the mission of Christian peacemaking is to confront a culture of violence and injustice, offering people better and more peaceful choices for settling disputes.

Gentleness means finding the most peaceful and caring, least violent and harmful solution to a problem. Gentleness should not be confused with weakness. Saint Francis de Sales said, "Nothing is as strong as gentleness, and nothing is as gentle as real strength."

ACTIVITY

Mapping a Path to Peace

Think about each of the following factors that contribute to a culture of violence. What should the Christian peacemaker's response be to each of them?

- Young people who drop out of school and can't find jobs are more likely to get involved in violent gang activity.
- The use of illegal drugs and alcohol contributes to domestic violence, fighting, and traffic deaths.
- Video games featuring extreme violence and sexism are growing in popularity among children and teens.
- Distrust among racial and ethnic groups leads to conflicts between police and local communities and may increase the potential for rioting.
- Bullying of students who are thought to be different goes beyond name calling to include violent attacks or psychological harassment that leads to suicide.
- Disrespectful attitudes toward sexuality lead to increases in date rape, abortion, underage pregnancy, child abuse, and sexually transmitted diseases.

Working for Justice

Pope Paul VI said, "If you want peace, work for justice." One way to do that is to identify the causes of problems and then think of practical steps to resolve them. Name three problems that disrupt the peace of your community. Identify the cause of each problem, and suggest a just solution.

Problem	Problem	Problem
Cause	Cause	Cause
Solution	Solution	Solution

✝ THE SOURCE OF PEACE

Pope Paul VI worked and prayed tirelessly for peace. Make his prayer your own.

Reader 1: O Lord, God of peace, you have created us and shown us your love so that we may share in your glory. We bless you and give you thanks because you have sent us Jesus, your well-beloved Son.

All: Through the mystery of his resurrection, you made him the worker of salvation, the source of peace, the bond of brotherhood.

Reader 2: We give thanks for the desires, efforts, and achievements stirred up by the Spirit of peace in our time, to replace hate by love, mistrust by understanding, indifference by interdependence.

All: Open our minds and hearts to the real demands of love, so that we may become peacemakers.

Reader 3: Remember, Father of mercy, all who struggle, suffer, and die to bring forth a world of closer relationship.

All: May your kingdom of justice, peace, and love come to people of every race and tongue. May the earth be filled with your glory.

Amen.

The exercises and activities on this page will help you know, love, and serve God better.

Know

Peace

"If you want peace, work for justice."
Pope Paul VI

Justice

Love

How does injustice make it difficult for people in your family or community to live happily and peacefully? Write two examples.

Serve

How can you replace violence with peace in your everyday life? Write three examples.

Heroes of Faith

John Leary

As a student at Harvard, John Leary lived among the poor and the homeless at a Catholic Worker house. He worked with Pax Christi, the international organization that seeks to bring about peace through justice and also protested against war, abortion, and the death penalty. His friends cherished John's gift of laughter, his generosity, and his simple goodness. A few weeks after graduating with honors, 24-year-old John Leary died of a heart attack. In his short life, John worked harder for peace than many people who outlived him, and left a model for those who would follow.

These projects and activities will help you keep this lesson alive all week long.

On your own

Make a list of ways in which you participate in small forms of injustice in your everyday life. For each example, think of one way in which you can act more justly.

With others

With your friends, form an *Alternatives to Violence* club. Look at the ways in which you support a culture of violence, such as paying to see or rent violent movies, playing violent video games, or fighting among yourselves. Pledge to choose nonviolent alternatives to these actions and to support one another in being peacemakers.

With your family

Ask family members how they define peace. Plan a family day (or afternoon, or even an hour!) of peace, during which you participate together in activities that restore your sense of peace or contribute to a more peaceful world.

Lord, make me an instrument of your peace!

GO ONLINE!
www.mhbenziger.com

Make a Difference

The call to be peacemakers and work for justice is so important to carrying out Jesus' mission that it forms an official ministry of the local, national, and global Church. In the United States, parish and diocesan offices of justice and peace, supported by the United States Conference of Catholic Bishops (USCCB), offer a variety of opportunities for making a difference in the world.

Many dioceses and parishes throughout the country have instituted a program called JustFaith. Supported by Catholic Charities and partially funded by the bishops' Campaign for Human Development, JustFaith uses small-group meetings, readings, videos, and guest speakers to *train prophets* in the Church's tradition of peacemaking and social justice. The process is life-changing. As participant Ed Cortas says:

> *In JustFaith I met Jesus. In the faces of the poor, I met Jesus. In the lives of courageous women and men fighting for justice, I met Jesus. In the struggles of my companion classmates, I met Jesus. And, like everyone who ever met Jesus, I am changed now.*

You can find out more about JustFaith at www.justfaith.org.

Where You Live

World peace and justice start where you live. Many parish and diocesan justice and peace ministries include programs specifically designed for young people, such as the workshops on environmental justice offered to middle school students at St. Charles Borromeo School by the Archdiocese of Santa Fe. To give your own ministry of peacemaking a jump start, contact your parish justice and peace commission or diocesan Office of Justice and Peace.

Parish and diocesan ministries of justice and peace help people sow the seeds of a better world.

Remember

1. How would Christians measure power and success if they follow Jesus' example?

Jesus showed that true power and success lie in humble service to others. All followers of Jesus are called in Baptism to a life of service, which often means holding beliefs that run counter to those of the world.

2. How can Christians practice Jesus' unifying ministry?

All Christians are called to end the divisions of racism, sexism, and other prejudices that keep people apart. In particular, Christians are called to work for ecumenism, or the reconciling of divisions among the followers of Jesus, and for interfaith understanding among people of all religious beliefs.

3. How are Christians called to give witness to their faith?

All followers of Jesus are called to witness to their faith in the words, actions, and choices of their everyday lives. This means standing up for one's beliefs, even when that is difficult. When Christian faith conflicts with political power, Christians may be called to witness by giving up their lives in martyrdom.

4. How can Christians be peacemakers?

The Church, following the example of Jesus, teaches that true peace cannot exist without justice. Christian peacemaking requires the followers of justice to find alternatives to violence and to work for the just treatment of all people.

Respond

Choose one of the following questions. Write a response. If you wish, share what you have written.

1. What group in your community or in the world do you think is most in need of service? What can you begin doing now to be of service to these people?

2. Where do your Christian values conflict most strongly with the messages you receive from society and the media? What kind of support would make it easier for you to stand up for your beliefs in this area?

3. What do you think poses the greatest danger to peace in your world? What practical steps can you take to begin removing this threat to peace?

Act

Choose one of the following projects, and make arrangements to carry it out with other young people in your parish community.

- Visit elderly parishioners who are homebound or living in care centers. Make cards with favorite Scripture verses to leave with the people you visit.
- Develop a series of dramatic skits to show young children alternatives to violence at home and at school. Present your skits to groups of younger children in your school or parish.
- Volunteer to provide hospitality—serving homemade cookies and lemonade, for example—to church members after services. Wear name tags identifying yourselves, and be ready to answer people's questions about your faith.

Share

Create a prayer service on the theme of commitment to service, witness, justice, and peace. Assign groups to choose readings and music; design the prayer environment; and develop prayers, pledges, and gestures of commitment. If possible, invite another group to join you when you celebrate the prayer service.

The words I have spoken to you are spirit and life.

John 6:63b

Vietnam From Maryknoll

I Am the Life

Chapter

Christian Life

Live as children of light, for light produces every kind of goodness and righteousness and truth.

Ephesians 5:8–9

Do You Know?

◆ How can you recognize a Christian?

Winners and Losers

Joe just received an award for never missing his turn as an altar server. When he is not serving, Joe always sits up front at Sunday Mass. He carries his Bible everywhere. During the week, Joe is often heard telling racist and sexist jokes. He and his friends pick on the boys in their class who aren't athletic.

Jess has a reputation for being a tough kid. Her older sister belongs to a gang, and Jess has been seen hanging out with these girls late at night. Jess struggles with her school work, but she usually turns it in on time and gets average grades. Every afternoon, Jess rides a bus across town to cook dinner for her grandmother, who lives alone.

Celina is one of the most popular girls in the seventh grade. Her parents are wealthy, and Celina always has the latest fashionable clothes and CDs. Recently, Celina has been spending most of her time with Ana, a new student from Guatemala. It's clear that Ana's family doesn't have much money. Her clothes come from the parish thrift shop. Celina's friends tell her she should dump Ana, because Ana is a loser. Celina dumps her old friends instead.

You Choose

Imagine that you go to school with Joe, Jess, Celina, and Ana. Which of these teens would you want to have as friends? Which would you avoid? Give reasons for your choices.

Make every effort to supplement your faith with virtue, virtue with knowledge, knowledge with self-control, self-control with endurance, endurance with devotion, devotion with mutual affection, mutual affection with love.

2 Peter 1:5–7

How Can You Tell?

Appearances, we all know, can be deceiving. People who appear to be *good* and *holy* can betray that appearance with sinful actions, and those who seem like losers in the world's eyes can have the hearts of winners. The crowds who listened to Jesus knew how easy it was to be swayed by people claiming to have the secret to eternal life. They asked how they could recognize the true prophets of God's reign. Jesus answered with a metaphor that the farmers in the crowd could easily understand:

> By their fruits you will know them. Do people pick grapes from thornbushes, or figs from thistles? Just so, every good tree bears good fruit, and a rotten tree bears bad fruit. A good tree cannot bear bad fruit, nor can a rotten tree bear good fruit.
>
> *Matthew 7:16–18*

Jesus wanted his followers to be easily recognized in the world—not necessarily by the words they spoke, or by some kind of outward badge of their faith, but by the way they lived their lives, even when no one was looking.

> Not everyone who says to me "Lord, Lord" will enter the kingdom of heaven, but only the one who does the will of my Father in heaven.
>
> *Matthew 7:21*

After Jesus had returned to his Father, the newly formed Christian churches had the same questions about how they could recognize authentic prophets, preachers, and fellow Christians. What did a real Christian life look like? This is how Paul answered the Colossians:

> Put on then, as God's chosen ones, holy and beloved, heartfelt compassion, kindness, humility, gentleness, and patience, bearing with one another and forgiving one another. And over all these put on love, that is, the bond of perfection. And whatever you do, in word or in deed, do everything in the name of the Lord Jesus.
>
> from *Colossians 3:12–17*

 If someone asked you how to recognize a true follower of Jesus, what would you say?

Keys to the Kingdom

Throughout the 2,000 years of the Church's history, people have looked with amazement at the way Christians have lived their lives. The followers of Jesus have been observed giving away their riches to meet the needs of the poor, reaching out to society's outcasts, and putting their lives on the line for the good of others. *What makes them live like this? What's their secret?*

The source of Christian living is no secret. God offers every person three incredible gifts that make it possible to live in amazing ways—even in the face of hardship, persecution, and death. At your Baptism, you said *Yes* to these three gifts and promised to use them to their fullest potential. These gifts of God, also known as **theological virtues,** are faith, hope, and love. They are not only the *secrets* of Christian living, but also the keys to God's eternal kingdom.

- **Faith** is the gift of believing and trusting in God. With that unshakable trust, Christians can face anything that comes along. Holding the key of faith, you can be sure that God believes in you, too.

- **Hope** is the gift of knowing that however painful and difficult life appears to be, God is in charge of the ending of the story. Holding the key of hope, you can be sure that God has unlimited joy in store for you.

- **Love** is the gift of seeing the very best in every person. Christian love is always ready to forgive and offers an embrace big enough for the whole world. Holding the key of love, you can be sure that God finds you completely lovable.

✝ THIS WE BELIEVE!

Christian life is guided by the theological virtues of faith, hope, and love and by the moral virtues of prudence, justice, temperance, and fortitude.

ACTIVITY

Taking the Keys

On each key, write one way it can help you "bear good fruit."

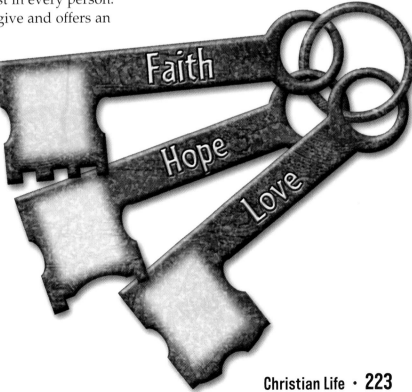

Hinge Habits

Faith, hope, and love are the keys to Christian life. But to make sure the door swings freely once the keys are turned, you need to make use of four other important qualities—the **cardinal virtues.** The word *cardinal* means "hinge." All the good habits and practices of Christian life depend on the cardinal virtues, just as a door depends on its hinges.

- **Prudence** is the virtue that helps you make wise choices. A person who is prudent sees the big picture, looks ahead to the consequences of choices, and refuses to be distracted by negative peer pressure. When you are prudent, you take time to weigh your actions and choices against what you know to be right.

- **Justice** is the virtue that helps you treat others as you would be treated. A person who is just makes sure that others get what they need and deserve as children of God, even when it means sacrificing his or her own desires. When you are just, you go beyond what is merely *fair* or *equal* and give preference to those most in need.

- **Temperance** is the virtue that helps you live a life of balance and moderation. A person who is temperate makes proper, not wasteful or abusive, use of God's gifts. When you are temperate, you avoid the temptation to be self-indulgent and to go for instant gratification.

- **Fortitude** is the virtue that helps you stay faithful to your Christian values. A person with fortitude hangs in for the long haul instead of giving up in times of trouble or inconvenience. When you have fortitude, you have the strength to endure life's challenges.

These cardinal virtues, also known as *moral virtues*, don't just show up whenever you need them. Just as the hinges of a door need frequent use and regular oiling to keep them swinging, the only way to grow in the cardinal virtues is to practice them every day.

VIRTUE

Prudence is the moral virtue that drives all other good habits and moral actions. People who are prudent make choices according to reason and conscience, guided by the Holy Spirit. They care about the consequences of their actions and are not impulsive.

ACTIVITY

Oiling the Hinges

Which of the four cardinal virtues do you need to practice the most? Write the name of the virtue in the oilcan, and add one way you can practice it this week.

Virtues in Action

On the drawer panels, list two ways you can put each cardinal virtue into action in your everyday life.

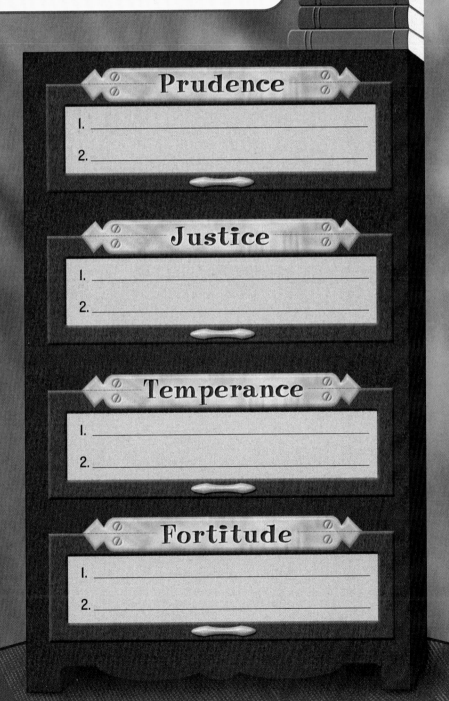

Prudence

1. _____
2. _____

Justice

1. _____
2. _____

Temperance

1. _____
2. _____

Fortitude

1. _____
2. _____

In the Land of the Living

Faith, hope, and love last beyond life. Pray this prayer based on Psalm 116 as a reminder that your Christian life is in God's hands.

All: I will walk in the presence of the Lord in the land of the living.

Group 1: Gracious is the Lord and just; yes, our Lord is merciful. The Lord keeps the little ones; I was brought low, and he saved me. The Lord has freed my soul from death, my eyes from tears, my feet from stumbling. I shall walk before the Lord in the land of the living.

All: I will walk in the presence of the Lord in the land of the living.

Group 2: How shall I make a return to the Lord for all the good God has done for me? The cup of salvation I will take up, and I will call upon the name of the Lord. Precious in the eyes of the Lord is the death of his faithful ones.

All: I will walk in the presence of the Lord in the land of the living.

The exercises and activities on this page will help you know, love, and serve God better.

Know

Christian Life
↓
Theological Virtues
↓
Faith   Hope   Love
↓
Cardinal Virtues
↓
Prudence   Justice   Temperance   Fortitude

Love

By what *good fruit* will people be able to recognize you as a follower of Jesus this week? Write three examples.

Serve

How will you practice the virtue of justice in the way you treat others this week? Write three examples.

Heroes of Faith

Dietrich Bonhoeffer

In the 1930s, a young Lutheran pastor watched in horror as the Nazis took over his native Germany. Dietrich Bonhoeffer, a committed pacifist, became involved in a plot to assassinate Adolf Hitler. Bonhoeffer was arrested and sentenced to death. From prison, he wrote letters that challenged the way some people viewed Christian life. Bonhoeffer believed that the Church was called to stand in the midst of the world, ministering to its suffering people not from a distance but in solidarity. On April 10, 1944, the thirty-nine-year-old Bonhoeffer was hanged by the Nazis.

These projects and activities will help you keep this lesson alive all week long.

On your own

Read the traditional prayers known as the Acts of Faith, Hope, and Love from a Catholic prayer book or missalette. Then, write your own short prayers asking God's help in living these gifts.

With others

With your friends, plan ways to be more temperate in your use of God's gifts. Find alternatives to overeating or unhealthy eating or dieting. Reduce the amount of food that you waste. Support one another in avoiding the use of alcohol, tobacco, and drugs.

With your family

One way to practice prudence is to heed the wisdom of people who are more experienced in Christian life. Ask family members for their advice on how to make wise moral choices and live as a follower of Jesus.

Holy Spirit, strengthen my faith, my hope, and my love!

GO ONLINE!
www.mhbenziger.com

Living Faith

Something to Believe In

Think of all the messages about belief, faith, and trust you hear every day:

"KEEP THE FAITH."

"I HAVE FAITH IN YOU."

"BELIEVE IT OR NOT!"

"TRUST ME, I KNOW WHAT I'M DOING."

"IT WAS *UNBELIEVABLE!*"

"BELIEVE YOU ME."

"PUT YOUR FAITH IN US."

"SHE INHERITED A TRUST FUND."

"IN GOD WE TRUST."

Add two of your own familiar sayings about belief, faith, and trust:

For all the talk about faith, many people today have a difficult time finding something to believe in or someone to trust. What factors get in the way of faith and trust?

WORD OF GOD

Faith is the realization of things hoped for and evidence of things not seen. By faith we understand that the universe was ordered by the word of God.

Hebrews 11:1, 3a

The Mustard Seed

Jesus had complete faith in God, his Father. Although his friends had seen that faith firsthand, they still had as much difficulty understanding it as most other people might. Like some people today, the disciples sometimes made the mistake of thinking of faith as a finite substance that could be measured out or earned. "Lord," they said, "increase our faith."

Jesus was silent for a moment. He must have wondered to himself whether his friends would ever get what he was saying—and living—about faith. But he patiently gave them yet another lesson. Pinching his thumb and forefinger together, as though holding something very tiny, Jesus said to them, "If you had faith the size of a mustard seed, you would say to this mulberry tree, 'Be uprooted and planted in the sea,' and it would obey you" *(Luke 17:5–6).*

Jesus was telling his friends that it is not the size of a person's faith that matters. Faith is infinite and cannot be measured. Rather, a person who has faith can accomplish far more than he or she could without this gift from God. According to another saying of Jesus that has become a proverb, "Faith can move mountains."

Although you cannot earn or deserve the gift of faith, which is offered to everyone, you can choose to cooperate with it. The faith Jesus wanted his followers to have is not a substance but an action. Faith means having total trust in God and acting on that trust.

When you live the gift of faith, you are able to believe in and commit yourself to God. You are given what you need in order to grow strong in faith through prayer, reading the Scriptures, and acting as a person of faith.

ACTIVITY

On the seed packet, write about a time when having faith enabled you to do more than you imagined was possible.

My Mustard Seed Moment

Not Just Lip Service

Some of the most practical advice about faith in the Bible comes from the New Testament letter attributed to James, the Apostle who led the Christian community in Jerusalem. This letter is addressed to Christians everywhere, and its wisdom holds true in every time.

James was concerned that people gave only lip service to the faith they professed. It was clear that some Christians were hypocrites—claiming to believe one thing, but acting in ways completely opposite to their beliefs. It is not enough, James wrote, just to "get religion." The words and the deeds of faith are equally important, and there should be no disharmony between what people say they believe and how they actually behave—their *works*.

THIS WE BELIEVE!

The gift of faith, the ability to place complete trust in God, is given to each person. Christians are called to live the gift of faith fully, as Mary did.

Be doers of the word and not hearers only. For if anyone is a hearer of the word and not a doer, he is like a man who looks at his own face in a mirror. He sees himself, then goes off and promptly forgets what he looked like. But the one who peers into the perfect law of freedom and perseveres, and is not a hearer who forgets but a doer who acts, such a one shall be blessed in what he does.

What good is it, my brothers, if someone says he has faith but does not have works? Can that faith save him? If a brother or sister has nothing to wear and has no food for the day, and one of you says to them, "Go in peace, keep warm, and eat well," but you do not give them the necessities of the body, what good is it? So also faith of itself, if it does not have works, is dead.

James 1:22–25, 2:14–17

ACTIVITY

Faith and Works

Think of three beliefs you have as a Christian. For each article of faith, write one work that will show harmony between what you believe and how you act.

What I Believe	How I Act
1.	
2.	
3.	

Fra Angelico, *Coronation of the Virgin*, Fifteenth Century

Mary's Faith

What does faith in action look like? The Church honors Mary, the mother of Jesus, as a model of faith. The Mother of God had moments of doubt and trouble, but she never lost her confidence in God. Here are some ways you can imitate Mary's total trust in God, even if the circumstances of your life differ from hers.

- **When you make important choices.** Mary was asked to be the mother of God's promised Messiah. She didn't hesitate to say yes, even though she didn't fully understand what God was asking of her *(Luke 1:38)*. How has faith helped you make an important decision?

_____

_____

- **When life doesn't go the way you planned.** After the panic of losing Jesus in Jerusalem and the joy of finding him in the Temple, Mary was confused by Jesus' words. Luke 2:51 says that Mary "kept all these things in her heart." When have you been helped by your faith to be patient?

_____

_____

Trust is confidence that remains unshaken by difficult circumstances. God alone is completely trustworthy; trust in oneself and in others is earned through faithful, caring, and responsible actions.

- **When there doesn't seem to be a solution.** The host ran out of wine at the wedding party in Cana. Mary wanted to do something to ease the host's embarrassment. At first, Jesus questioned Mary's request for help. But she persisted, and Jesus worked his first public miracle *(John 2:1–11)*. When has faith given you the courage to persevere?

_____

_____

- **When even God seems absent.** Among a handful of others, Mary stood at the cross as her son died an agonizing death. She did not abandon him or her faith, and she welcomed Jesus' friends as her own children *(John 19:25–27)*. How can faith help you see God's will and God's love even in the darkest times?

_____

_____

Keeping the Faith

Being faithful doesn't have to involve struggling with big theological questions. Tell how you would put your faith into practice in each of the following situations.

You need just $5 more to buy the video game you've been saving for. You know where your mom keeps her purse, and you know she doesn't always keep track of how much cash is in her wallet.

A classmate you don't like very much makes a big mistake while solving a math problem on the board.

$$X = \$9,000 \div \tfrac{3}{4}$$
$$X = \$13,000$$

Your dad reminds you that it's your turn to do the dishes just as your favorite TV show comes on. Your sister is already recording another program for a school project.

You don't make the cut for the school track team, even though it is your dream to be an Olympic runner.

PRAYERS OF FAITH

The Psalms are songs of faith. These prayers were known and sung by Jesus and are part of the Church's liturgical heritage. They celebrate the many moods of faith.

Use each of these Psalm verses as a meditation starter or the inspiration for your own prayer, or read the whole Psalm.

Whenever I lay down and slept, the LORD preserved me to rise again *(Psalm 3:6).*

How long, LORD? Will you utterly forget me? How long will you hide your face from me? *(Psalm 13:2).*

Even when I walk through a dark valley, I fear no harm for you are at my side *(Psalm 23:4).*

In you, LORD, I take refuge. Into your hands I commend my spirit; you will redeem me, LORD, faithful God *(Psalm 31:2, 6).*

A clean heart create in me, God, renew in me a steadfast spirit *(Psalm 51:12).*

The exercises and activities on this page will help you know, love, and serve God better.

Know

Faith + Works = Life in Christ

Love

Who are your models of faith? List three people who show you how to trust in God, and tell how they do it.

Serve

How will you put your faith into action this week? Write three examples.

Heroes of Faith

Flannery O'Connor

The American writer Flannery O'Connor is best known for her short stories and novels. The most powerful influence in Flannery O'Connor's life was her deep Catholic faith. She knew that in the twentieth century, it was sometimes easier for people not to believe than it was to try to reconcile faith in God with the injustices and tragedies of modern life. She wrote, "I think there is no suffering greater than what is caused by the doubts of those who want to believe. I know what torment this is, but I can only see it, in myself anyway, as the process by which faith is deepened."

CHAPTER 22
HOME and FAMILY

These projects and activities will help you keep this lesson alive all week long.

On your own

Write a prayer that expresses your faith in God.

With others

Find out more about the titles under which Mary is honored as a model of faith in your parish, diocese, or ethnic community. What do these descriptions of Mary tell you about how to live your faith?

With your family

Choose one way your family can put its faith into action this week for the good of others.

Yes, Lord,
I have come to
believe that you are
the Messiah,
the Son of God.

GO ONLINE!
www.mhbenziger.com

Christian Hope

> Be strong and take heart, all you who hope in the LORD.
>
> *Psalm 31:25*

Do You Know?

◆ What reasons do Christians have for hope?

Seeds of Hope

My family has been farming this same rich black Iowa soil for more than one hundred years. My mother's great-grandparents Jan and Annalise settled this land, breaking through the thick prairie sod with a plow pulled by oxen. They came from Holland to the United States to fulfill a dream. They wanted a bright future for their children. They put their hope in God.

Farming is never easy. All spring, you plow and till the fields until the weather is right for planting. All summer long, you weed, cultivate, and irrigate the fields, praying each night for rain—but not too much rain. When the weather is right, the crop is bountiful and the harvests are joyful celebrations. When the weather fails, so do the crops. Those harvests are sad times, as farmers wonder whether they can hang on for another year.

Although I'm only thirteen, I know that I will be a farmer like my parents before me. I will plant the seed and tend it. I will celebrate when the first green stalks push out of the ground. And I will give thanks to God at the harvest, because for another year God's promise is fulfilled. I am a farmer. I am a person of hope.

A Harvest of Hope

Consider your own life. Where do you see signs of hope?

THIS WE BELIEVE!

Hope is a gift from God. Moved by the example of Jesus' life and teachings, Christians are called to share hope with others.

In Joyful Hope

Christian hope is rooted in faith in God and has much in common with the farmer's trust in the arrival of the harvest season. The Letter of James used this agricultural image to describe the state of hope in which Christians are to anticipate the coming of God's reign in its fullness:

Be patient, therefore, brothers, until the coming of the Lord. See how the farmer waits for the precious fruit of the earth, being patient with it until it receives the early and the late rains. You too must be patient. Make your hearts firm, because the coming of the Lord is at hand.

James 5:7–8

The kind of hope Christians are called to have does not require proof. In fact, Christian hope is its own testament to the reason for hope. As Saint Paul wrote from his prison cell in Rome, the gift of hope is needed most precisely when there doesn't seem to be any reason for it. If things are going well, and the future is assured, hope is unnecessary. But if you can't see clearly through a fog of fear or grief, hope gives you vision.

For in hope we were saved. Now hope that sees for itself is not hope. For who hopes for what one sees? But if we hope for what we do not see, we wait with endurance.

Romans 8:24–25

What is it that Christians wait for? What harvest requires your patient endurance? Certainly, Christian hope anticipates changes for the better in this life: a relative will recover from an illness, a parent will find a job, or the sun will come out after a long rainstorm. Hope gives you the ability to wait out these and other difficult times. But as a theological virtue, hope looks even further than the future you can imagine, beyond this world to the harvest of souls at the end of time. As Catholics pray at every Mass, "we wait in joyful hope for the coming of our Savior, Jesus Christ."

ACTIVITY

Today, Tomorrow, Forever

Complete the chart by writing three things for which you hope.

What I Hope For		
In the present	**In the future**	**In the world to come**

People of Hope

Christians are living signs of hope. No matter how bad a situation may seem, they see that God's love is always there for them. This message of hope is too good to keep to themselves, so Christians find countless ways to bring hope to others.

At Chicago's Bonaventure House, the residents were accustomed to being dismissed as so-called hopeless cases. They're poor. They're homeless. Many had been addicted to drugs or had worked as prostitutes. And now they all live with HIV. But at Bonaventure House, the Alexian Brothers, Franciscans, and other volunteers who live with and care for the residents see them as children of God with lives of hope ahead of them. That's how God sees them, too.

Children should be living signs of hope. Yet millions of children today suffer from diseases, poverty, homelessness, crimes, violence, and sexual abuse. The terrible conditions they face could fill these children with despair and make them old before their time. In cities and towns all over the world, Salesian priests, religious, and lay volunteers follow the example of their founder, Saint John Bosco. They work to welcome these children into loving homes and give them back their childhood.

What events or circumstances make it difficult for people to be hopeful?

Encouragement literally means "putting a new heart into someone." When you are encouraging, you give people reason to hope in times of trouble. You support people in making a new start, learning from failure, and not giving up.

Dialog Box

◆ What are two of the biggest problems in your community? How could people of hope help resolve these problems?

◆ How are people of hope at work right now in your parish or neighborhood?

◆ How can you be a person of hope?

Give Birth to Hope

St. Anne's Maternity Home in Los Angeles began as a shelter for pregnant, unwed teens. This important outreach ministry provides prenatal care, encouragement to talk things through with family members, and options for their own and their children's future. The people who work at St. Anne's have extended their mission of hope to other important areas, such as providing education in the responsible use of God's gift of sexuality and working to place children in loving adoptive homes. St. Anne's home gives birth to hope.

Imagine that you have been locked behind bars in a prison for more than a year. How would you feel? Thousands of young teens experience similar feelings of fear and abandonment every day. Detention ministers volunteer to visit children in jails and juvenile detention centers. They listen to these young people, pray with them, and work with them to break the hopeless cycle of crime and imprisonment.

Words of Hope

When people feel down, sometimes all they need to feel better are words of hope. What words of hope would you offer in the following situations?

Your friend is feeling depressed about her grades. Her parents are upset about her poor performance in school. She has confided in you that she may run away from home rather than show her parents her latest report card.

_____

_____

You run into Joe in the hall after school. He looks terrified. A bully from another class has threatened to beat him up.

_____

_____

Margaret's mom died of cancer last year. She was the one Margaret always talked to when she needed help. Now Margaret feels all alone. Her dad is very busy, and she doesn't want to bother him because she knows how much he misses her mom, too.

_____

_____

Fill My Heart With Hope

The Christophers are a group of Catholics whose motto is "It is better to light one candle than to curse the darkness." Through their everyday activities, the Christophers bring the light of hope into the world. Here is a prayer by Father James Keller, the group's founder:

Lord, help me to be a doer, not a talker.
Help me to say "It can be done," not
  "It can't be done."
Help me to improve, not merely disapprove.
Help me to get into the thick of things,
  not just sit on the sidelines.
Help me to point out what's right with the world,
  not always what's wrong.
Help me to light candles, not blow them out.
Lord, fill my heart with hope
that looks for good in people,
  with hope that discovers what can be done,
  with hope that pushes ahead,
  with hope that opens doors,
  with hope that carries on.
Amen!

The exercises and activities on this page will help you know, love, and serve God better.

Know

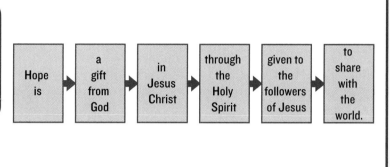

Hope is → a gift from God → in Jesus Christ → through the Holy Spirit → given to the followers of Jesus → to share with the world.

Love

How can you share the gift of hope this week with the people you love? Write three examples.

Serve

Write three ways you can provide encouragement to people who need a boost at school this week.

Heroes of Faith

Saint Barnabas

Barnabas is introduced in the Acts of the Apostles as Joseph. Having heard the message of Jesus from the Apostles, Joseph sold his property and gave the money to the Christian community. He wanted to make sure Jesus' message of hope reached every corner of the world. Because of his help in their missionary efforts, the Apostles gave Joseph the nickname Barnabas, which means "son of encouragement." Barnabas lived up to his new name, not only by offering monetary support but also by becoming a missionary himself. Tradition says he gave his life as a martyr.

HOME and FAMILY

These projects and activities will help you keep this lesson alive all week long.

On your own

Give yourself a list of things to hope for and look forward to over the next three months. Practice waiting in joyful hope.

With others

With a friend, put together a tape or CD of songs that give you hope and encouragement. Share the music with someone who is feeling down.

With your family

Plant a small garden or start a few houseplants from seeds. As each family member puts seeds into the soil, he or she should share a prayer of hope for your family.

My soul, be at rest in God alone, from whom comes my hope.

GO ONLINE!
www.mhbenziger.com

Love One Another

One Word, Many Uses

Rosie walked home, deep in thought. She had just one more day to write her essay on the meaning of the word *love*, and she had no idea how to begin.

Rosie remembered leaving home in the morning. Her mom had handed her a lunch bag as usual, before jumping in the car to head for her job. Rosie's mom called to her, just as she did each morning, "I love you."

At lunch, Rosie had listened as her friend Sara talked about her fifteen-year-old cousin, who was pregnant. "Her boyfriend told her that if she didn't have sex with him, it meant she didn't love him," Sara said.

Passing the corner market, Rosie heard a little boy whine, "But Mom, you have to buy me that candy bar! I love chocolate so much!"

After Rosie let herself into the apartment, her dog Sasha greeted her. Sasha jumped up excitedly and licked Rosie's face. Rosie laughed. "I love you, too, Sasha," she said, grabbing the dog's leash from its hook on the wall. "Let's go for a run in the park!"

Love, love, love, Rosie thought. All these different ways to use the same word. Which was the real one, the right definition? How could she tell?

Lots of Love

Make a list of the different ways you use or hear other people use the word *love*. Circle the items on your list that you think describe real love.

We have come to know and to believe in the love God has for us. God is love, and whoever remains in love remains in God and God in him.

1 John 4:16

Do You Know?

◆ How does Christian love show itself?

Paul's Definition

Paul knew that the people of Corinth were an unruly bunch, but he loved them just the same. They took to Christianity with a passion not found in many other places Paul had visited. But because of that passion, the Corinthians tended to go to extremes. Paul heard that the Corinthians now even argued about which of them had the greatest faith and the best leadership skills and which of them loved God best.

Paul thought about love and what it meant in his own life. He struggled to find a definition of real love that would be simple and clear enough to cut through the Corinthians' quarreling. This is what he wrote:

> *Love is patient, love is kind. It is not jealous, love is not pompous, it is not inflated, it is not rude, it does not seek its own interests, it is not quick-tempered, it does not brood over injury, it does not rejoice over wrongdoing but rejoices with the truth. It bears all things, believes all things, hopes all things, endures all things.*
>
> *1 Corinthians 13:4–7*

WORD OF GOD

So faith, hope, love remain, these three; but the greatest of these is love.

1 Corinthians 13:13

Of all the attempts to define love, Paul's words remain the most powerful in their directness.

Paul's definition of love works for every kind of relationship, from the love of parents and children to the bonds of friendship to the deep attraction that moves people to commit to marriage. In ancient Greek, these different forms of love had different names: *philia* for the love of family and friends, and *eros* for sexual passion. Paul's words encompass these everyday human relationships, but also transcend them to describe the kind of love the Greeks called *agape*—selfless, all-giving, concerned only for the good of others. This is the love to which all Christians are called, the greatest of the theological virtues.

ACTIVITY

Your Letter to Youth

Using Paul's definition, give the youth of today an example of how they can demonstrate real love in action.

In Deed and Truth

How does Christian love show itself? Like all the virtues, love is recognized by its fruits. That means love can't just be something you say, or sing about, or sign above your name on a valentine. Real love, like real faith and real hope, has to be brought to life in actions that demonstrate unselfish care for others.

The writer of the New Testament letters of John took love so seriously that he insisted there is no difference between love and God—and no difference between hatred and death. In his first letter to the early Christians, John wrote that real love is a life-and-death matter:

> *We know that we have passed from death to life because we love our brothers. Whoever does not love remains in death. Everyone who hates his brother is a murderer, and you know that no murderer has eternal life remaining in him. The way we came to know love was that he laid down his life for us; so we ought to lay down our lives for our brothers. If someone who has worldly means sees a brother in need and refuses him compassion, how can the love of God remain in him? Children, let us love not in word or speech but in deed and truth.*
>
> *1 John 3:14–18*

THIS WE BELIEVE!

Love is the fullness of Christian life. Christians are judged by how well they love others and are called to a life of eternal happiness and love with God.

Strong words! Yet Jesus himself said that all people would be judged at the end of time not on how many prayers they had memorized, or on how radically they had fasted, or on how much money they had made, but very simply on how well they had shown real love to those most in need of it.

God's gift of love is behind every good choice you make, every temptation you overcome, every wall you break down between people, and every kind action you perform. As a follower of Jesus and a child of God, you have the grace of knowing that you are never unloved or alone. You have more than enough love to give away.

ACTIVITY

Looking for Love

In small groups, come up with two skits—one that shows real love "in deed and in truth" and one that shows a wrong message about love that you receive from the media or from other kids.
Perform your skits for the whole group, and see if people can tell real love from false messages.

Love Is Forever

In his letter to the Corinthians, Paul made a surprising suggestion. Two of the three theological virtues will eventually pass away, he wrote, and only one will remain. At the end of time, when God's reign of justice and peace comes into its fullness, there will be no more need for faith—because the reality of God's reign will be clearly visible to everyone. There will be no more need for hope—because the waiting will at last be over. All that will remain is love, because God *is* love.

The message of love's everlasting power over death has sustained generations of believers through the loss of loved ones. Every Mass of Christian Burial, for example, is both an opportunity for shared mourning and a celebration of love. The smaller, yet just as painful deaths that humans undergo—separation, divorce, illness, political or economic oppression—are also endurable because of the knowledge that real love never fails. Even the separation of death is only temporary, because God calls all people to be reunited in love with him forever in heaven.

This may sound too idealistic if you have never experienced the power of love to overcome suffering. But Paul, who knew all about the terrible things that human life can hold, was able to write with confidence from his prison cell as he faced execution:

> *We know that all things work for good for those who love God, who are called according to his purpose. What will separate us from the love of Christ? Will anguish, or distress, or persecution, or famine, or nakedness, or peril, or the sword? No, in all these things we conquer overwhelmingly through him who loved us. For I am convinced that neither death, nor life, nor angels, nor principalities, nor present things, nor future things, nor powers, nor height, nor depth, nor any other creature will be able to separate us from the love of God in Christ Jesus our Lord.*
>
> *Romans 8:28, 35, 37–39*

Charity is unselfish love that rejoices in making sure that the needs of others are met. Christian charity sees every person through God's eyes, as lovable and worthy of respect.

ACTIVITY

L-O-V-E

Using the letters of the word *love* as the first letters of each line, write a four-line reminder to yourself that love is forever.

L _____

O _____

V _____

E _____

Glimpses of Heaven

Artists and poets have struggled for centuries to picture the glories of heaven. But you can get a glimpse of heaven any time you see real love, because heaven *is* love. Look at each picture. Tell how each is a sign of love and a glimpse of heaven.

Pilgrims in This World

This whole year, you and your class have journeyed together as followers of Christ. Although this school year is ending, your pilgrimage of faith, hope, and love will continue throughout your life. Pray this prayer of Pope Clement XI today and every day of your journey.

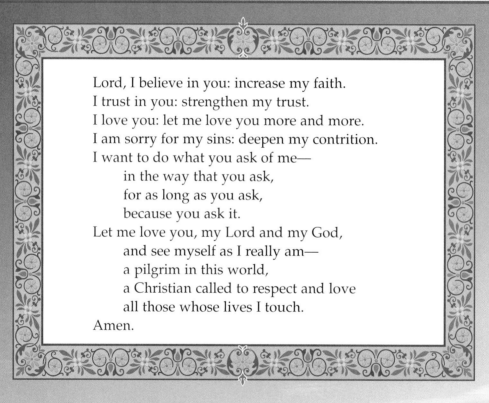

Lord, I believe in you: increase my faith.
I trust in you: strengthen my trust.
I love you: let me love you more and more.
I am sorry for my sins: deepen my contrition.
I want to do what you ask of me—
    in the way that you ask,
    for as long as you ask,
    because you ask it.
Let me love you, my Lord and my God,
    and see myself as I really am—
    a pilgrim in this world,
    a Christian called to respect and love
    all those whose lives I touch.
Amen.

The exercises and activities on this page will help you know, love, and serve God better.

Know

Life Forever with God

Love of God

Love of Neighbor

The Way to Heaven

Love

Write three ways you will grow in love for God and others this summer.

Serve

Write three things you have learned about yourself this year that will help you serve others as a follower of Jesus.

Heroes of Faith

Dante Alighieri

The fourteenth-century Italian poet Dante Alighieri is best known for his *Divine Comedy*, a three-part epic poem about his visionary journey from hell through purgatory to heaven. Love is the driving force of Dante's vision. As a young man, Dante saw a girl named Beatrice crossing a bridge. He fell in love at first sight, though only in his imagination; the two met just briefly, and Beatrice died at the age of 24. In the *Divine Comedy*, it is the spirit of Beatrice—whose name means "giver of blessed happiness"—who guides Dante into the presence of God.

These projects and activities will help you keep this lesson alive all week long.

On your own

Look back over this year's religion class. Make a list of questions you still have and ideas you want to continue to explore. Plan how you can keep growing in faith over the school break.

With others

Make plans to connect with members of your class or youth group over the break. Try to get together for at least one meal, attend Mass together at least once, and carry out at least one service project during your time off.

With your family

Plan a special way to show your love for each family member this week.

Jesus, help me grow in love!

GO ONLINE!
www.mhbenziger.com

Make a Difference

Your power to make a difference as a follower of Jesus does not end with the school year. You can take responsibility for continuing to grow in faith, hope, and love during your time off. One good resource for continuing your religious education is the Web site for Catholic young people in grades six through twelve run by Disciples Now Ministries. At this Web site, www.DisciplesNow.com, you can find the following useful resources:

- Information on the traditions, history, and teachings of the Roman Catholic Church
- Reflections on the weekly lectionary readings
- Dialogue and discussion on current events and other topics of interest to Catholic teens
- Direct links to local parishes, schools, diocesan offices, and national Catholic organizations
- Ideas for Christian service

At the Disciples Now Web site, you can also access the archives of *Youth Update*, the popular monthly newsletter for Catholic teens from St. Anthony Messenger Press. You can even volunteer to be a *Youth Update* teen reviewer.

Web sites for Catholic teens can help you keep growing in faith, hope, and love over the school break.

Looking Ahead

The Disciples Now Web site is just one starting place. Brainstorm with your group about ways to continue your faith journey over the summer.

This summer I will continue to

- Know God by
- Love God by
- Serve God by

Remember

1. **What three theological virtues help Christians live as followers of Jesus?**

   The theological virtues of faith, hope, and love are gifts from God. When people cooperate with these gifts, they are better able to live as followers of Jesus.

2. **What are the cardinal virtues? What do they do?**

   The four cardinal, or "hinge," virtues are prudence, justice, temperance, and fortitude. These moral virtues guide all good actions and choices. Prudence helps you make wise choices. Justice helps you treat others with respect. Temperance helps you live a balanced life. Fortitude gives you the strength to overcome temptation and negative peer pressure.

3. **How are Christians called to live the gift of faith?**

   Christians are called to put their full trust in God. They are to live their faith not only by professing what they believe in words but also by living their beliefs through the actions of justice and service.

4. **What does the gift of hope help Christians do?**

   The gift of hope helps Christians live their faith and share their love even in times of difficulty. Hope allows people to be confident that good will triumph not only during their life but also at the end of time.

5. **Why is love the most important theological virtue?**

   God is love. Love guides all Christian actions and choices. At the end of time, all people are judged on how well they have loved others, especially those most in need. Those who have responded to God's love by loving others will be welcomed into heaven, God's eternal reign of justice, love, and peace. Those who have consciously rejected God's love will endure hell, the eternal absence of God's love.

Respond

Choose one of the following questions. Write a response. If you wish, share what you have written.

1. What difference does being a Catholic Christian make in your life? How does your faith shape who you are?

2. Many young people today have trouble finding reasons to be confident in the future. How can you be a messenger of hope to young people who feel hopeless?

3. What advice would you give another teen who asked you how to identify true love?

Act

Make plans with members of your group to continue growing in faith, hope, and love during the school break. Here are some suggestions.

Faith

• Attend Mass together. After Mass, share breakfast and talk about the Scripture readings.

• Rent a movie that deals with themes of faith. Watch it together and discuss what you have seen.

• Attend a church fair or ethnic festival in your community. Find out more about how other people live their faith.

Hope

• Volunteer to visit patients in a children's hospital, parishioners who are homebound, or elderly people in a care center. If you can't visit, write notes or make and send greeting cards.

• Clean up a playground or park. Be sure to use safety precautions and recycle materials where possible.

Love

• Treat your family to a picnic. Take responsibility for bringing the meal, taking care of younger siblings, organizing games, and cleaning up.

• Clean out attics, closets, and garages. Take outgrown clothes and toys and furniture in good condition to a shelter for homeless families. Or have a yard sale and give the proceeds to a charitable organization.

Share

Plan an end-of-the-year celebration. Include a Mass or prayer service, a shared meal or snacks, and a time for talking about what you have learned and how far you have traveled on your pilgrimage of faith this year.

Looking Back

1. What does it mean to be a disciple? Who were the Apostles?

Disciples (from a word that means "learners") are followers of Jesus. Jesus chose twelve of his disciples as special companions. These twelve are known as the Apostles (from a word meaning "one who is sent") because Jesus sent them to share his mission and message with the world.

2. Who are the members of Jesus' human family?

Mary is the mother of Jesus. Her husband, Joseph, is the adoptive father of Jesus. Jesus, Mary, and Joseph are known as the Holy Family. Mary's cousin Elizabeth, Elizabeth's husband Zachariah, and their son John (later John the Baptist) are members of Jesus' extended family.

3. Why is Jesus known by the titles Son, Messiah, and Lord?

Jesus, who is God and human, is the Son of God (the Second Person of the Blessed Trinity) and the son of Mary. Christians believe that Jesus is the Messiah (the "anointed one") sent by God to save humanity from sin and death. Jesus is Lord (a title of honor given both to God and to human authorities) because of his divine mission and his powerful teaching authority.

4. Why is the Church called *apostolic*?

The Church carries on the mission of the Apostles, led by the bishops and the pope who are the successors of the Apostles.

5. In what way can the Church be understood to be a sacrament?

The Church is the Body of Christ. Jesus is present in the Church through the working of the Holy Spirit. Through the members of the Church, Jesus becomes present to the whole world.

6. How do followers of Jesus become members of the Body of Christ?

Christians are initiated into the Body of Christ through the sacraments of initiation: Baptism, Confirmation, and Eucharist. These sacraments take away sin, fill people with sanctifying grace, and make people members of the Church.

7. What actions does Jesus accomplish in the Eucharist and, through us, in the world?

Through the Eucharist, Jesus builds community, heals and forgives, shares Good News, gives thanks to his Father, offers himself in sacrifice for the good of others, and becomes truly present in the lives of his people. We are sent forth to live these Eucharistic actions in the world.

8. **Why did Jesus die on the cross?**

   Jesus gave up his life in loving sacrifice to win for all people salvation from sin and death.

9. **What central event of our Christian faith gives hope that death will be the beginning of new life with God? When do we celebrate this event?**

   Jesus' resurrection, celebrated solemnly at Easter and at every Sunday Mass, teaches us that death is not the end. God has the power to offer us eternal life.

10. **What gift did Jesus promise to his followers to help them continue his work?**

    Jesus promised that the Holy Spirit would come to be with the Apostles forever to protect, comfort, and teach them.

11. **When did the Apostles receive the Holy Spirit?**

    The Apostles received the Holy Spirit on the morning of Pentecost, about ten days after Jesus had returned to his Father in heaven.

12. **What gifts of the Holy Spirit help Christians carry out their mission to "make disciples of all nations"? When do Christians receive these gifts?**

    The gifts of the Holy Spirit are wisdom, understanding, right judgment, courage, knowledge, reverence, and wonder and awe. These gifts are given in the sacrament of Confirmation.

13. **How does Jesus' teaching ministry continue?**

    Jesus continues to teach and guide the Church through the Scriptures, the Word of God, especially as they are shared in the Liturgy of the Word at Mass and explained in the homily. The magisterium, the Church's teaching authority, is guided by the Holy Spirit in interpreting the Word of God and applying it to the circumstances of today.

14. **How do Christians live a moral life?**

    Every person has been given the gift of free will by God and can choose between right and wrong. These are moral choices. Christians are guided by their conscience, which is formed by studying the Scriptures and the teachings of the Church, in making moral choices. The Holy Spirit offers grace through the sacraments to grow in virtue.

15. **What happens in the sacrament of Reconciliation?**

    In the sacrament of Reconciliation, or Penance, a person who is sorry for having sinned confesses his or her sins to the priest, expresses contrition, accepts a penance, and is absolved of sin by the priest in the name of God and through the Church. The sacrament reconciles the sinner to God and to the community.

16. Which two sacraments celebrate special ways of living out one's baptismal call or vocation?

The sacraments of Marriage and Holy Orders celebrate vocations to married life and to ordained ministry. These vocations are particularly important to the life of the Church, although all people are called to love and serve as Jesus did.

17. How can Christians practice Jesus' unifying ministry?

All Christians are called to end the false divisions of racism, sexism, and other prejudices that keep people apart. In particular, Christians are called to work for ecumenism, or the reconciling of sinful division among the followers of Jesus, and for interfaith understanding among people of all religious beliefs.

18. How are Christians called to give witness to their faith?

All followers of Jesus are called to witness to their faith in the words, actions, and choices of their everyday lives. This means standing up for one's beliefs, even when it is difficult. When Christian faith conflicts with political power, Christians may be called to witness by giving up their lives in martyrdom.

19. How can Christians be peacemakers?

The Church, following the example of Jesus, teaches that true peace cannot exist without justice. Christian peacemaking requires the followers of justice to find alternatives to violence and to work for the just treatment of all people.

20. What three theological virtues help Christians live as followers of Jesus?

The theological virtues of faith, hope, and love are gifts from God. When people cooperate with these gifts, they are better able to live as followers of Jesus.

21. What are the cardinal virtues? What do they do?

The four cardinal, or "hinge," virtues are prudence, justice, temperance, and fortitude. These moral virtues guide all good actions and choices. Prudence helps you make wise choices. Justice helps you treat others with respect. Temperance helps you live a balanced life. Fortitude gives you the strength to overcome temptation and negative peer pressure.

22. Why is love the most important theological virtue?

God is love. Love guides all Christian actions and choices. At the end of time, all people are judged on how well they have loved others, especially those most in need. Those who have responded to God's love by loving others will be welcomed into heaven, God's eternal reign of justice, love, and peace. Those who have consciously rejected God's love will endure hell, the eternal absence of God's love.

Seasons of Faith

Learning to Celebrate

The Church earnestly desires that all the faithful be led to that full, conscious, and active participation in liturgical celebrations called for by the very nature of the liturgy. Such participation by the Christian people is their right and duty by reason of their baptism.

Constitution on the Sacred Liturgy, # 14

Liturgical Language

What Does This Say?

Steve slammed his book on his desk and stared at the computer screen in front of him. He was really stumped. His assignment was to develop a message in a secret code, and Steve didn't have a clue how to begin.

When he opened his book again, a folded sheet of paper fell out. It looked like a note, but most of it was unreadable. Only five words were in English. The message began, "Dear Steve," and it was signed, "See ya? Susan." A note from Susan—too much to hope for! But what did it say? Steve looked at the paper again:

Dpvme xf cf dpnqvufs gsjfoet?

A=B, Z=A

What was Susan trying to tell him?

When friends gather to talk about the latest gadget, or when the group buzzes about the latest movie, everyone wants to be included in the conversation. No one wants to be left out because he or she isn't familiar with the topic, isn't up on the slang, or hasn't seen the latest film in question. When you attend Mass, or another liturgical service do you ever feel confused or distracted because you don't understand what is going on? Learning the language and understanding the ritual actions will make you feel more at home.

The Language of Liturgy

The Catholic Church has a language all its own—the language of liturgy. It is a language of symbols and ritual actions that are shared by people all over the world. Learning this liturgical language is key to understanding your unique identity as a Catholic Christian.

The language of the Church includes sights, sounds, smells, tastes, touches, actions, and gestures that are common to all of us. It is a combination of signs, symbols, and actions: bread and wine, dark and light, water and blessing, offering and processing, fire and ashes, assembly and leader, posture and gesture, altar and lectionary, music and word, oil and incense, and so much more. All these elements of everyday life are used in worship of God. Through the liturgy, these elements are made holy, and so are you. Week after week, year after year, you use these signs, symbols, and actions to express your understanding of God's presence in your life and in the life of the Church. This vocabulary of signs, symbols, and actions becomes a part of who you are and how you act in the world. You bring your life to liturgy, and liturgy brings you life!

What are some symbols or ritual actions that are used in everyday life?

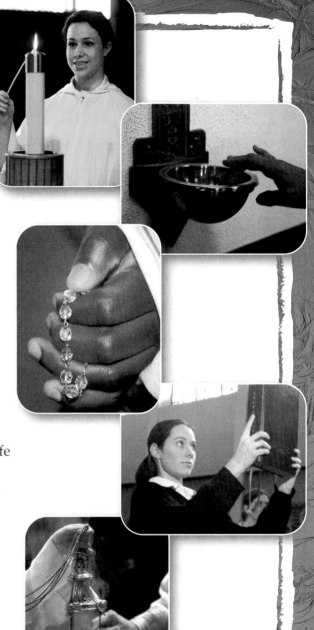

Signs, Symbols, and Actions

Consider the following feasts or celebrations of the Church. What signs, symbols, or actions are used or could be used in each of these celebrations? How do the signs, symbols, or ritual actions express the meaning of the celebration?

Palm Sunday

Pentecost

Epiphany

A wedding

The feast of St. Francis of Assisi

Know Where You Are Going

Planning Makes It Happen

The day of the class trip finally arrived. After months of careful planning and hard work, the class was finally gathered. Danielle had looked forward to this trip and was excited to be on her way. She was ready for any adventures they might have. Even as they waited for everyone to arrive, she clicked away with her camera. She intended to capture the moments on film so that when she returned she could relive the trip forever.

Have you ever planned a trip or some other event? What did you have to consider and plan for?

Suppose your class or group was asked to plan a prayer service. Would you know how to make it happen?

What you do in liturgy makes you who you are as Catholic Christians. You need:

- Desire and motivation to enter into the prayer wholeheartedly
- Appropriate structures, skills, and tools so that you know what to expect, know your part, and if you are responsible for planning a liturgy, know how to put it together
- Consistent practice to improve your skills
- Community with which to plan and pray

Knowing the structure of prayer will make your planning easier. It's very simple. Prayer time needs a beginning, a middle, and an end. Keep that in mind as you plan.

Structure of Liturgical Prayer

Effective prayer has a structure like other events in your life. Consider the following structure of liturgical prayer:

- Gathering: This is a way to call people to prayer. You can begin with music, the Sign of the Cross, an opening dialogue, an invitation to prayer such as "Let us pray," or any combination of these.
- Prayer: This is the heart of the prayer service. It may contain simple rituals, such as the lighting of a candle, readings from Scripture, a shared reflection on the readings, intercessions or petitions, the Lord's Prayer, and other prayers.
- Dismissal: This is a sending forth. Prayer should not be forgotten the moment it is over. The dismissal might suggest ways to continue living the prayer, a blessing, a concluding song, and a final "Amen."

Writing Prayers

You may be puzzled when it comes to actually writing your own prayers for a service. Again, you need a beginning, a middle, and an end. Here is a formula developed by Sister Kathleen Hughes, R.S.C.J., to get you started. It is called "You, Who, Do, Through." Now, how does it work?

You: Begin by addressing God, for example: "Generous God," "Loving Creator," "Spirit of God," "Forgiving God."

Who: Name what God has done. "You give us life and love," or "We praise you for the gifts you have given us," or "You call us to be united with one another."

Do: Tell God what you want or need. "Help us to," "Make us more loving," "Forgive us," or "Bless Joe as he goes into surgery."

Through: You make this prayer through Jesus. "We ask this through Jesus Christ, our Lord. Amen."

Signs, Symbols, and Actions

Using the formula, practice writing prayers for various occasions and for various needs.

Prepare the Way

As it is written in Isaiah the prophet:
"Behold, I am sending my messenger ahead of you; he will prepare your
way. A voice of one crying out in the desert: 'Prepare the way of the
Lord, make straight his paths.'" John the Baptist appeared in the desert
proclaiming a baptism of repentance for the forgiveness of sins.

Mark 1:2–4

The season of Advent is four weeks of intense listening to that voice crying in the wilderness asking you to prepare a way for God, who will bring peace to all of creation. In the first week of the season, the voices in Scripture cry out about God's judgment and use phrases that invite you into the excitement of this coming of God: "Wake from sleep." "Stay awake." "Be on guard."

In the second week of Advent, the voices proclaim hope and comfort in God's promises: "Justice shall flourish in his time, and fullness of peace forever." "The wolf shall be a guest of the lamb."

In week three of Advent, the feelings intensify and the voices announce that God *IS* present: "Be strong." "Rejoice always."

Finally, the fourth week of Advent sings out the fulfillment of God's promises: "God is with us." "Let the Lord enter."

The voice that cried out through the person of John the Baptist and other prophets is still heralding the Good News of God's promise through your voice, and through the voices of all the members of the Church. Both the lector at Mass who stands up to proclaim the readings and the presider who stands to proclaim the Gospel become the voice crying out and raising hope and comfort in the hearts of the people. That powerful presence of God in the Word is proclaimed at Mass and in any prayer is when the Church gathers. The lector is the vehicle by which God's Word becomes present to all who are listening. Like John the Baptist, the lector announces that God is here.

Proclaiming the Word of God

Think about the last time you had to give an oral presentation in school or for any event. Do you remember how well you needed to know your subject? How carefully you needed to choose the right words to communicate to your listeners? How directly you needed to speak to them with eye contact and enthusiasm? Did you have to think about how you would stand and how you would use your hands, head, arms, and all of your body?

How you use your body when you speak tells your listener a lot about you and your subject. If you are interested in your subject, your listener will hear that, not just in your words, but through the tone of your voice and the movement of your body.

Communication is the ability to express not just words but the thoughts and feelings behind the words. This is what a lector does when proclaiming the Scriptures.

The tools of good communication that affect how you proclaim Scripture include:

- Studying the reading until you know the sentence and phrase structures as though they were your own
- Practicing the reading aloud until the words and thoughts connect with your own feelings and, in fact, seem to be your own
- Enunciating the words clearly
- Speaking with energy and enthusiasm
- Looking directly into the eyes of your listener(s)
- Observing the body language of those who are listening to you

John the Baptist cried out to people what he heard God saying in his heart. All his words and actions proclaimed God's presence. You, as a lector, must do the same. As a lector, you proclaim God's presence through the words of Scripture.

Parish Connection

This Sunday when you go to Mass, listen carefully to the lector. Are you able to understand every word? Does it sound as though the lector means and understands what he or she is proclaiming?

Be a Proclaimer!

Practice proclaiming various Scripture passages with your classmates. Each person should read the passage several times individually before getting up to proclaim the passage to the class. Critique one another as you go through this activity.

Christmas Time

Did you know that Christmas is a season? It doesn't begin right after Thanksgiving the way the retailers would have you believe. The Christmas season starts on Christmas Eve and extends for several weeks.

During the season of Christmas, the Scriptures tell the story of the birth of Jesus of Nazareth. The joy of this event was first revealed to the shepherds, the poor and lowly ones of society. Later, it was revealed to the people of all nations, as represented by the Magi. Epiphany, the feast celebrating the coming of the Magi, is the peak of the Christmas season.

The season of Christmas also celebrates the Holy Family of Jesus, Mary, and Joseph, honors Mary as the Mother of God, and ends with the celebration of Jesus' Baptism by John.

How is this message of Christmas communicated to you today? What are the sights, smells, feelings, and sounds of Christmas? What part does music play in expressing the story?

Music Tells the Story

Imagine Christmas without music! Throughout time, the story of Christmas has been told over and over in many ways, and through many cultures, all over the Earth. Music is a powerful way that this story has been kept alive. During Christmastime, the music of the season is everywhere—radio, TV, special concerts, and even street corners. It helps us celebrate the joy of the season. Music flows from the very heart of the Christmas story—"O come all ye faithful. O come let us adore him."

Say It With Music

Music in liturgy is meant to express in song the heart of the celebration, the mood of the season, and even to retell the Scripture proclaimed. Music is prayer.

When you plan a prayer service or a Mass, music will most likely be a part of it. How will music affect the spirit of the prayer? Ask yourself these questions:

- What are you celebrating?
- Who is the assembly (the people gathered for prayer)?
- What style of music will this assembly relate to?
- What music resources do you have? In other words, what songbooks will be available to everyone? Remember that the music you choose should be specifically for worship and prayer, not the latest popular song.

Make a list of possible songs to use. Be sure that your list starts with familiar songs. As you examine each song on your list more closely, ask yourself:

- What feelings does the song evoke? Does it reflect the prayer time for which you are preparing? (Music for a funeral will differ from music for a wedding.)
- Read the words of the song. Do they express the reason for the celebration? Do they reflect the liturgical season?
- Which key moments in the prayer will be sung? What songs on your list will fill those moments? (Will you sing a gathering song, a meditation?)
- What ritual responses (such as the responsorial psalm, the Gospel Acclamation or Alleluia, the Holy, Holy, and other Mass parts) will you sing?
- Be sure that your opening song is strong enough to focus everyone on the reason for the prayer, and that your closing song helps everyone hold on to and remember the prayer time.

Taking care to select the music will make your celebration more meaningful.

EXPERIENCING LITURGY

The Christmas season looks like this:

December 24—25
Christmas Eve and Day

Sunday after Christmas
Holy Family

January 1
Mary, the Mother of God

Sunday between January 2 & 8
Epiphany

Sunday after Epiphany
Baptism of the Lord

What's in a song?

Select a liturgical season or event. Look through your parish song books or listen to recordings of liturgical music to find appropriate songs that could be used for the season or feast. What do the words of the song communicate? What feelings are evoked? Why would the song you selected be a good choice to sing?

A Sign of Faith

Ash Wednesday

The first day of the Lenten season is called Ash Wednesday because on this day the Church has a long tradition of marking the forehead of each member of the community with blessed ashes in the shape of a cross.

In the early Church, Lent was the time when public sinners, who were sorry for their sins, prepared to be reconciled with the church community. This reconciliation took place on Holy Thursday. The community gathered to pray over the penitents who were robed in sack cloth, a fabric similar to burlap. The bishop blessed the penitents and sprinkled them with ashes using these words from the Book of Genesis 3:19: "Remember that you are dust and unto dust you shall return." They were then sent out to pray, fast, and do good works. Eventually, this practice of repentance and being marked with a cross of ashes was extended to the whole church as a reminder that Lent is a special time to renew and deepen the baptismal commitment.

This is just one way that the sign of the cross is used to mark a person. Can you think of other times when the sign of the cross is made over someone or is used to mark someone? See how many instances of persons being marked by the cross you can name.

The Mark of Faith

At your Baptism, you were marked with the simple but powerful sign of the cross. The sign of the cross marks you as a follower of Christ.

We use the sign of the cross to bless ourselves, to bless others, to bless objects we use, to bless moments in our lives, and to mark sacramental anointing. What does it mean to *bless?* Blessing is a simple ritual using words and actions to request that God remember you and remain with you. You, in turn, are reminded that God is always with you. Using the sign of the cross in blessing acknowledges that it is through Christ that Christians come closer to God.

When you bless a person, you may extend your hand over him or her as the blessing prayer is said or you may make the sign of the cross on the person's hands or forehead.

Look at the photos on these pages. How are blessings being given in each of the situations?

Signing With the Cross

Discuss with your classmates what occasions in daily life you could mark with a blessing. You might want to offer a blessing over a sports team before an important game, for a student who has a new brother or sister in the family, over your class as it starts off on a field trip, or for a student celebrating his or her birthday. Together, make a list of different events or people for whom you would like to offer a blessing. Then, choose one item on your list and create the words and actions for a blessing.

Easter Vigil

This Is the Night

The people gather in darkness. A hush falls over the assembly as we witness the lighting of the Easter fire. A new Paschal Candle is lit, and from that light, all those present begin lighting the candles they carry. Flickering lights are seen as the people of God process into the darkened church, dispelling some of the darkness that surrounds them.

A strong voice fills the night as the Exsultet, a special proclamation that tells the meaning of Easter, is sung. Then, it is once again quiet as we wait for the story of salvation to be told beginning with the Creation in Genesis. After the last reading from the Old Testament, the Church breaks into song. Bells are rung, lights come on, beautiful flowers appear, and the night is filled with excitement.

Then comes the special moment. Tonight, my friend Tina will be baptized and confirmed, and will receive Eucharist.

A blessing is said over the water in the font and the Paschal Candle is plunged into the water as the priest says, "We ask you, Father, with your Son, to send the Holy Spirit upon the waters of this font." You can hear the water pouring in the font as Gina and the other elect are washed clean with the waters of Baptism. Then, we are all sprinkled with the water as we renew our own baptismal promises.

Tina is dressed in a white robe, and I can almost smell the oil of Confirmation as it is poured and smoothed over her forehead. Soon, Tina will receive the Body and Blood of Christ for the first time.

I am so proud and happy to be a part of this wonderful and holy night.

A Feast for the Senses

We are a sensual people. We see, hear, smell, touch, and feel. The Easter Vigil, more than any other liturgy, involves all our senses.

Recall an Easter Vigil you have attended or go back to the description just given and name all the ways the senses are involved.

Using Your Senses

The Easter Vigil is a feast for the senses. Not all prayers are or need to be so rich in symbol, movement, and ritual actions, but a good balance of all of these will draw people into the prayer.

When planning a prayer service, be aware of the varied ways of praying and the many ways of involving the whole body in the prayer experience. As you plan, keep the following in mind:

- **Environment** Where will the service take place? What do you need to do to enhance the space? Will you use wall hangings or other artwork? Where will participants sit or stand? What do you have to do to make the space more inviting?

- **Prayer table** The prayer table is the focal point. What color cloth will you drape it with? What symbols will be placed on or around it? The prayer table doesn't have to be a table. You can stack different size boxes and drape them with cloth.

- **Movement and Actions** Think of all the different ways you can have the participants move. They can stand, sit, kneel, walk, or use arm and hand movements and gestures. Consider acting out the Scripture or using mime to express a prayer.

- **Sounds** Music isn't the only sound you can use in prayer. A soft chime, a rain stick, or nature sounds can help focus the participants. Rhythm instruments can move people to sing, clap, or move their bodies.

- **Smells** Consider using incense or a scented candle, if allowed. Scented oil can also be used for anointing.

Involve the Senses

Plan a seasonal prayer service or a saint's feast day. Brainstorm with your group all the ways you can involve the senses in the prayer. Go overboard in your brainstorming and then pare it back if need be. Remember, to be effective, all the elements must blend together to draw the participants into prayer. Also remember that this is prayer, not a performance.

Processions

Good liturgy depends on actions and gestures that have special meaning. One of those actions is the procession. A procession is a time-honored tradition used in many countries and cultures on religious occasions. Catholics gather in procession to honor Mary, the Saints, and special Christian feasts. Often accompanied by music, prayers, and readings, processions highlight the meaning of a particular liturgy.

Processions differ in tone depending on the season or event. Some occasions call for a solemn procession, such as carrying the consecrated bread to the altar of repose on Holy Thursday or praying the Stations of the Cross. Other processions are very festive with banners, ribbons, and musical instruments, when a joyous event is being celebrated. Often statues are carried in procession, especially when celebrating Mary or one of the Saints.

Walking in procession is more than just an ordinary walk. When you process, your heart moves with your body. You move from your everyday life and situations into a holy space and time. People gathered for a procession move together to a designated place of honor, such as an altar or shrine, to pray, praise, and give thanks to God.

When have you taken part in a procession? What was the occasion? What was the purpose of the procession?

Movement in Prayer

In the Mass, there are moments when processions are a part of the prayer:

- At the gathering
- When the Gospel Book is taken to the ambo before the proclamation of the Gospel
- When the bread and wine are brought forward
- When the people go to Communion
- At the closing or end of Mass

Besides procession, there are other movements that take place. Various *postures* are used in prayer.

Standing:

- For the gathering rites
- Whenever God is addressed by name—during the opening prayer, the general intercessions, the prayer over the gifts and the prayer after Communion
- For the proclamation of the Gospel

Sitting:

- During the readings and the homily
- Meditation after Communion

Kneeling:

- During the Eucharistic Prayer
- After receiving Communion (optional)

Gestures are used to punctuate prayer. Hands are held in the orans position during the praying of the Lord's Prayer. The priest uses hand gestures in a variety of ways— hands extended toward the assembly, hands palm down over the bread and wine as he calls forth the Holy Spirit, hands extended over the community in blessing. Bowing is a gesture used as a sign of reverence and respect.

You might recall times when you clapped during the singing of a hymn or used other actions to accompany the singing.

Procession, gesture, and posture are all an important part of prayer. It means the whole body is entering into the prayer and is fully engaged.

Parish Connection

At Mass this weekend, pay particular attention to all the movement (processions, posture, gestures) that takes place. What movements are done by the priest and other ministers? What movements are done by the community?

Many Cultures, Many Processions

Do some research as a class. Investigate how various cultures celebrate with processions. (Consider May Crowning processions, Las Posadas, the Way of the Cross, Good Friday, saint's feast days, etc.) Where do the processions take place? Who participates?

Plan a procession as part of your next prayer service.

Planning Guide for Liturgical Celebrations

This planning guide provides information and an outline that will help you plan a liturgical celebration.

Liturgical Season _____

Feast, or event being celebrated _____

Participants _____

Who will take part in this prayer service?

Prayer space _____

Where will the prayer take place? In the Church, classroom, outdoors?

Environment _____

What decor is needed? What symbols would be appropriate? Liturgical color?

Movement or ritual action _____

Will you have a procession? Gesture or movement? Special rituals?

Prayer leader _____

Who can best lead the prayer service with reverence, confidence, and dignity?

Lector _____

Who can proclaim the Word of God with reverence, clarity, and enthusiasm?

Other ministers _____

What other ministers will be needed: greeters, altar servers, candle bearers, and so on?
Be sure to practice with all the ministers.

Other notes _____

_____

_____

Planning Guide for a Liturgy of the Word

This is the basic structure for a Liturgy of the Word. (If you are planning for a Eucharistic Liturgy, note the added points for planning.)

Gathering _____

How will you call everyone to prayer? What gathering song will you sing?

Opening Prayer _____

This is prayed by the prayer leader (presider).

Reading 1 _____

Responsorial Psalm _____

Reading 2 _____

Gospel Acclamation _____

If not sung it is omitted.

Gospel _____

Reflections/Homily _____

Intercessions or litany _____

The Lord's Prayer _____

Closing Prayer _____

Concluding Song _____

If you are planning for a Eucharistic Liturgy, you will also need to plan for

- Preparation of the Gifts and song
- Sung Acclamations within the Eucharistic Prayer:
  Holy, Holy,
  Memorial Acclamation
  Great Amen
- Fraction Rite: Lamb of God
- Communion Procession Song

GLOSSARY

ENGLISH

Amen   Hebrew for "Let it be so!" The term is used by both Jews and Christians to say they believe and will put into practice everything they have spoken.

Angels   Spiritual supernatural beings created by God; messengers of God. The three archangels named in the Bible are Gabriel, Michael, and Raphael.

Annunciation   The Church feast that honors the angel's announcement to Mary that she was to be the Mother God.

Anointing of the Sick   The sacrament of healing by which the seriously sick and the dying receive the care of the Church and the grace of God's healing love.

Apostle   One of the twelve first followers of Jesus. Jesus chose the Apostles to continue his mission. An apostle is one who is sent to do the work of the kingdom.

Ark of the Covenant   The special container for the tablets of the Law; the sign of God's presence with the Israelites.

Atonement   Making amends for an offense.

Babylonian Exile   The period of time the Jews were forced to live in Babylon.

Baptism   A sacrament of initiation. It gives new life in Christ, takes away sin, and makes one an adopted child of God.

Basilica   A Greek word that means "royal house." It is the title of honor given to certain special churches.

Beatitudes   Short sayings that Jesus told the people in his Sermon on the Mount. The word means "blessedness" or "happiness."

Bible   The book of God's Word, the Scriptures. The word *bible* means "book," but the Bible is actually a whole collection of books.

Bishop   The leader or shepherd of a diocese; the highest level of Holy Orders.

Blessed Trinity   Three Persons in one God: the Father, the Son, and the Holy Spirit.

Blessing   The condition or happiness and peace that comes from being in God's favor, living as God wants.

Catechumens   Unbaptized people who are preparing to join the Christian community through the sacraments of initiation.

Catholic   A member of the Church. Catholics are also called Christians. The word *catholic* is a mark of the Church that shows the Church is open to everyone.

SPANISH

Amén   Palabra hebrea que significa "¡Así sea!" La usan los judíos y los cristianos para decir que creen y que van a poner en práctica todo lo que han hablado.

Ángeles   Espíritus puros creados por Dios; mensajeros de Dios. Los tres arcángeles que se nombran en la Biblia son Gabriel, Miguel y Rafael.

Anunciación   Una fiesta de la Iglesia, que honra el anuncio del ángel a María de que iba a ser la Madre del Señor.

Unción de los enfermos   El sacramento de curación por medio del cual los enfermos y los moribundos reciben la gracia del amor sanador de Dios.

Apóstol   Uno de los doce primeros seguidores de Jesús. Jesús eligió a los Apóstoles para que continuaran su misión. Un apóstol es aquél al que se envía para realizar el trabajo del Reino.

Arca de la Alianza   Una caja especial para las tablas de la Ley; el signo de la presencia de Dios entre los israelitas.

Expiación   Reparar el mal que uno ha hecho.

Exilio en Babilonia   El período de tiempo en el que se forzó a los judíos a vivir en Babilonia.

Bautismo   Un sacramento de iniciación que da nueva vida en Cristo, quita el pecado, y hace a uno un hijo adoptado de Dios.

Basílica   Una palabra griega que significa "casa real". Es el título honorífico que se da a ciertas iglesias especiales.

Bienaventuranzas   Frases cortas que Jesús dijo a la gente en su Sermón de la montaña. La palabra significa "beatitud" o "felicidad".

Biblia   El libro de la Palabra de Dios, las Escrituras. La palabra biblia significa "libro", pero la Biblia es una completa colección de libros.

Obispo   El líder de los pastores de una diócesis; el nivel más alto del orden sacerdotal.

Santísima Trinidad   Tres Personas en un solo Dios: Padre, Hijo y Espíritu Santo.

Bendición   La condición de felicidad y paz que proviene de estar en el favor de Dios, viviendo como Dios quiere.

Catecúmenos   Personas sin bautizar que se están preparando para unirse a la comunidad cristiana por medio de los sacramentos de la iniciación.

Católico(a)   Un miembro de la Iglesia. Los católicos también se llaman cristianos. La palabra católica es un atributo o cualidad de la Iglesia que muestra que está abierta a todo el mundo.

Christ   A title for Jesus that means "the anointed or chosen one of God."

Church   The Church is the gathering of the People of God from all over the earth. It is also the building where Christians gather for common prayer.

Communion   Receiving Jesus Christ in the Holy Eucharist.

Communion of Saints   The unity of all baptized people, living and dead, who believe in Jesus and follow his way.

Confession   Telling one's sins to the priest in the sacrament of Reconciliation.

Confirmation   A sacrament of initiation. Confirmation completes the grace of Baptism by an outpouring of the gifts of the Holy Spirit which seals or confirms the baptized with Christ and the Church.

Conscience   The ability to judge when an action is right or wrong.

Conversion   Making a complete change. Turning away from sin and going back to God.

Courage   Moral strength to resist temptation and opposition, and to endure difficulties, hardship, or danger.

Covenant   A sacred and loving promise and relationship.

Deacon   An ordained minister who helps the priest and the bishop to serve the Christian community.

Diocese   A portion of the universal Church made up of a number of parishes in a certain area, led by a bishop.

Disciple   A person who believes in and follows Jesus. A disciple also helps others know and follow Jesus.

Ecumenical council   A formal gathering of all the bishops with the pope for the purpose of clarifying Church teaching. There have been twenty-one such councils in the history of the Church. The most recent was Vatican II in the early 1960s.

Encyclical   A letter written by the pope to the whole Church about some important matter of faith or practice.

Epistles   A Greek word for "letters." The New Testament letters written by Saint Paul and other Christian leaders to the early faith communities are called the Epistles.

Eucharist   A sacrament of initiation. At the celebration of the Eucharist, you receive the Body and Blood of Jesus. Another name for the Eucharist is the Mass. The word *eucharist* means "thanksgiving."

Evangelist   Someone who brings good news to others. The writers of the four Gospels are called evangelists.

Cristo   Un título para Jesús, que significa "el Ungido o Elegido de Dios".

Iglesia   La Iglesia es la unión del Pueblo de Dios de todo el mundo. La iglesia es también el edificio donde los cristianos se reúnen para la oración en común.

Comunión   La acción de recibir a Jesu Cristo en la Eucaristía.

Comunión de los santos   La unidad de todas las personas, vivas y muertas, que han creido y creen en Jesús y han seguido y siguen su camino.

Confesión   Contar los pecados al sacerdote en el sacramento de la reconciliación.

Confirmación   Un sacramento de iniciación. La confirmación completa la gracia del bautismo mediante el traspaso de los dones del Espíritu Santo, que sellan o confirman al bautizado con Cristo y la Iglesia.

Conciencia   La capacidad de juzgar cuándo una acción es buena o mala.

Conversión   Cambiar por completo. Alejarse del pecado y volver a Dios.

Fortaleza   Fuerza moral para resistir la tentación y la oposición, y para afrontar las dificultades o el peligro.

Alianza   Una promesa de relación sagrada y amorosa.

Diácono   Un ministro ordenado que ayuda al sacerdote y al obispo a servir a la comunidad cristiana.

Diócesis   Una parte de la Iglesia universal formada por un cierto número de parroquias de cierta zona, liderada por un obispo.

Discípulo(a)   Una persona que cree en Jesús y lo sigue. Un discípulo también ayuda a los demás a seguir a Jesús.

Concilio ecuménico   Una reunión formal de todos los obispos con el papa, con el propósito de aclarar las enseñanzas de la Iglesia. En la historia de la Iglesia se han realizado 21 de estos concilios. El más reciente fue el Vaticano II a comienzos de los años sesenta del siglo pasado.

Encíclica   Una carta que escribe el papa para toda la Iglesia sobre algún tema importante de fe o de práctica.

Epístolas   Palabra griega que significa "cartas". Se llaman Epístolas las cartas del Nuevo Testamento que Pablo y otros líderes cristianos escribieron a las Iglesias jóvenes.

Eucaristía   Un sacramento de iniciación o unión a la Iglesia, en el que celebras y recibes el Cuerpo y la Sangre de Cristo. Se lo llama también misa. La palabra eucaristía significa "acción de gracias".

Evangelista   Alguien que trae la Buena Nueva. Se llama evangelistas a los que escribieron el Evangelio.

Everlasting life Life with God forever; the gift of grace received through Jesus' death and resurrection.

Evil That which is against God's kingdom; the effects of sin in the world. Evil is the opposite or the absence of good.

Exodus A Greek word that means "departure"; the name of the second book of the Bible. Exodus tells the story of how God led the Israelites out of slavery in Egypt.

Faith Belief in God who reveals himself. Faith involves the mind and the will. The Church and Scripture form one's faith.

Father The name Jesus used for God to show that God cares for all people like a loving parent does.

Fidelity Keeping one's promises; faithfulness to the covenant.

Free will The ability God gives you to choose. You can choose either right or wrong.

Genesis A Greek word that means "in the beginning"; the name of the first book of the Bible. Genesis tells the origin of the world and of God's People.

Gentile A name for anyone not born into the people of Israel.

Gospel A New Testament account of the life and the teachings of Jesus. The word *gospel* means "good news."

Heaven Being happy with God forever.

Hebrew Scriptures The Jewish sacred writings, which contain the story of God's loving relationship with Israel. In the Christian Bible, the Hebrew Scriptures are contained in the Old Testament.

Hebrews One of the earliest names for God's People.

Heritage Something precious passed on from one's ancestors. Christians share a heritage of faith with Jews because both faiths descend from Abraham and Sarah.

Holiness, Holy Living as Jesus did. All people are called to be holy.

Holy Orders The sacrament that celebrates the call to serve the faith community as an ordained priest, deacon, or bishop.

Holy Spirit The third Person of the Blessed Trinity; the personal love of the Father and the Son for each other, who is present in the world.

Hope One of the three theological virtues. Hope is the expectation and the trust that God will always be with you.

Hosanna A Hebrew word that means "Lord, save us!"

Idolatry The act of substituting some person or object for God in order to worship it. Even money, pleasure, or power can be an idol.

Vida eterna La vida con Dios para siempre; el don o regalo de la gracia recibido por medio de la muerte y la resurrección de Jesús.

Mal Lo que está en contra del Reino de Dios; los efectos del pecado en nuestro mundo. El mal es lo opuesto al bien o su ausencia.

Éxodo Una palabra griega que significa "salida"; el nombre del libro de la Biblia que cuenta cómo Dios sacó a los israelitas de la esclavitud en Egipto.

Fe Adhesión personal a Dios que revela. Fe implica a la mente y la voluntad. Escritura y la Iglesia forman la fe.

Padre El nombre que Jesús usaba para Dios para indicar que Dios cuida a todas las personas como lo hace un padre amoroso.

Fidelidad Cumplir las promesas hechas; lealtad a la alianza.

Libre albedrío La capacidad que Dios te da para elegir lo que está bien o lo que está mal.

Génesis Una palabra que significa "comienzo u origen", el nombre del primer libro de la Biblia, que cuenta los orígenes del Pueblo de Dios.

Gentil Un nombre para cualquiera que no haya nacido dentro del pueblo de Israel.

Evangelio El Nuevo Testamento explica la vida y las enseñanzas de Jesús. La palabra evangelio significa "Buena Nueva".

Cielo Ser feliz para siempre con Dios.

Escrituras hebreas Los escritos sagrados judíos que contienen la historia de la relación amorosa de Dios con Israel. En las Biblias cristianas es el Antiguo Testamento el que contiene las Escrituras hebreas.

Hebreos Uno de los primeros nombres del Pueblo de Dios.

Herencia Algo precioso que se recibe de los antepasados. Los cristianos comparten una herencia de fe con los judíos, porque la fe de los dos pueblos desciende de Abraham y Sara.

Santidad, Santo Vivir como lo hizo Jesús. Todas las personas están llamadas a ser santas.

Sacramento del orden El sacramento que celebra el llamado a servir al pueblo de Dios con la ordenación como sacerdote, diácono o obispo.

Espíritu Santo La tercera Persona de la Santísima Trinidad. El amor personal entre el Padre y el Hijo, que está presente en el mundo.

Esperanza Una de las tres virtudes teologales. La esperanza es la confianza en que Dios estará siempre con nosotros.

Hosanna Una palabra hebrea que significa "Señor, ¡sálvanos!"

Idolatría El acto de sustituir a Dios por alguna persona o cosa para rendirle culto. Incluso el dinero, el placer o el poder pueden ser ídolos.

Inspiration The guidance of the Holy Spirit that led the biblical writers to set down the truth of God's Word in the language and the culture of their times.

Israel The name given to Jacob by God and later used to identify the People of God and the kingdom of Abraham's descendants. The modern country of Israel carries the name of the biblical kingdom.

Israelites The name for the People of God from the time of Jacob onward. Those who settled in the northern kingdom were called Israelites.

Jerusalem The holy city of God's People. Today, Jerusalem is sacred to Jews, Christians, and Muslims.

Jews The people of the tribe of Judah, the name of the southern kingdom. Jesus was a Jew.

Judges The military and tribal leaders of the Israelites after their entry into the Promised Land. The Judges were sent by God to defend Israel.

Judgment At the end of time when Jesus comes again to bring the kingdom of God. All people, living and dead, will be judged on how well they have followed the Law of God. This is called the Last Judgment. At the time of death, each person also faces a personal judgment. For the faithful Christian, the final judgment is a source of hope, not fear.

Justice A moral virtue. Justice is the firm will to give God and neighbor their due. Justice promotes the common good.

Kerygma The proclamation of the basic teaching of the faith: that Jesus Christ, the Son of God, was born of Mary, taught about the reign of God, died, and rose again.

Kingdom of God The reign of God or the power and love of God working in your life and in the world. It is justice, peace, and joy. It is God ruling in your heart and in the community.

Lectionary The book that contains the Scripture readings used in the Liturgy of the Word.

Lector A person who performs the liturgical ministry of proclaiming the Scriptures in the Liturgy of the Word.

Liturgical year The cycle of seasons and feasts celebrated by the Church.

Liturgy The Church's public worship, including the Mass, the sacraments, and the Divine Office.

Liturgy of the Eucharist The part of the Mass for remembering, giving thanks, and taking part in the death and resurrection of Jesus. It includes the Eucharistic Prayer and Holy Communion.

Liturgy of the Hours The Divine Office. The daily prayer of the Church is composed of psalms, prayers, and readings from Scripture.

Inspiración La orientación del Espíritu Santo que llevó a los autores bíblicos a escribir la verdad sobre la Palabra de Dios en el lenguaje de su tiempo.

Israel El nombre que Dios le dio a Jacob y que más tarde se usó para identificar al Pueblo de Dios y al reino de los descendientes de Abraham. Israel, el país de hoy día, lleva el nombre del reino bíblico.

Israelitas El nombre del Pueblo de Dios desde el tiempo de Jacob en adelante. Se llamó israelitas a aquellos que se instalaron en el reino del norte.

Jerusalén La ciudad sagrada del Pueblo de Dios, sagrada para los judíos, los cristianos y los musulmanes.

Judíos Gente de la tribu de Judea, el nombre del reino del sur. Jesús era judío.

Jueces Los líderes militares y tribales de los israelitas después de su entrada en la Tierra prometida. Dios envió a los jueces para defender a Israel.

Juicio Cuando Jesús vuelva para traer el Reino de Dios. Todas las personas, vivas y muertas, serán juzgadas según cómo hayan seguido la Ley de Dios. A esto se llama el Juicio Final. En el momento de la muerte, cada persona también enfrenta un juicio personal. Para el cristiano o cristiana el juicio es una fuente de esperanza, no de temor.

Justicia Una virtud moral. Justicia es la voluntad de darle a Dios y nuestro prójimo su debido. Promueve el bueno común.

Kerigma La proclamación de la enseñanza básica de la fe: que Jesucristo, el Hijo de Dios, nació de María, enseñó acerca del Reino de Dios, murió y resucitó.

Reino de Dios El reinado de Dios; la presencia de Jesús en nuestra vida y en nuestro mundo. Es justicia, paz y alegría. Es cuando Dios gobierna en nuestro corazón y en la comunidad.

Leccionario El libro que contiene las lecturas de la Escritura que se usan en la liturgia de la Palabra.

Lector Una persona que ejerce el ministerio litúrgico de la proclamación o comunicación en voz alta de las Escrituras en la liturgia de la Palabra.

Año litúrgico El ciclo de estaciones y fiestas que la Iglesia celebra.

Liturgia El culto público de la Iglesia, que incluye la misa, los sacramentos y el Oficio divino.

Liturgia Eucarística Parte de la misa para recordar, agradecer y compartir la muerte y resurrección de Jesús. Incluye la Oración Eucarística y la Sagrada Comunión.

Liturgia de las Horas El Oficio divino; la oración diaria de la Iglesia, que se compone de salmos, oraciones y lecturas de la Escritura.

Liturgy of the Word   The part of the Mass during which the Scripture readings, the homily, the Creed, and the prayer of the faithful take place.

Magisterium   The teaching authority of the Church, made up of the pope and the bishops, the successors of the Apostles.

Manna   The Hebrew word for the miraculous "bread from heaven" with which God fed the Israelites in the desert.

Marks of the Church   The four characteristics of the Church that are mentioned in the Nicene Creed: the Church is one, holy, catholic, and apostolic.

Marriage   The sacrament that celebrates the lifelong vow, or covenant, made between a man and a woman. They promise to live together in love and to be open to having children.

Martyr   A follower of Jesus who dies for his or her faith. The term comes from the Greek word for "witness."

Matzoth   The unleavened bread eaten especially at Passover.

Meditation   Quiet mental prayer in which you try to understand more deeply what God teaches and wants.

Mercy   The loving-kindness shown to one who offends.

Messiah   The Hebrew word for God's anointed or chosen one; the savior promised by God. Jesus is the Messiah.

Ministry   The work of helping people live in holiness. Ministry is done primarily through the preaching of God's Word and the celebration of the sacraments by those who have received Holy Orders. The work lay people do is also called ministry.

Miracle   A supernatural sign of God's power and love. Jesus performed miracles to show God's goodness.

Mission   The work a person is called to do. Jesus' mission was to share the kingdom of God with all people. As a follower of Jesus, you have the same mission.

Morality   Living according to God's Law. Morality is cooperation with God's grace in order to live a good life and to do what is right.

New covenant   God's relationship with the followers of Jesus; the promise to open the kingdom of God to all people.

New Testament   The part of the Christian Bible that contains the Gospels, the Acts of the Apostles, the Letters, and Revelation.

Old Testament   The part of the Christian Bible that contains the Hebrew Scriptures and other sacred writings from before the time of Jesus.

Liturgia de la Palabra   La parte de la misa en la que tienen lugar la lectura de las Escrituras, la homilía, el Credo y la Oración de los Fieles.

Magisterio   La autoridad docente o de la enseñanza de la Iglesia, que forman el papa y los obispos, los sucesores de los Apóstoles.

Maná   La palabra hebrea para el "pan del cielo" milagroso con el cual Dios alimentó a los israelitas en el desierto.

Atributos de la Iglesia   Cuatro características especiales de la Iglesia que se mencionan en el Credo de Nicea-Constantinopla: la Iglesia es una, santa, católica y apostólica.

Matrimonio   El sacramento que celebra la promesa o alianza de por vida entre un hombre y una mujer para vivir juntos amándose y educando a sus hijos, si pueden tenerlos.

Mártir   Un(a) seguidor(a) de Jesús que muere por su fe. Proviene de la palabra griega para decir "testigo".

Matzoth   Pan sin levadura que se come especialmente en la Pascua judía.

Meditación   Oración mental silenciosa en la que tratas de entender con mayor profundidad lo que Dios enseña y desea.

Misericordia   Bondad que se demuestra al que ofende.

Mesías   La palabra en hebreo para designar al Ungido o Elegido de Dios; el salvador que Dios prometió. El Mesías es Jesús.

Ministerio   La tarea de ayudar a la gente a vivir en santidad. La hacen principalmente aquellos que han recibido el sacramento del orden, o en ciertos casos las personas laicas, por medio de la prédica de la Palabra y la celebración de los sacramentos.

Milagro   Un signo sobrenatural del poder y el amor de Dios. Jesús hacía milagros para demostrar la bondad de Dios.

Misión   El trabajo que se manda hacer a una persona. La misión de Jesús es compartir el Reino de Dios con todas las personas. Ahora participas de la misión de Jesús.

Moralidad   Viviendo según la ley de Dios. Moralidad es la cooperación con la gracia de Dios para vivir una vida buena y hacer bien.

Nueva Alianza   Relación de Dios con los seguidores de Jesús; la promesa de abrir el Reino de Dios a todas las personas.

Nuevo Testamento   La parte de la Biblia cristiana que contiene los Evangelios, los Hechos de los Apóstoles, las Cartas y el Apocalipsis.

Antiguo Testamento   La parte de la Biblia cristiana que contiene las Escrituras hebreas y otros escritos sagrados anteriores a la época de Jesús.

Original Sin The first sin. Adam and Eve, the first man and woman, disobeyed God, choosing to follow their own will instead. Original sin also describes the pull everyone feels toward doing things that are wrong.

Parable A special kind of teaching story that is used to make a moral or a religious point. Jesus often used parables to tell about God's kingdom.

Parish A community of Catholics who pray, learn, and serve together. The ordained leader of the parish is called the pastor.

Paschal Mystery The death, resurrection, and ascension of Jesus.

Passion The arrest, trial, suffering, and death of Jesus. The passion is commemorated during Holy Week.

Passover The Jewish feast of Unleavened Bread, which commemorates the Israelites' passage from slavery in Egypt to freedom.

Pastoral Letters Letters written by a bishop or a group of bishops to give advice on matters of Church teaching, practice, contemporary issues, and social justice.

Penance A way to make up for sin and to practice making better choices. A penance is given by the priest in Reconciliation.

Penitential rite The part of the Mass in which the people ask forgiveness for sins from God and the community.

Pentateuch A Greek word for the first five books of the Sacred Scriptures. Jews call these books the Torah, or the Law.

Pentecost The Church feast that celebrates the sending of the Holy Spirit to the disciples. It is celebrated fifty days after Easter.

Pope The leader of the Catholic Church on earth. As the successor of Saint Peter, the pope is the Bishop of Rome. The word *pope* comes from the Latin word for "father."

Prayer The raising of the mind and heart to God. Prayer can be any thoughts, words, or actions that show a person's love for God. Prayer can be formal or spontaneous. The four purposes of prayer are adoration, thanksgiving, petition, and contrition.

Priest An ordained minister who builds up and guides the Church in the name of Christ by preaching the Word of God, celebrating the sacraments, and serving the community.

Profession of faith A formal declaration of beliefs. The Apostles' Creed and the Nicene Creed are two examples of traditional Christian professions of faith.

Promised Land The biblical name for Canaan, the land God promised to the children of Abraham and Sarah.

Pecado original El pecado que cometieron los primeros hombres cuando eligieron seguir su propia voluntad en lugar de obedecer a Dios. También describe el impulso que todos sentimos de hacer cosas que no son correctas.

Parábola Una clase especial de narración didáctica, frecuentemente con un final sorpresivo, que Jesús usaba para hablar sobre el Reino de Dios.

Parroquia Una comunidad de católicos que rezan, aprenden y sirven juntos. El líder ordenado de la parroquia se llama pastor.

Misterio pascual La muerte, la resurrección, y la ascensión de Jesús.

Pasión El arresto, el juicio, el sufrimiento y la muerte de Jesús, que se conmemoran durante la Semana Santa.

Pascua judía La fiesta judía del pan ácimo o sin levadura, que conmemora el paso de los israelitas de la esclavitud a la libertad.

Cartas pastorales Cartas que escribe un obispo o grupo de obispos para aconsejar sobre asuntos de doctrina o ideas religiosas de la Iglesia, práctica de la doctrina y justicia social.

Penitencia Una manera de enmienda del pecado y de práctica para hacer elecciones mejores, que da el sacerdote en la reconciliación.

Rito de la penitencia La parte de la misa cuando pedimos perdón a Dios y a la comunidad por nuestros pecados.

Pentateuco Una palabra griega para los cinco primeros libros de la Biblia; en hebreo estos libros se llaman la Torá, o la Ley.

Pentecostés Una fiesta de la Iglesia, que celebra el envío del Espíritu Santo a los discípulos, que se festeja 50 días después de la Pascua.

Papa El líder de la Iglesia católica en el mundo. Como sucesor de San Pedro, el papa es el obispo de Roma. La palabra papa proviene de la palabra latina para decir "padre".

Oración La elevación de la mente y el corazón a Dios. La oración puede ser hablada, cantada o dicha en silencio. Puede ser formal o espontánea. Los cuatro propósitos de la oración son la adoración, la acción de gracias, la petición y la contrición.

Sacerdote Un ministro ordenado que fortalece y guía la Iglesia en el nombre de Cristo, por medio de la prédica de la Palabra de Dios y la celebración de los sacramentos, entre otras cosas.

Profesión de fe Una declaración de creencia. Dos profesiones de fe cristianas tradicionales son el Credo de los apóstoles y el Credo de Nicea-Constantinopla.

Tierra prometida El nombre bíblico para Canaán, la tierra que Dios prometió a los hijos de Abraham y Sara.

Prophet   A person who calls others to follow God's Word and to be fair and just. John the Baptist is generally regarded as the final prophet of the Old Testament.

Prudence   Thinking ahead and using common sense to see whether something you want to do will have good or bad results.

Psalm   A sacred song used in worship. The Book of Psalms in the Bible is a collection of 150 of these songs.

Rabbi   The Hebrew word for "teacher." A rabbi is the spiritual and educational leader of a Jewish community, or synagogue.

Reconciliation   The sacrament that celebrates God's loving forgiveness and reunites you with God and the Church.

Resurrection   The Christian mystery of Jesus being raised from the dead. Christians believe in the final resurrection of the body, when all faithful people will rise to new life in Christ at the end of the world.

Revelation   God's communication of himself, by which he makes known his power and love through words and deeds, expressed in the person of Jesus, the Scriptures, and the tradition of the Church. Revelation is also the name of the last book of the Bible.

Sabbath   A day of rest and worship. Christians celebrate Sunday as a Sabbath day, or the Lord's Day.

Sacraments   Special signs and celebrations of God's life and love. Through the sacraments, the faith community receives grace—a share in God's life and friendship.

Sacred Scripture   Holy writings. The Bible is the Christian Scripture.

Sacred tradition   From the Latin word for "handing on." The tradition is the collected teachings of the Church, handed down through the centuries. God is revealed in Scripture and in tradition.

Sacrifice   Something precious offered to God out of love and worship.

Saint   Holy people who love Jesus and who help others follow him are called saints. Saints receive the reward of eternal life with God. Some people, after death, are given the title saint. These saints are the heroes of the Church.

Salvation   God's great act of love and mercy. God sent Jesus to save the world from sin and death.

Salvation history   The story of God's saving love as told in the Scriptures.

Sanctuary   From a Latin word meaning "holy place." In Catholic churches, the sanctuary is the area around the altar.

Profeta   Una persona que convoca o llama a los demás para seguir la Palabra de Dios, y para ser honrados y justos. El último profeta de la Antigua Testamento fue Juan el Bautista.

Prudencia   Ser previsor y usar el sentido común para ver si lo que quieres hacer tendrá buenos o malos resultados.

Salmo   Una canción sagrada que se usa en el culto. El Libro de los Salmos de la Biblia es una colección de 150 de estas canciones.

Rabbi   La palabra hebrea para decir "maestro". Un rabbi es el líder espiritual y pedagógico de la comunidad judía o una sinagoga.

Reconciliación   El sacramento que celebra el perdón bondadoso de Dios y que te reúne con Dios y con la Iglesia.

Resurrección   El misterio cristiano de Jesús que resucitó de entre los muertos. Los cristianos creen en la resurrección del cuerpo, cuando todo el pueblo fiel resurgirá a una vida nueva al final de los tiempos.

Revelación   La comunicación que hace Dios de sí mismo, por medio de la cual hace conocer su poder y amor a través de palabras y acciones, y que se expresa en la persona de Jesús, en las Escrituras y en la Tradición de la Iglesia. También el último libro de la Biblia.

Sabbat   Un día para el descanso y el culto. Los cristianos celebran el domingo como día sabático, o día del Señor.

Sacramentos   Signos o representaciones y celebraciones especiales de la vida y el amor de Dios. A través de los sacramentos recibes la gracia: participación en la vida de Dios.

Sagrada Escritura   Escritos sagrados. La Escritura cristiana es la Biblia.

Tradición sagrada   Proviene de la palabra latina para decir "transmitir". La Tradición son las enseñanzas de la Iglesia reunidas, transmitidas a través de los siglos. Dios se revela en la Escritura y la Tradición.

Sacrificio   Algo precioso que se ofrece a Dios por amor y culto.

Santo(a)   Se llaman santos(as) las personas puras que aman a Jesús y que ayudan a los demás a seguirlo. El título de santo(a) se da a algunas personas después de que mueren. Estos santos o santas son los héroes de la Iglesia.

Salvación   El gran acto de amor y misericordia de Dios; al enviar a Jesús para salvar el mundo del pecado y la muerte.

Historia de la salvación   La historia del amor sanador de Dios como se relata en las Escrituras.

Santuario   Una palabra que significa "lugar santo". En las iglesias católicas, el santuario es la parte anterior del tabernáculo.

Scribes People who studied the Law of God and commented on the Scriptures to help others understand them.

Second Coming The glorious return of Jesus at the end of the world. At that time, Jesus will judge all people, living and dead, and bring the fullness of God's kingdom.

Seder A Jewish ceremonial meal in commemoration of the exodus from Egypt.

Shalom The Hebrew word for the peace, holiness, and wholeness of God's kingdom. When used as a greeting, the term means "I wish you God's peace."

Sin Sin is a deliberate choice to do what you know is wrong. Such choices separate you from God and the community. Reconciliation with God and the community comes through the sacrament of Penance.

Son of God The title given to Jesus to show that he is both God and human.

Son of Man A biblical title for the Messiah, used by Jesus to describe himself.

Soul The spiritual basis of each human being. It is God's gift of everlasting life or spirit within you. Body and soul are not separate. Together they make up the human person.

Stewardship Showing care for one another and for all creation.

Synagogue A Jewish house of worship and religious study.

Synod A gathering of bishops meeting to advise the pope on important matters. A synod can be local, national, or worldwide.

Synoptic A Greek word that means "seeing together." The Gospels of Matthew, Mark, and Luke are called the synoptic Gospels because of their similarities.

Temple The central place of worship for the Jews, located in Jerusalem.

Ten Commandments The Law given by God to Moses on Mount Sinai as part of the covenant with Israel.

Theological Virtues Habits that lead you to God. The three theological virtues are faith, hope, and love.

Torah The Hebrew title for the first five books of the Bible.

Trust To place your faith and hope in someone. Christians trust God.

Unity Oneness in Jesus Christ. The movement for unity among separate Christian churches is called ecumenism.

Vocation A call from God to serve him and others in a particular way. Marriage, Holy Orders, belonging to a religious community, and living as a single lay person are some examples of Christian vocations.

Escribas Personas que estudiaban la Ley de Dios y comentaban las Escrituras para ayudar a los demás a entenderlas.

Segunda venida El regreso glorioso de Jesús al final de los tiempos, momento en el cual juzgará a todas las personas y traerá la plenitud del Reino de Dios.

Séder Una comida ceremonial judía en conmemoración del éxodo de Egipto.

Shalom La palabra hebrea para la paz, la santidad y la integridad del Reino de Dios. Cuando se usa como saludo, significa "Que la paz de Dios esté contigo".

Pecado El pecado es una elección deliberada para hacer lo que sabes que está mal. Tales elecciones te separan de Dios y la comunidad. La reconciliación con Dios y la comunidad viene por medio del sacramento de la reconciliación.

Hijo de Dios El título dado a Jesús para indicar que es Dios y es hombre.

Hijo del Hombre Un título bíblico para el Mesías, que Jesús usó para describirse a sí mismo.

Alma La base espiritual de cada ser humano. Es el don de Dios de vida eterna o el espíritu en tu interior. Cuerpo y alma no están separados. Juntos forman la persona humana.

Administración Demostrar preocupación por las otras personas y por toda la creación.

Sinagoga Una casa judía para el culto y el estudio religioso.

Sínodo Una reunión de obispos que se encuentran para aconsejar al papa sobre asuntos importantes. Un sínodo puede ser local, nacional o mundial.

Sinóptico Una palabra griega que significa "vistos juntos". Los Evangelios de Mateo, Marcos y Lucas se llaman evangelios sinópticos debido a sus similitudes.

Templo El lugar de culto central para los judíos, ubicado en Jerusalén.

Diez Mandamientos La Ley que Dios dio a Moisés en el monte Sinaí como parte de la Alianza con Israel.

Virtudes teologales Hábitos que te conducen a Dios. Las tres virtudes teologales son la fe, la esperanza y el amor.

Torá Una palabra hebrea para los cinco primeros libros de la Biblia.

Confiar Depositar tu fe y tu esperanza en alguien. Los cristianos confían en Dios.

Unidad Ser uno en Jesucristo. El movimiento de unidad entre las iglesias cristianas separadas se llama ecumenismo.

Vocación Un llamado de Dios para servir a Él y a los demás de una determinada manera. Son ejemplos de vocación el matrimonio, el orden sacerdotal, el unirse a una comunidad religiosa y el vivir como laico célibe.

Vows   Sacred promises.

Wisdom   The gift of the Holy Spirit that allows you to see as God sees. It is also the name of one of the books of the Old Testament.

Witness   To tell others what you believe about Jesus by what you say and do.

Works of Mercy   Practices and actions that help bring about God's kingdom by caring for and serving other people.

Worship   The prayers, honor, and praise that people give to God alone.

Zion   The name of the hill on which the Jerusalem Temple stood; a symbol for the capital city of God's kingdom.

Votos   Promesas sagradas.

Sabiduría   El don del Espíritu Santo que nos permite ver como Dios ve. También es el nombre de uno de los libros del Antiguo Testamento.

Dar testimonio   Contar a los demás, con lo que dices y haces, lo que crees acerca de Jesús.

Obras de caridad   Prácticas que ayudan a traer el Reino de Dios por medio del servicio a los demás.

Culto   Las oraciones, la honra y las alabanzas que la gente da sólo a Dios.

Sión   El nombre de la colina en donde se levantaba el templo de Jerusalén; un símbolo para la ciudad capital del Reino de Dios.

The faith community of

_____

is proud to announce that

_____

has completed a yearlong study of
Christ Jesus, the Way.

This adopted child of God has shown growth in
knowledge,
love,
and service.

Because of this fine work,
the young person
receives the warm congratulations
of this faith community.
We are your family in Christ Jesus, the Way.

_____

(Signed)

Illustrations David Barnette: 68; Charles Beyl: 233, 245; Sally Wern Comport: 4, 86, 141; Jim Conaway: 166, 188, 210, 230; Byron Gin: 66; Leonid Gore: 139; Jennifer Hewitson: 5, 47, 55, 63, 71, 83, 91, 99, 107, 119, 127, 135, 143, 155, 163, 171, 179, 191, 207, 215, 227, 235, 243; Susan Jaekel: 58, 69, 113; Susan Keeter: 49; Anni Matsick: 78; Jane McCreary: 101; Bob Pepper: 165; Jaclyne Scardova: 52, 106, 203; Mark Schroder: 42; NJ Taylor: 114; Mike Tofanelli: 209, 237, 260; Jack White: 95, 122, 202; Paula Wiggins: 203.

Photographs Alexian Brothers Bonaventure House: 239; Alinari/Art Resource: 266; AP/Wide World Photos: 203; John E. Argauer/USA/Maryknoll: 170; Arte & Immagini/ Corbis: 115, 123; Arte & Video Immagini Italia/Corbis: 232; Craig E. Barcal/Maryknoll: 220; Billy Barns/PhotoEdit: 190; Dave Bartruff/Corbis: 224; Peter Beck/Corbis: 237; John J. Beeching/Maryknoll: 112; Bettmann/Corbis: 152; Denis Boissavy/Taxi/Getty Images: 221; Brand X Pictures/ Getty Images: 77; Cameraphoto/Art Resource: 126; Mryleen Ferguson Cate/Index Stock: 160; Myrleen Ferguson Cate/ PhotoEdit: 26, 80, 116, 154, 168, 174, 239; Myrleen Ferguson Cate/PictureQuest: 54; Chabruken/Image Bank/Getty Images: 104; Ken Chernus/Taxi/Getty Images: 250; Royalty-Free/Corbis: 77, 173; Corbis Sygma/Corbis: 196; Coy Photo/Maryknoll: 79; Richard Cummins/Corbis: 26; Bob Daemmrich/Stock Boston/PictureQuest: 137, 272; Thomas Danaher/Maryknoll: 40; Mary Kate Denny/ Photo Edit: 241; Digital Vision/Getty Images: 140; Duomo/ Corbis: 167; Susi Eggenberger/Seeds of Peace: 73; Chad Ehlers/Stock Connection/PictureQuest: 82; Joseph Fedora/ Maryknoll: 5, 89; Curt Fisher: 41; Tony Freeman/PhotoEdit: 194, 242; Jeff Greenberg/PhotoEdit: 211; Photo Researchers Inc./Jeff Greenberg/Diana Gongora: 62; Brian Hagiwara/ FoodPix/Getty Images: 193; Will Hart/PhotoEdit: 157; K. Horgan/ESA/Tony Stone Images: 217; Richard Hutchings/ Photo Edit: 113; The Image Bank/Getty Images: 131; Robert Jones/Corbis: 117; Jose Luis Pelaez/Corbis: 247; Michael Keller/Corbis: 175; George D. Lepp/Corbis: 129; Rob Lewine/The Stock Market: 93; Dan Loh/AP Photo: 145; Maryknoll: 195; Ryan McVay/PhotoDisc: 43; John J. Moran/Maryknoll: 98; William F. Mullan/Maryknoll: 184; Amy Neunsinger/StockFood: 193; Michael Newman/ PhotoEdit: 80, 121, 140, 185, 246; Nimatallah/Art Resource: 94; Alan Oddie/PhotoEdit: 175; Allen Lee Page/Corbis: 221; Photodisc: 226; Photodisc Blue/Getty Images: 140, 205; Photodisc Green/Getty Images: 117, 185, 201, 211, 245; Amy Beth Pitura/Maryknoll: 181; Betty Press/Woodfin Camp/PictureQuest: 109; Readio Magazine: 206; M. Regali/Maryknoll: 37; Roger Ressmeyer/ Corbis: 178; Olivier Ribardiere/Taxi/Getty Images: 197; Galen Rowell/Corbis: 158; Rubberball Productions/Getty Images: 173, 185; William R. Sallaz/Image Bank: 177; Scala/Art Resource, NY: 138; James L. Shaffer/Shaffer Photography: 29, 61, 87, 97; Nancy Sheehan/PhotoEdit: 242; Ron Sherman/Stock Boston/PictureQuest: 129; Rhoda Sidney/PhotoEdit: 240; Frank Siteman/Index Stock Imagery: 51; Ariel Skelley/Corbis: 149, 175; Steve Skjold/ Photo Edit: 140; Solzberg Studio/StockFood: 193; Sean Sprague/Maryknoll: 36, 76, 176, 234; Mary Steinbacher/ Photo Edit: 117; Elaine Sulle/ImageBank: 97; SuperStock/ PictureQuest: 253; Terry Sutherland: 124; LWA-Dann Tardif/ Corbis: 177; Thinkstock/Getty Images: 140, 173; Kevin T. Thomas/Maryknoll: 195; Joseph W. Towle/Maryknoll: 39; Peter Turnley/Corbis: 212; Rudi Von Briel/PhotoEdit/ Diana Gongora: 162; Joseph Weclawik/Maryknoll: 148; Jim West/Impact Visuals: 242; Eric Wheater/Maryknoll: 31; Bill Wittman: 8, 9, 10, 12, 16–17, 18, 19, 20, 21, 22, 25, 30, 31, 32, 34, 38, 90, 261, 262, 263, 264, 267, 268, 269, 270, 271; Cary Wolinsky/Stock Boston/PictureQuest: 272; David Young-Wolff/PhotoEdit: 57, 177, 204, 222; David Young-Wolff/PhotoEdit/PictureQuest: 201; David Young-Wolff/Stone/Getty Images: 221, 229; Kwame Zikomo/ SuperStock: 4, 125.